LITERARY CRITICISM

LITERARY CRITICISM

An Introduction to
Theory and Practice

CHARLES E. BRESSLER
Houghton College

Prentice Hall Englewood Cliffs, New Jersey 07632

Library of Congress Cataloging-in-Publication Data

BRESSLER, CHARLES E.
   Literary criticism : an introduction to theory and practice /
Charles E. Bressler.
   p. cm.
   Includes bibliographical references (p.) and index.
   ISBN 0–13–533001–7 (pbk.)
   1. Criticism. I. Title.
PN81.B666 1994
801'.95—dc20   93–24166
                                                    CIP

ACQUISITIONS EDITOR: Alison Reeves
EDITORIAL/PRODUCTION SUPERVISION
   AND INTERIOR DESIGN: Hilda Tauber
PRODUCTION COORDINATOR: Herb Klein
COVER DESIGN: Violet Lake Studio

 © 1994 by Prentice-Hall, Inc.
A Paramount Communications Company
Englewood Cliffs, New Jersey 07632

Printed in the United States of America
10 9 8 7 6 5 4 3 2 1

ISBN 0-13-533001-7

Prentice-Hall International (UK) Limited, *London*
Prentice-Hall of Australia Pty. Limited, *Sydney*
Prentice-Hall Canada Inc., *Toronto*
Prentice-Hall Hispanoamericana, S.A., *Mexico*
Prentice-Hall of India Private Limited, *New Delhi*
Prentice-Hall of Japan, Inc., *Tokyo*
Simon & Schuster Asia Pte. Ltd., *Singapore*
Editora Prentice-Hall do Brasil, Ltda., *Rio de Janeiro*

For my best friend and loving wife,
Darlene

Contents

To the Instructor   *xi*

Acknowledgments   *xv*

1 Criticism, Theory, and Literature   1

What Is Literary Criticism?   *3*
What Is Literary Theory?   *4*
What Is Literature?   *7*
Further Reading   *9*

2 A Historical Survey of Literary Criticism   11

Plato (*ca.* 427–347 B.C.)   *11*
Aristotle (384–322 B.C.)   *13*
Horace (65–8 B.C.)   *16*
Longinus (First Century A.D.)   *17*
Dante Alighieri (1265–1321)   *17*
Sir Philip Sidney (1554–1586)   *18*
John Dryden (1631–1700)   *19*
Alexander Pope (1688–1744)   *20*
William Wordsworth (1770–1850)   *21*
Hippolyte Adolphe Taine (1828–1893)   *23*
Matthew Arnold (1822–1888)   *25*
Henry James (1843–1916)   *27*
Modern Literary Criticism   *29*
Further Reading   *30*

3 New Criticism   31

Introduction   *31*
Historical Development   *32*
Assumptions   *34*
Methodology   *37*
Further Reading   *40*
STUDENT ESSAY: Browning's Self-Revealing Duke   *40*

4 Reader-Response Criticism   45

Introduction   *45*
Historical Development   *47*
Assumptions   *50*
Methodology   *51*
Further Reading   *54*
STUDENT ESSAY: "Young Goodman Brown" and Me   *54*

5 Structuralism   58

Introduction   *58*
Historical Development   *59*
Assumptions   *62*
Methodology   *64*
Further Reading   *67*
STUDENT ESSAY: A Structuralist Look at Glaspell's
    Trifles   67

6 Deconstruction   71

Introduction   *71*
Historical Development   *72*
Assumptions   *75*
Methodology   *77*
Further Reading   *82*
STUDENT ESSAY: A Deconstructor's View of "Young
    Goodman Brown"   *83*

7 Psychoanalytic Criticism   87

Introduction   *87*
Historical Development   *89*

Assumptions   94
Methodology   95
Further Reading   96
STUDENT ESSAY: A Psychoanalytic View of Glaspell's
        Trifles   97

8 Feminism   102

Introduction   102
Historical Development   104
Assumptions   106
Methodology   108
Further Reading   110
STUDENT ESSAY: Feminist Criticism and Susan Glaspell's
        Trifles   110

9 Marxism   114

Introduction   114
Historical Development   115
Assumptions   118
Methodology   121
Further Reading   122
STUDENT ESSAY: A Marxist Interpretation of "My Last
        Duchess"   123

10 New Historicism   127

Introduction   127
Historical Development   129
Assumptions   130
Methodology   133
Further Reading   135
STUDENT ESSAY: Hawthorne's Ambiguity: A New
        Historical Point of View   136

Literary Selections   143

Nathaniel Hawthorne, "Young Goodman Brown"   144
Robert Browning, "My Last Duchess"   153
Susan Glaspell, *Trifles*   155

Glossary   166

Bibliography   185

References   188

Index   201

To the Instructor

Literary Criticism is designed as a supplemental text for introductory literature courses. It will enable students to approach literature from a variety of practical and theoretical positions, and equip them with a working knowledge of how critics and readers develop and articulate interpretations. It provides an overview of the concerns of literary theory and outstanding schools of criticism. In addition, this text may also be useful for those undergraduate students studying literary theory and criticism or those first-year graduate students who have had little or no exposure to literary theory.

This book holds to several basic premises. First, it assumes that there is no such thing as an innocent reading of a literary work: Whether our responses are emotional and spontaneous or well-reasoned and highly structured, all such interactions are based on some underlying factors that cause us to respond to a text in a particular fashion. What elicits these responses or how a reader makes sense or meaning out of a text is what really matters. Literary theory questions our responses, our interpretations, and our assumptions, beliefs, and feelings. To understand why we respond to a text in a certain way, we must first understand literary theory and criticism.

Second, since our reactions to any literary work or indeed any printed material have theoretical bases, I have assumed that all readers have a literary theory. Consciously or unconsciously, we as readers have developed a mind-set concerning our expectations when reading any text, be it a novel, a short story, a poem, or any other type of literature. Somehow, as Jonathan Culler maintains, we make sense out of printed material. The methods and techniques we use to frame our personal interpretations of any text directly involve us in the process of literary criticism and theory, and automatically make us practicing literary critics.

My third assumption rests on the observation that each reader's literary theory is either conscious or unconscious, complete or incomplete, informed or ill-informed, eclectic or unified. Since an unconscious, incomplete, ill-informed and eclectic literary theory often leads to illogical, unsound, and haphazard interpretations, I believe that a well-defined, logical, and clearly articulated theory will enable readers to develop their own personal methods of interpretation, permitting them to order, clarify, and justify their personal appraisals of a text in a consistent and logical manner.

More frequently than not, however, readers cannot articulate their own literary theory and have little knowledge of the history and development of the ever-evolving principles of literary criticism. It is the goal of this book to introduce students to literary theory and criticism, its historical development, and the various theoretical positions or schools of criticism that will enable them as readers to make conscious, informed, and intelligent choices concerning their own methods of literary interpretation.

Chapter 1 introduces the basic concerns of literary theory and criticism and defines various theoretical terms. After making students aware that literary theory and criticism exist, I present a working definition of literature itself. Such a definition, I hope, will become the starting point for each student's personal definition of literature and for his or her exploration of multiple interpretations of a text.

Chapter 2 places literary theory and criticism in historical perspective. Starting with Plato and ending with Henry James, students are exposed to some of the leading theorists and literary critics from the Greeks to the beginning of the twentieth century. Since this is an introductory and not an advanced text, students will read about Plato, Aristotle, and Alexander Pope, for example, rather than reading these authors' primary texts. I hope that the individual discussions of each theorist or critic will arouse students' interest and lead them to read some primary works by the authors who address their concerns and stimulate their fancy.

In chapters 3 through 10 I discuss individually eight major schools or theoretical positions that have developed in the twentieth century: New Criticism, Reader-Response Criticism, Structuralism, Deconstruction, Psychoanalytic Criticism, Feminism, Marxism, and New Historicism. To maintain consistency, each of these chapters is organized identically. We begin with a brief Introduction that presents a few of the major beliefs or tenets of that particular school or theoretical position. Next comes the Historical Development, followed by the Assumptions section that sets forth the philosophical principles upon which the school of criticism is based. In the following section, Methodology, we discuss the procedures used by adherents of that school or theoretical position. The methodology sections serve as a "how to" manual for explaining the techniques used by various critics to formulate an interpretation of a text based on their philosophical assumptions. Each chapter closes with an essay written by a college junior, in which the student applies the principles and methods of the school of criticism under discussion to one of the three primary texts included at the end of the book. I have chosen not to edit the students' essays in order to let other students critique and evaluate them.

The three literary works that appear are Nathaniel Hawthorne's short story "Young Goodman Brown," Robert Browning's poem "My Last Duchess," and Susan Glaspell's one-act play *Trifles.* By including these selections in the volume, we provide easy access and enable readers to judge for themselves the success and strengths of the student essays.

A detailed Glossary defines the key terms highlighted in the text. In addition, the Glossary provides an overview of the eight schools of twentieth-century criticism covered, and will be most helpful for teaching and reinforcing important theoretical terms and concepts.

At the back of the book we provide a detailed Bibliography divided into two parts. The first part lists introductory and general surveys of literary criticism that supplement this book. The second part lists theoretical sources for more advanced students who may wish to further their knowledge. Finally, the References section cites the works consulted during the writing of this book, chapter by chapter, and may be useful for further research.

Instructors should keep in mind that this is an introductory text aimed at college undergraduates who are beginning their study of literature and literary theory. For this reason the explanations of the various schools of criticism should not be considered as exhaustive. Instead, each chapter should be viewed as a first step toward an understanding of some rather difficult concepts, principles, and methodologies. After reading each chapter, it is hoped that the students will continue their own investigations of literary theory and criticism by reading advanced theoretical texts and the primary works of both theoretical and practical critics.

Acknowledgments

The creation of any book usually involves the author's relationships with a variety of people. This text is no exception. To the members of my literary criticism class who first inspired me to write a text they could understand, I say thank you. To Houghton College, for granting me a sabbatical that allowed the time to study and research literary theory, I express my appreciation. To my students in literary criticism who heard many parts of this text in lecture form, I thank you for your patience, your questions, and your suggestions. Thanks are also due to Sue Crider, Bruce Brenneman, Larry Mullen, Willis Beardsley, and Ben King—my colleagues and friends—who read various parts of the manuscript and offered helpful insights and constructive criticism. I am particularly grateful to Kevin Eaton, Kathleen Stockin, Dwayne Piper, and Julie Claypool—the four students whose essays appear in this text. I also wish to thank Janet M. Ellerby, University of North Carolina at Wilmington, and Douglas R. Butler, College of St. Rose, Albany, for reviewing the manuscript and making helpful suggestions. To Alison Reeves, Hilda Tauber, and the editorial staff at Prentice Hall, I am grateful for the superb editing and professional advice. Most of all I express my love and appreciation to my wife, Darlene, and my daughter, Heidi, for freeing me from many of life's daily chores and demands so that I could study, research, and write. Without their support this text simply would not exist. Because of the input of my friends and family, this is a better work. Any mistakes, errors in judgment, or other flaws must be attributed to the author alone.

Criticism, Theory, and Literature

Once I said to myself it would be a thousand times better for Jim to be a slave at home where his family was, as long as he'd *got* to be a slave, and so I'd better write a letter to Tom Sawyer and tell him to tell Miss Watson where he was. But I soon give up that notion, for two things: she'd be mad and disgusted at his rascality and ungratefulness for leaving her, and so she'd sell him straight down the river again; and if she didn't, everybody naturally despises an ungrateful nigger, and they'd make Jim feel it all the time, and so he'd feel ornery and disgraced. And then think of *me*! It would get all around that Huck Finn helped a nigger to get his freedom; and if I was to ever see anybody from that town again I'd be ready to get down and lick his boots for shame. That's just the way: a person does a low-down thing, and then he don't want to take no consequences of it. Thinks as long as he can hide it, it ain't no disgrace. That was my fix exactly. The more I studied about this the more my conscience went to grinding me, and the more wicked and low-down and ornery I got to feeling. And at last, when it hit me all of a sudden that here was the plain hand of Providence slapping me in the face and letting me know my wickedness was being watched all the time from up there in heaven, whilst I was stealing a poor old woman's nigger that hadn't ever done me no harm, and now was showing me there's One that's always on the lookout, and ain't agoing to allow no such miserable doings to go only just so fur and no further, I most dropped in my tracks I was so scared. Well, I tried the best I could to kinder soften it up somehow for myself by saying I was brung up wicked, and so I warn't so much to blame; but something inside of me kept saying, "There was the Sunday school, you could a gone to it; and if you'd a done it they'd a learn't you there that people that acts as I'd been acting about that nigger goes to everlasting fire."

It made me shiver. . . .

Adventures of Huckleberry Finn, Chapter 31

In this climactic scene from Mark Twain's novel, the protagonist, Huckleberry Finn, must decide whether or not he should inform Miss Watson of the location of Jim, her runaway slave. Having helped Jim escape from Miss Watson's homestead and having spent several days and nights with Jim floating down the Mississippi River on a raft, Huck has become Jim's friend, eating, playing, and even philosophizing with him about the creation of the stars and moon. In the midst of their adventures both on and off the raft, Huck and Jim meet up with two scoundrels, the Duke and the Dauphin. Through a series of events hatched by these tricksters, Jim is once again sold into slavery, this time for forty dollars. Knowing Jim's present fate, Huck must decide if he should write Jim's lawful owner and tell her that her slave is being held at Silas Phelps' farm, or simply keep quiet about Jim's whereabouts.

In this scene, we, the readers, watch Huck struggle with his decision. Along with Huck, we too wonder if Jim should be returned to his home and family, since, as Huck notes, Jim has "got to be a slave" anyway. At first Huck decides that he should not write Miss Watson, for two reasons: (1) She will be so angry at Jim for his "ungratefulness" for leaving her and for causing her such trouble in the first place that she may decide to sell him to another owner or simply choose to keep him, in which case Jim would feel "ornery and disgraced" in his town, for "everybody naturally despises an ungrateful nigger"; and (2) Huck's letter would stigmatize him as one who helped a slave get his freedom, forever shaming him in the eyes of his townsfolk. At first, we may accept Huck's reasoning as logical, but upon closer scrutiny we may be startled at Huck and his society. Do they not treat Jim and other blacks as property, as something to be owned, and not as people? Or perhaps we need to ask if Twain himself is presenting an accurate picture of the white, middle-class American view of blacks in the 1850s. Is the author's analysis of his society and its people's feelings, beliefs, and prejudices true to life, or is Twain simply inserting his own opinions in the mouths of his characters? Furthermore, we may wonder how Twain's contemporary audience responded to this scene. Did they nod their heads in agreement with Huck Finn and his analysis of the townsfolk and Miss Watson, or did they declare that Twain himself was simply fictionalizing and "playing with the truth" to enhance his own viewpoint or even to promote the sale of his novel?

As Huck continues his internal debate, he experiences an epiphany: Providence, he thinks, is "slapping him in the face" for stealing a poor lady's slave. Troubled by his conscience, he declares that "One" up in heaven has been noting his wickedness, and he, Huckleberry Finn, is without excuse. Like Huck, we too question his so-called wickedness. Is he really a thief for snatching Jim from slavery? Is the source of his troubling conscience "someone" in heaven or simply the internalized molding influences and dictates of his society? Indeed, is there really a "someone" in heaven in the first place? And does Twain himself posit the existence of a god in heaven or not? Moreover, should Twain's beliefs concerning the existence of any god influence or concern us, the readers?

By answering any or all of the above questions or any other question evoked by Twain's text, we have become practicing literary critics.

What Is Literary Criticism?

Matthew Arnold, a nineteenth-century literary critic, describes literary criticism as "a disinterested endeavor to learn and propagate the best that is known and thought in the world." Implicit in this definition is that **literary criticism** is a disciplined activity that attempts to study, analyze, interpret, and evaluate a work of art. By necessity, Arnold would argue, this discipline attempts to formulate aesthetic and methodological principles on the basis of which the critic can evaluate a text.

When we consider its function and its relationship to texts, literary criticism is not usually considered a discipline in and of itself, for it must be related to something else—that is, a work of art. Without the work of art, the activity of criticism cannot exist. And it is through this discerning activity that we can explore those questions that help define our humanity, evaluate our actions, or simply increase our appreciation and enjoyment of both a literary work and our fellow human beings.

When analyzing a work of art, literary critics ask basic questions concerning the philosophical, psychological, functional, and descriptive nature of a text. Since the time of the Greek philosophers Plato and Aristotle, the answers to these questions have been seriously debated. By asking questions of Twain's or any other text, and by contemplating answers, we too can become participants in this debate. Whether we question if Huckleberry Finn is committing sin by not sending a letter to Miss Watson, or whether we attempt to discover the chief influences working on Huck's conscience, we are participating in an ongoing discussion of the value, worth, and enjoyment of Twain's novel while simultaneously engaging in literary criticism and functioning as practical literary critics.

Traditionally, literary critics involve themselves in either theoretical or practical criticism. **Theoretical criticism** formulates theories, principles, and tenets regarding the nature and value of art. By citing general aesthetic and moral principles of art, theoretical criticism provides the necessary framework for practical criticism. **Practical criticism** (known also as **applied criticism**) then applies the theories and tenets of theoretical criticism to a particular work—*Huckleberry Finn*, for example. It is the **practical critic** who defines the standards of taste and explains, evaluates, or justifies a particular piece of literature. A further distinction is made between the practical critic who posits that there is one and only one theory or set of principles a critic may utilize when evaluating a literary work—the **absolutist critic**—and the **relativistic critic,** who employs various and even contradictory theories in critiquing a piece of literature. The basis, however, for either kind of critic, or for any form of criticism, is literary theory. Without theory, practical criticism could not exist.

What Is Literary Theory?

When reading *Huckleberry Finn,* we necessarily interact with the text, asking specific, text-related questions, such as What are Huck's personal feelings for Jim? What was the concept of slavery during Huck's times? What was Jim's concept of self-worth? Such questions involve us in practical criticism. What we tend to forget during the actual reading process is that we have read other literary works. Our response to any text, then—or the principles of practical criticism we apply to it—is largely a conditioned or programmed one—that is, how we arrive at meaning in fiction is in part determined by our past experiences. Consciously or unconsciously, we have developed a mind-set or framework concerning our expectations when reading a novel, a short story, a poem, or any other type of literature. In addition, what we choose to value or uphold as good or bad, moral or immoral, or beautiful or ugly within a given text actually depends on this ever-evolving framework. To articulate this framework and piece together the various elements of our practical criticism into a coherent, unified body of knowledge is to formulate our **literary theory.**

Since anyone who responds to a text is already a practicing literary critic, every reader espouses some kind of literary theory. Each reader's theory, however, may be conscious or unconscious, complete or incomplete, informed or ill-informed, eclectic or unified. An incomplete, unconscious, and therefore unclear literary theory leads to illogical, unsound, and haphazard interpretations. On the other hand, a well-defined, logical, and clearly articulated theory enables readers to develop a method whereby they can establish principles that enable them to justify, order, and clarify their own appraisals of a text in a consistent manner.

A well-articulated literary theory assumes that an innocent reading of a text or a sheerly emotional or spontaneous reaction to a work cannot exist, for theory questions the assumptions, beliefs, and feelings of readers, asking why they respond to a text in a certain way. According to a consistent literary theory, a simple emotional or intuitive response to a text does not explain the underlying factors that caused such a reaction. What elicits that response, or how the reader makes meaning out of the text, is what matters.

How we as readers make meaning out of or from the text will depend upon the mental framework that each of us has developed concerning the nature of reality. This framework or **worldview** consists of "the assumptions or presuppositions that we all hold (either consciously or unconsciously) concerning the basic makeup of our world." We all struggle, for example, to find answers to such questions as these: What is the basis of morality or ethics? What is the meaning of human history? Is there an overarching purpose for humanity's existence? What are beauty, truth, and goodness? Is there an ultimate reality? Interestingly, our answers to these and other questions do not remain static, for as we interact with other people, with our environment, and with our own personal philosophies, we continue to grapple with these issues, often changing our ideas. But it is our answers that largely determine our response to a literary text.

Upon such a conceptual framework rests literary theory. Whether that framework is well-reasoned, or simply a matter of habit and past teachings, readers respond to works of art via their worldview. From this philosophical core of beliefs spring their evaluations of the goodness, the worthiness, and the value of art itself. Using their worldviews either consciously or unconsciously as a yardstick by which to measure and value their experiences, readers will respond to individual works of literature, ordering and valuing each separate or collective experience in the work based on the system of beliefs housed in their worldviews.

During the act of reading, this process becomes evident, for when we are reading, we are constantly interacting with the text. According to Louise M. Rosenblatt's text *The Reader, the Text, the Poem* (1978), during the act or "event" of reading:

> a reader brings to the text his/her past experience and present personality. Under the magnetism of the ordered symbols of the text, the reader marshals his/her resources and crystallizes out from the stuff of memory, thought, and feeling a new order, a new experience, which he/she sees as the poem. This becomes part of the ongoing stream of the reader's life experience, to be reflected on from any angle important to him/her as a human being.

Accordingly, Rosenblatt declares that the relationship between the reader and the text is not linear, but **transactional;** that is, it is a process or event that takes place at a particular time and place in which the text and the reader condition each other. The reader and the text transact or interact, creating meaning, for meaning does not exist either solely within the reader's mind or solely within the text, Rosenblatt maintains, but in the interaction between them. To arrive at an interpretation of a text, readers bring their own "temperament and fund of past transactions to the text and live through a process of handling new situations, new attitudes, new personalities, [and] new conflicts in value. They can reject, revise, or assimilate into the resource with which they engage their world." Through this transactional experience, readers consciously and unconsciously amend their worldview.

Since no literary theory can account for all the various factors included in everyone's conceptual framework, and since we, as readers, all have different literary experiences, there can exist no **metatheory**—no one overarching literary theory that encompasses all possible interpretations of a text suggested by its readers. There can exist, then, no one correct literary theory, for in and of itself, each literary theory asks valid questions to and about the text, and no one theory is capable of exhausting all legitimate questions to be asked about any text.

The kinds of valid questions asked by the various literary theories often differ widely. Espousing separate critical orientations, each theory focuses primarily on one element of the interpretative process, although in practice different theories may utilize several areas of concern in interpreting a text. For example, one theory stresses the work itself, believing that the text alone contains all the necessary information to arrive at an interpretation. This theory isolates the text from its historical and/or sociological setting and concentrates on the various literary forms found in the text, such as figures of speech, word choice, and style. Another theory attempts to place a text in its historical, political, sociological, religious, and economic setting. By placing the text in historical perspective, this theory asserts that its adherents can arrive at an interpretation that both the text's author and its original audience would support. Still another theory directs its chief concern toward the text's audience. It asks how the readers' emotions and personal backgrounds affect a text's interpretation. Whether the primary focus of concern is psychological, linguistic, mythical, historical, or any other critical orientation, each literary theory establishes its own theoretical basis and then proceeds to develop its own methodology whereby readers can apply this theory to an actual text.

Although each reader's theory and methodology for arriving at a text's interpretation will differ, sooner or later groups of readers and critics declare allegiance to a similar core of beliefs and band together, thereby "founding" different **schools of criticism.** For example, those critics who believe that social and historical concerns must be highlighted in a text are known as Marxist critics, whereas reader-response critics concentrate on the reader's personal reactions to the text. Since new points of view concerning literary works are continually evolving, new schools of criticism and therefore new literary theories often develop. The most recent school to emerge in the 1980s and 1990s, New Historicism, declares that a text must be analyzed through historical research that assumes that history and fiction are inseparable. The members of this school, known as New Historicists, hope to shift the boundaries between history and literature and thereby produce criticism that accurately reflects what they believe to be the proper relationship between the text and its historical context.

Since the various schools of criticism (and the theories on which they are based) ask different questions about the same work of literature, these theoretical schools provide an array of seemingly endless options from which readers can choose to broaden their understanding not only of the text but also of their society, their culture, and their own humanity. By embracing literary theory, we can thus learn not only about literature but also about tolerance for other people's beliefs. By rejecting or ignoring theory, we are in danger of canonizing ourselves as literary saints who possess divine knowledge and can therefore supply the one and only correct interpretation for a work of literature. To be against literary theory is also to be against "self-examination—against raising and exploring questions about how texts and selves and societies are formed and maintained and for whose benefit." By embracing literary theory and literary criticism (its practical application), we can participate in the seemingly endless historical conversation and debate concerning the nature of humanity and its concerns as expressed in literature itself.

What Is Literature?

Since literary criticism presupposes that there exists a work of literature to be interpreted, we could assume that formulating a definition of what literature is would be simple. But not so. For centuries, writers, literary historians, and others have debated about but failed to agree on a definition for this term. Many assume that literature is simply anything that is written, thereby declaring a city telephone book, a cookbook, and a road atlas to be literary works along with *David Copperfield* and *Huckleberry Finn.* Derived from the Latin *littera,* meaning "letter," the root meaning of *literature* refers primarily to the written word and seems to support this broad definition. Such a definition, however, eliminates the important oral traditions upon which much of our literature is based. For example, Homer's *Iliad* and *Odyssey,* the English epic *Beowulf,* and many Native American legends could not, by this definition, be considered literature.

To solve this problem, others choose to define literature as an art, thereby leaving open the question of its being written or oral. This further narrows its meaning, equating literature with works of the imagination or creative writing. By this definition, written works such as a telephone book or a cookbook can no longer be considered literature, being replaced or superseded by poetry, drama, fiction, and other types of imaginative writing.

Although such a narrowing and an equating of the definition of literature to art seemingly simplifies what can and cannot be deemed a literary work, such is not the case. That the Banana Republic clothes catalogue is imaginative (and colorful) writing is unquestioned, but should it be considered a work of literature? Or should Madonna's "book" entitled *Sex* or the lyrics of the rap song "Cop Killer" be called a literary work? Is Madonna's text or the rap song an imaginative or a creative work? If so, can or should either of them be considered a work of literature? Defining and narrowing the definition of literature as being a work of art does not immediately provide consensus or a consistent rule concerning whether or not a work can or should be considered a work of literature.

Whether one accepts the broad or the narrow definition, many argue that a text must possess particular qualities before it can be considered literature. For example, the artist's creation or secondary world often mirrors the author's primary world, the world in which the creator lives and moves and breathes. Since reality or the primary world is highly structured, so must be the secondary world. To achieve this structure, the artist must create plot, character, tone, symbols, conflict, and a host of other elements or parts of the artistic story, with all of these literary elements working in a dynamic interrelationship to produce a literary work. It is the presence of these elements, some would argue, that determines whether or not a piece of writing is literature.

Still other critics add the "test of time" criterion to their list of the essential components of literature. If a work like Dante's *The Divine Comedy* withstands the passage of time and is still being read centuries after its creation, it is deemed valuable and worthy to be called literature. This criterion also denotes literature's functional or cultural value: if people value a written work, for whatever reason, they frequently decree it to be literature whether or not it contains the prescribed or so-called essential elements of a text.

What this work may contain is a peculiar aesthetic quality that distinguishes it as literature from other forms of writing. **Aesthetics,** that branch of philosophy that deals with the concept of the beautiful, strives to determine the criteria for beauty in a work of art. Theorists like Plato and Aristotle declare that the source of beauty is inherent within the art object itself, while other critics such as David Hume decree that beauty is in the eye of the beholder. And some twentieth-century theorists argue that one's perception of beauty in a text rests in the dynamic relationship between the object and the perceiver at a given moment in time. Wherever the criteria for judging the beauty of a work of art finally reside, most critics agree that a work of literature does possess an appealing aesthetic quality.

While distinguishing literature from other forms of writing, this appealing aesthetic quality directly contributes to literature's chief purpose: the telling of a story. While it may simultaneously communicate facts, literature's primary aim is to tell a story. The subject of this story is particularly human, describing and detailing a variety of human experiences, not stating facts or bits and pieces of information. Literature does not, for example, define the word *courage,* but shows us a courageous character acting courageously. By so doing, literature concretizes an array of human values, emotions, actions, and ideas in story form. And it is this concretization that allows us, the readers, to experience vicariously the lives of a host of characters. Through these characters we observe people in action, making decisions, struggling to maintain their humanity in often inhumane circumstances, and embodying for us a variety of values and human characteristics that we may embrace, discard, enjoy, or detest.

Is literature, then, simply a story that contains certain aesthetic and literary qualities that all somehow pleasingly culminate in a work of art? Put another way, is a literary work ontological?—that is, does it exist in and of itself, or must it have an audience, a reader, before it becomes literature? Although any answer is debatable, most would agree that an examination of a text's total artistic situation would help us make our decision. This total picture of the work involves such elements as the work itself (an examination of the fictionality or secondary world created within the story), the artist, the universe or world the work supposedly represents, and the audience or readers. Although readers and critics will emphasize one, two, or even three of these elements while deemphasizing the others, such a consideration of a text's artistic situation immediately broadens the definition of literature from the narrow concept that it is simply a written work that contains certain qualities to a definition that must include the dynamic interrelationship of the actual text and the readers. Perhaps, then, the literary competence of the readers themselves helps determine whether a work should be considered literature. If this is so, then a literary work may be more functional than ontological, its existence and therefore its value being determined by its readers and not by the work itself.

Overall, the definition of literature really depends on the school of criticism which the reader and/or critic espouses. For formalists, for example, the text and the text alone will contain certain qualities that make a particular piece of writing literature. But for reader-response critics, the interaction and psychological relationships between the text and the reader will help determine whether a document should be deemed literary.

However one decides to define literature, unquestionably this art form provides many hours of pleasure for readers through the imaginative creation of secondary worlds via the vehicle of words.

Further Reading

Daiches, David. *Critical Approaches to Literature*. Longman: New York, 1981.

Danziger, Marlies, and W. Stacy Johnson. *An Introduction to Literary Criticism*. Boston: D. C. Heath, 1961.

Eagleton, Terry. *Literary Theory: An Introduction*. Minneapolis: University of Minnesota Press, 1983.

Sire, James. *The Joy of Reading: A Guide to Becoming a Better Reader.* Portland, OR: Multnomah Press, 1978.

Staton, Shirley F., ed. *Literary Theories in Praxis.* Philadelphia: University of Pennsylvania Press, 1987.

Stevens, Bonnie, and Larry Stewart. *A Guide to Literary Criticism and Research.* Fort Worth: Holt, 1992.

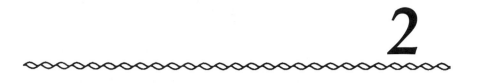

A Historical Survey of Literary Criticism

Questions concerning the value, the structure, and even the definition of literature undoubtedly arose in all cultures as people heard or read works of art. Such practical criticism probably began with the initial hearing or reading of the first literary works. It was the Greeks of the fifth century B.C., however, who first articulated and developed the philosophy of art and life that serves as the foundation for most theoretical and practical criticism. These fifth-century Athenians questioned the very act of reading and writing itself, while pondering the purpose of literature. In so doing, these early critics began a debate concerning the nature and function of literature that continues to the present day. What they inaugurated was the formal study of literary criticism.

From the fifth century B.C. to the present, various critics such as Plato, Dante, Wordsworth, and a host of others have developed principles of criticism that have had a major influence on the ongoing discussion of literary theory and criticism. By examining these critics' ideas, we can gain an understanding of and participate in this critical debate, while simultaneously acquiring an appreciation for and a working knowledge of both practical and theoretical criticism.

Plato (*ca.* 427–347 B.C.)

Alfred North Whitehead, a modern British philosopher, once quipped that "all of Western philosophy is but a footnote to Plato." Although others have indeed contributed to Western thought, it was Plato's ideas, expressed in his *Republic, Ion, Crito,* and other works, that laid the foundation for many, if not most, of the pivotal issues of both philosophy and literature: the concepts of truth, beauty, and goodness; the nature of reality; the structure of society; the nature and relations of being (ontology); questions concerning how we know what we know (epistemology); and ethics and morality. Since Plato's day, such ideas have been debated, debunked, or simply accepted. None, however, have been ignored.

Before Plato, only fragmentary comments concerning the nature or value of literature can be found. In the plays and writings of the comic dramatist Aristophanes, a contemporary of Plato, a few tidbits of practical criticism arise, but no clearly articulated literary theory. It is Plato who systematically begins the study of literary theory and criticism.

The core of Platonic thought resides in Plato's doctrine of essences, ideas, or forms. Ultimate reality, he states, is spiritual. This spiritual realm, "The One," is composed of "ideal" forms or absolutes that exist whether or not any mind posits their existence or reflects their attributes. It is these ideal forms that then give shape to our physical world, for our material world is nothing more than a shadowy replica of the absolute forms found in the spiritual realm. In the material world we can therefore recognize a chair as a chair because the ideal chair exists in this spiritual realm and preceded the existence of the material chair. Without the existence of the ideal chair, the physical chair, which is nothing more than a shadowy replica of the ideal chair, could not exist.

Such an emphasis on philosophical ideals earmarks the beginning of the first articulated literary theory and becomes the foundation for literary criticism. Before Plato and his Academy, Greek culture ordered its world through poetry and the poetic imagination; that is, by reading such works as the *Iliad* and the *Odyssey,* the Greeks saw good characters in action performing good deeds. From such stories, they formulated their theories of goodness and other similar standards. Such narratives became a framework or mode for discovering truth. With the advent of Plato and his Academy, however, philosophical inquiry and abstract thinking usurp the narrative as a method for discovering truth. Not by accident, then, Plato placed above his school door the words "Let no one enter here who is not a geometer." Like Plato himself, all his students had to value the art of reason and abstraction as opposed to the presentational mode for discovering truth.

Such metaphysical reasoning not only usurps literature's role as an evaluating mode for discerning truth but actually condemns it. If ultimate reality rests in the spiritual realm, and the material world is a shadowy replica of the world of ideals, then according to Plato and his followers, poets (those who compose imaginative literature) are merely imitating an imitation when they write about any object in the material world. Accordingly, Plato declares that a poet's craft is "an inferior who marries an inferior and has inferior offspring"; now the poet is two steps or degrees removed from reality itself. These imitators of reality, says Plato, cannot be trusted.

While condemning poets for producing art that is nothing more than a copy of a copy, Plato also argues that poets produce their art irrationally, relying on untrustworthy intuition rather than reason for their inspiration. He writes, "For the poet is a light and winged and holy thing, and there is no invention in him until he has been inspired and is out of his senses, and then the mind is no longer in him." Because such inspiration opposes reason and asserts that truth can be attained intuitively, Plato condemns all poets.

Since poets are both untrustworthy and damned, no longer can their works be the basis of the Greeks' morality or ethics. For Plato argues that in the poets' works, lies abound concerning the nature of ultimate reality. In the *Iliad,* for example, the gods lie and cheat and are one of the main causes of suffering among humans. Even the mortals in these works steal, complain, and hate each other. Such writings, contends Plato, set a bad example for Greek citizens and may even lead normally law-abiding people into paths of wickedness and immorality. In the *Republic,* Plato ultimately concludes that such people, the poets, must be banished.

In a later work, Plato seemingly recognizes society's need for poets and their craft to "celebrate the victors" of the state. Only those poets, however, "who are themselves good and also honorable in the state" can and will be tolerated. Plato thus decrees poetry's function and value in his society: to sing the praises of loyal Greeks. Poets must be supporters of the state or risk banishment from their homeland. Being mere imitators, these artisans and their craft must be rigorously censored.

By linking politics and literature in a seemingly moral and reasoned worldview, Plato and his Academy founded a complex theory of literary criticism that initiated the ongoing debate concerning the value, nature, and worth of the artist and of literature itself.

Aristotle (384–322 B.C.)

Whereas literary criticism's concern with morality began with Plato, its emphasis on the elements or characteristics of which a work is composed began with Aristotle, Plato's famous pupil. Rejecting some of his teacher's beliefs concerning the nature of reality, Aristotle opts for a detailed investigation of the material world.

The son of a medical doctor from Thrace, Aristotle reveled in the physical world. After studying at the Academy and mastering the philosophy and the techniques of inquiry taught there, he founded the Lyceum, a school of scientific and philosophical thought and investigation. Applying his scientific methods of investigation to the study of literature, Aristotle answers Plato's accusations against "poetry" in a series of lectures known as the *Poetics*. Unlike **exoteric works** meant for general publication, the *Poetics* is an **esoteric work,** one meant for private circulation to those who attended the Lyceum. It therefore lacks the unity and coherence of Aristotle's other works, but it remains one of the most important critical influences on literary theory and criticism.

Aristotle's *Poetics* has become the cornerstone of Western literary criticism. By applying his analytic abilities to a definition of tragedy, Aristotle began in the *Poetics* a discussion of the components of a literary work that continues to the present day. Unfortunately, many critics and scholars mistakenly assume that the *Poetics* is a "how-to manual," defining and setting the standards for literature (particularly tragedy) for all time. Aristotle's purpose, however, was not to formulate a series of absolute rules for evaluating a tragedy, but to state the general principles of tragedy as he viewed them in his time while simultaneously responding to many of Plato's doctrines and arguments.

Even his choice of title, the *Poetics,* reveals Aristotle's purpose, for in Greek the word *poetikes* means "things that are made or crafted." Like a biologist, Aristotle will dissect tragedy to discover its component or crafted parts.

At the beginning of the *Poetics,* Aristotle notes that "epic poetry, tragedy, comedy, dithyrambic poetry, and most forms of flute and lyre playing all happen to be, in general, imitations." All seemingly differ in how and what they imitate, but nevertheless, Aristotle agrees with Plato that all the arts are imitations. In particular, the art of poetry exists because people are imitative creatures who enjoy such imitation. Plato contends that such pleasure can undermine the structure of society and all its values, but Aristotle disagrees. His disagreement is basically a metaphysical argument concerning the nature of imitation itself. While Plato posits that imitation is two steps removed from the truth or realm of the ideal (the poet imitating an object that is itself an imitation of an ideal form), Aristotle contends that poetry is more universal, more general than things as they are. For "it is not the function of the poet to relate what has happened, but what may happen—what is possible according to the law of probability or necessity." It is the historian, not the poet, who writes of what has already happened. The poet's task, declares Aristotle, is to write of what could happen. "Poetry, therefore, is a more philosophical and a higher thing than history: for poetry tends to express the universal, history the particular." In arguing that poets present things not as they are but as they should be, Aristotle rebuffs Plato's concept that the poet is merely imitating an imitation, for Aristotle's poet, with his emphasis on the universal, actually attains nearer to the ideal than does Plato's.

But not all imitations by poets are the same, for "writers of greater dignity imitated the noble actions of noble heroes; the less dignified sort of writers imitated the actions of inferior men." For Aristotle, "comedy is an imitation of base men . . . characterized not by every kind of vice but specifically by 'the ridiculous,' some error or ugliness that is painless and has no harmful effects." It is to tragedy written by poets imitating noble actions and heroes that Aristotle turns his attention.

Aristotle's definition of **tragedy** has perplexed and frustrated many a reader:

> Tragedy is, then, an imitation of a noble and complete action, having the proper magnitude; it employs language that has been artistically enhanced by each of the kinds of linguistic adornment, applied separately in the various parts of the play; it is presented in dramatic, not narrative form, and achieves, through the representation of pitiable and fearful incidents, the catharsis of such pitiable and fearful incidents.

When put in context with other ideas in the *Poetics*, such a complex definition highlights Aristotle's chief contributions to literary criticism:

1. Tragedy, or a work of art, is an imitation of nature that reflects a higher form of art exhibiting noble characters and noble deeds, the act of imitation itself giving us pleasure.

2. Art possesses form; that is, tragedy, unlike life, has a beginning, a middle, and an end, with each of the parts being related to every other part. A tragedy, then, is an organic whole with all its various parts interrelated.

3. In tragedy, concern for form must be applied to the characters as well as the structure of the play, for the tragic hero must be "a man who is not eminently good and just, yet whose misfortune is brought about not by vice or depravity, but by some error or frailty. He must be one who is highly renowned and prosperous." In addition, all tragic heroes must have a tragic flaw or **hamartia** that leads to their downfall in such a way as not to offend the audience's sense of justice.

4. The tragedy must have an emotional effect on its audience and "through pity and fear" effect a **catharsis**—that is, by the play's end, the audience's emotions should be purged, purified, or clarified (what Aristotle really meant by catharsis is debatable).

5. The universal, not the particular, should be stressed, for unlike history, which deals with what happens, poetry (or tragedy) deals with what could happen and is therefore closer to perfection or truth.

6. The poet must give close attention to diction or language itself, be it in verse, prose, or song, but ultimately it is the thoughts expressed through language that are of the utmost concern.

Interestingly, nowhere in the *Poetics* does Aristotle address the didactic value of poetry or literature. Unlike Plato, whose chief concern is the subject matter of poetry and its effects on the reader, Aristotle emphasizes literary form or structure, examining the component parts of a tragedy and how these parts must work together to produce a unified whole.

From the writings of these two philosopher-artists, Plato and Aristotle, issue the concerns, questions, and debates that have spearheaded the development of most literary schools of criticism. By addressing different aspects of these fifth-century Greeks' ideas and concepts, a variety of literary critics from the Middle Ages to the present have formulated theories of literary criticism that force us to ask different but equally legitimate questions of a text. But the shadows of Plato and Aristotle loom over much of what these later theorists espouse.

Horace (65–8 B.C.)

With the passing of the glory that was Greece and its philosopher-artists comes the grandeur of Rome and its chief stylist, Quintus Horatius Flaccus or simply Horace. A friend of Emperor Augustus and of many members of the Roman aristocracy, Horace enjoyed both the wealth and the influence of these associates. In a letter to the sons of one of his friends and patrons, Maecenas, Horace articulated what became the official canon of literary taste during the Middle Ages, the Renaissance, and through much of the neoclassic period. By reading this letter and his *Ars Poetica* or *The Art of Poetry,* any Roman aristocrat, any medieval knight, even Alexander Pope himself could learn the standards of good or proper literature.

Although Horace was probably acquainted with Aristotle's works, his concerns are quite different. Whereas both Plato and Aristotle decree that poets must, and do, imitate nature, Horace declares that poets must imitate other poets, particularly those of the past. Less concerned with metaphysics than his predecessors, Horace establishes the practical dos and don'ts for a writer. To be considered a good writer, he maintains, one should write about traditional subjects in novel ways. In addition, the poet should avoid all extremes in subject matter, word choice, vocabulary, and style. Gaining mastery in these areas can be achieved by reading and following the examples of the classical Greek and Roman authors. For example, since authors of antiquity began their epics in the middle of things, all epics must begin **in medias res.** Above all, writers should avoid appearing ridiculous and must therefore aim their sights low, not attempting to be a new Virgil or a new Homer.

Literature's ultimate aim, declares Horace, is to be *dulce et utile,* or sweet and useful; the best writings, he argues, both teach and delight. To achieve this goal, poets must understand their audience: the learned reader may wish to be instructed, while others may simply read to be amused. The poet's task is to combine both usefulness and delight in the same literary work.

Often oversimplified and misunderstood, Horace opts to give the would-be writer practical guidelines for the author's craft while leaving unchallenged many of the philosophical concerns of Plato and Aristotle. For Horace, a poet's greatest reward is the adulation of the public.

Longinus (First Century A.D.)

Although his date of birth and his national origin remain controversial, Longinus garners an important place in literary history for his treatise "On the Sublime." Probably a Greek, Longinus often peppers his Greek and Latin writings with Hebrew quotations, making him the first literary critic to borrow from a different literary tradition and earning him the right to be called the first comparative critic in literary history.

Unlike Plato, Aristotle, and Horace, who focus respectively on a work's essence, the constituent parts of a work, and literary taste, Longinus concentrates on single elements of a text, and he is the first critic to define a literary classic.

One cannot accurately judge a literary work, he argues, unless one is exceedingly well-read. A well-read critic can evaluate and recognize what is great or what Homer calls "sublime": "For that is really great which bears a repeated examination, and which it is difficult or rather impossible to withstand, and the memory of which is strong and hard to efface." Homer asserts that all readers are innately capable of recognizing the sublime, for "Nature has appointed us men to be no base or ignoble animals . . . for she implants in our souls the unconquerable love of whatever is elevated and more divine than we." When our intellects, our emotions, and our wills harmoniously respond to a given work of art, we know we have been touched by the sublime.

Until the late seventeenth century, few people considered Longinus' "On the Sublime" important or had even read it. By the eighteenth century, however, its significance was recognized, and it was quoted and debated by most public authors. Emphasizing the author, the work itself, and the reader's response, Longinus' critical method foreshadows New Criticism, reader-response, and other schools of twentieth-century criticism.

Dante Alighieri (1265–1321)

Born in Florence, Italy, during the Middle Ages, Dante is the only significant contributor to literary criticism since Longinus and the appearance of his "On the Sublime" approximately 1,000 years earlier. Like Longinus, Dante is concerned with the proper language for poetry.

Banished from his native Florence for political reasons, Dante wrote many of his works in exile, including his masterpiece, *The Divine Comedy*. As an introduction to the third and last section of this *Commedia*, entitled the *Paradiso*, Dante wrote a letter to Can Grande Della Scala explaining his literary theory. Known today as *Letter to Can Grande della Scala*, this work argues that the language spoken by the people (the vulgar tongue or the vernacular) is an appropriate and beautiful language for writing.

Until the publication of Dante's works, Latin was the universal language, and all important works—histories, church documents, and even governmental decrees—were written in this official church tongue. Only frivolous or popular works appeared in the "vulgar" language of the common people. But in his *Letter*, Dante asserts and establishes that the vernacular is an excellent and acceptable vehicle for works of literature.

In the *Letter* Dante also notes that he utilizes multiple levels of interpretation or symbolic meaning in *The Divine Comedy*. Since the time of St. Augustine and throughout the Middle Ages, the church fathers had followed a tradition of allegoric reading of scripture that interpreted many of the Old Testament laws and stories as symbolic or as allegories of Christ's actions. Such a semiotic interpretation—a reading of signs—had been applied only to scripture. Until Dante's *Commedia* no secular work had employed these principles of symbolic interpretation.

Praising the lyric poem and simply ignoring a discussion of genres, Dante establishes himself as the leading, if not the only, significant critic of the Middle Ages. Thanks to his declaring the common tongue an acceptable vehicle of expression for literature, literary works found an ever-increasing audience.

Sir Philip Sidney (1554–1586)

The paucity of literary criticism and theory during the Middle Ages is more than made up for by the abundance of critical activity during the Renaissance. One critic of this period far excels all others—Sir Philip Sidney.

As the representative scholar, writer, and gentleman of Renaissance England, Sidney is usually considered the first great English critic-poet. His work *An Apology for Poetry* (sometimes called *Defence of Poesy*) is the "epitome of the literary criticism of the Italian Renaissance" and the first influential piece of literary criticism in English history. With Sidney begins the English tradition and history of literary criticism.

In his critical theory as evidenced in *An Apology for Poetry*, Sidney is eclectic, borrowing and frequently amending the theories of Plato, Aristotle, Horace, and a few of his contemporaries among Italian critics. He begins his criticism by quoting from Aristotle; he writes, "Poesy therefore is an art of imitation, for so Aristotle termeth it in his word *mimesis,* that is to say, a representing, counterfeiting, or figuring forth"; but eight words later he adds a Horatian note, declaring poesy's chief end to be "to teach and delight." Like Aristotle, Sidney values poetry over history, law, and philosophy; but he takes Aristotle's idea one step further by declaring that poetry, above all the other arts and sciences, embodies truth.

Unlike his classical forefathers, Sidney best personifies the Renaissance period when he dictates his literary precepts. After ranking the different literary genres and declaring all to be instructive, he decrees poetry to excel all. Other genres he mocks (tragicomedy, for example) and adds more dictates to Aristotelian tragedy by insisting on unity of action, time, and place.

Throughout *An Apology for Poetry,* Sidney stalwartly defends poetry against those who would view it as a mindless or even immoral activity. At the essay's end, a passionate and somewhat platonically inspired poet places a curse on all those who do not love poetry. Echoes of such emotionality reverberate throughout the centuries in English literature, especially in British romantic writings.

John Dryden (1631–1700)

Poet laureate, dramatist, and critic, John Dryden more than any other English writer embodies the spirit and ideals of neoclassicism, the literary age that follows Sidney and the Renaissance. Dr. Samuel Johnson attributes to Dryden "the improvement, perhaps the completion of our meter, the refinement of our language, and much of the correctness of our sentiments." The most prolific writer of the Restoration, Dryden excelled in almost all genres. His lasting contribution to literary criticism, *An Essay of Dramatic Poesy,* highlights his genius in most of these genres.

The structure of Dryden's *An Essay of Dramatic Poesy* reflects his brilliance: during a naval battle between the English and the Dutch, four men are floating down a barge on the Thames River, each supporting a different aesthetic theory among those prominently espoused in Renaissance and neoclassic literary criticism. The Platonic and Aristotelian debate concerning art's being an imitation of nature begins the discussion. Nature, argues one debater, must be imitated directly, while another declares that writers should imitate the classical authors such as Homer, for such ancient writers were, after all, the best imitators of nature. Through the voice of Neander, Dryden presents the merits of both positions.

A lengthy discussion then ensues over the Aristotelian concept of the three unities of time, place, and action within a drama. Should the plot of a drama take place during one 24-hour cycle (time)? And in one location (place)? Should it be only a single plot with no subplots (action)? The position that a drama must keep the three unities unquestionably wins the debate.

Other concerns center on (1) the language or diction of a play, with the concluding emphasis being placed on "proper" speech; (2) issues of decorum—i.e., whether violent acts should appear on the stage, with the final speaker declaring it would be quite "improper"; (3) the differences between the English and French theaters, with the English drama winning out for its diversity, its use of the stage, and its Shakespearian tradition; and (4) the value of rhymed as opposed to blank verse in the drama, with rhymed verse being the victor—although Dryden later recanted this position and wrote many of his tragedies in blank verse.

Being a reflection of his age, Dryden sides with politesse, clarity, order, decorum, elegance, cleverness, and wit as controlling characteristics of literary works.

Alexander Pope (1688–1744)

Born into a Roman Catholic family in Protestant-controlled England, born a healthy infant but quickly deformed and twisted in body by spinal tuberculosis, and born at the beginning of the Neoclassic Age and becoming its literary voice by age 20, Alexander Pope embodies in his writings eighteenth-century thought and literary criticism. His early poems, such as *The Rape of the Lock*, "Eloisa to Abelard," and "Pastorals," establish him as a major British poet, but with the publication of his *Essay on Criticism*, he becomes for all practical purposes the "literary pope" of England.

Unlike previous literary critics and theorists, Pope in this essay directly addresses the critic rather than the poet, while simultaneously codifying neoclassic literary theory and criticism. Toward the end of the essay he does, however, speak to both critics and poets.

According to Pope, the golden age of criticism is the classical age, the age of Homer, Aristotle, Horace, and Longinus. They are the writers who discovered the rules and laws of a harmonious and ordered nature. It is the critic and poet's task first to know and then to copy these authors and not nature, for "to copy nature is to copy them [the classical authors]."

Pope asserts that the chief requirement of a good poet is that the poet possess natural genius coupled with a knowledge of the classics and an understanding of the rules of poetry (literature). Such knowledge must be tempered with politeness and grace, for "Without good breeding truth is disapproved / That only makes superior sense beloved."

Natural genius and good breeding being established, the critic/poet must then give heed, says Pope, to certain rules. To be a good critic or poet, one must follow the established traditions as defined by the ancients. Not surprisingly, Pope decrees what these rules are and how they should be applied to eighteenth-century verse. Great concern for poetic diction, the establishment of the heroic couplet as a standard for verse, and the personification of abstract ideas, for example, became fixed standards, while emotional outbreaks and free verse were *extraordinaire* and were considered unrefined.

Governed by rules, restraint, and good taste, poetry, as defined by Pope, seeks to reaffirm truths or absolutes already discovered by classical writers. The critic's task is clear: to validate and maintain classical values in the ever-shifting winds of cultural change. In effect, the critic becomes the custodian and defender of good taste and cultural values.

By affirming the imitation of the classical writers and through them of nature itself, and by establishing the acceptable or standard criteria of poetic language, Pope grounds his criticism in both the **mimetic** (imitation) and **rhetoric** (patterns of structure) literary theories. By the end of the 1700s, however, a major shift in literary theory occurs.

William Wordsworth (1770–1850)

By the close of the eighteenth century, the world had witnessed several major political rebellions—among them the American and French revolutions—along with exceptional social upheavals and prominent changes in philosophical thought. During this age of rebellion, a paradigmatic shift occurred in the way people viewed the world. Whereas the eighteenth century had valued order and reason, the emerging nineteenth-century worldview emphasized intuition as a proper guide to truth. The eighteenth-century mind likened the world to a great machine with all its parts operating harmoniously, but to the nineteenth-century perception the world was a living organism that was always growing and eternally becoming. Whereas the cities housed the centers of art and literature and set the standards of good taste for the rationalistic mind of the eighteenth century, the emerging nineteenth-century citizen saw a rural setting as the place where people could learn about and discover their inner selves. And, devaluing the empirical and rationalistic methodologies of the previous century, the nineteenth-century thinker believed that truth could be attained by tapping into the core of our humanity or our transcendental natures.

Such radical changes found their spokesperson in William Wordsworth. Born in Cockermouth, Cumberlandshire, and raised in the Lake district of England, Wordsworth completed his formal education at St. John's College, Cambridge, in 1791. After completing his grand tour of the Continent, he published *Descriptive Sketches* and then met one of his literary admirers and soon-to-be friends and coauthors, Samuel Taylor Coleridge. In 1798, Wordsworth and Coleridge published *Lyrical Ballads,* a collection of poems that heralded the beginning of British romanticism. In the ensuing 15-year period, Wordsworth wrote most of his best poetry, including *Poems in Two Volumes, The Excursion, Miscellaneous Poems,* and *The Prelude.* But it is *Lyrical Ballads* that ushers in the Romantic Age in English literature.

In an explanatory "Preface" written as an introduction to the second edition of *Lyrical Ballads,* Wordsworth espouses a new vision of poetry and the beginnings of a radical change in literary theory. His purpose, he notes, is "to choose incidents and situations from common life, and . . . describe them in language really used by men in situations . . . the manner in which we associate ideas in a state of excitement." Like Aristotle, Sidney, and Pope, Wordsworth concerns himself with the elements and subject matter of literature, but changes the emphasis: common men and women will people his poetry, not kings, queens, and aristocrats, for in "humble and rustic life" the poet finds that "the essential passions of the heart find a better soil in which they can attain their maturity, are less under restraint, and speak a plainer and more emphatic language."

Not only does Wordsworth suggest a radical change in subject matter, but he also dramatically shifts focus concerning poetry's "proper language." Unlike Pope and his predecessors, Wordsworth chooses "language really used by [people]"—everyday speech, not the inflated poetic diction of heroic couplets, the complicated rhyme schemes, and the convoluted figures of speech placed in the mouth of the typical eighteenth-century character. Wordsworth's rustics, like Michael and Luke in his poetic narrative *Michael,* will speak in the simple, everyday diction of their trade.

In addition to reshaping the focus of poetry's subject and language, Wordsworth redefines poetry itself: "For all good poetry is the spontaneous overflow of powerful feelings." Unlike Sidney, Dante, and Pope, who decree that poetry should be restrained, controlled, and reasoned, Wordsworth now highlights poetry's emotional quality. Imagination, not reason or disciplined thought, becomes its core.

After altering poetry's subject matter, language, and definition, Wordsworth than redefines the role of the poet. The poet is no longer the preserver of civilized values or proper taste, but "he is a man speaking to men: a man . . . endowed with more lively sensibility, more enthusiasm and tenderness, who has a greater knowledge of human nature and a more comprehensive soul than are supposed to be common among mankind." And this poet "has acquired a greater readiness and power in expressing what he thinks and feels, and especially those thoughts and feelings which, by his own choice, or from the structure of his own mind, arise in him without immediate external excitement." Such a poet need no longer follow a prescribed set of rules, for this artist may freely express his or her own individualism, valuing and writing about those feelings which are peculiarly the artist's.

Since Wordsworth defines poetry as "the spontaneous overflow of powerful feelings . . . [taking] its origin from emotion recollected in tranquility," his new kind of poet crafts a poem by internalizing a scene, circumstance or happening and "recollects" that occasion with its accompanying emotions at a later time when the artist can shape that remembrance into words. Poetry, then, is unlike biology or one of the other sciences, for it deals not with something that can be dissected or broken down into its constituent parts, but primarily with the imagination and feelings. Intuition, not reason, reigns.

But what of the reader? What part does the audience play in such a process? Toward the end of the "Preface," Wordsworth writes, "I have one request to make of my reader, which is, that in judging these poems he would decide by his own feelings genuinely, and not by reflection upon what will probably be the judgment of others." Wordsworth apparently hopes that his readers' responses and opinions of his poems will not depend on those critics who would freely dispense their evaluations. Wordsworth wants his readers to rely on their own feelings and their own imaginations as they grapple with the same emotions the poet felt when he first saw and then later "recollected in tranquility" the subject or circumstances of the poem itself. Through poetry, declares Wordsworth, the poet and the reader share such emotions.

This subjective experience of sharing emotions leads Wordsworth away from the preceding centuries' mimetic and rhetorical theories of criticism and toward a new development in literary theory: the **expressive school**—those critics who emphasize the individuality of the artist and the reader's privilege to share in this individuality. By expressing such individuality and valuing the emotions and the imagination as legitimate concerns in poetry, Wordsworth lays the foundation for English romanticism and broadens the scope of literary criticism and theory for both the nineteenth and twentieth centuries.

Hippolyte Adolphe Taine (1828–1893)

Wordsworth's romanticism, with its stress on intuition as a guide to learning ultimate truth and its belief that emotions and the imagination form the core of poetry's content, dominated literature and literary criticism throughout the first three decades of the nineteenth century, and its influence still continues today. With the rise of the Victorian era in the 1830s, reason, science, and a sense of historical determinism began to supplant romantic thought. The growing sense of historical and scientific determinism finally found its authoritative voice and culminating influence, in literary criticism and in many other disciplines, in Charles Darwin and his text *The Origin of Species*, published in 1859. Humankind was now demystified, for we finally knew our origins and understood our physiological development; science, it seemed, had provided us with the key to our past, an understanding of our present, and would help us determine our future if we relied upon the scientific method in all our endeavors.

Science's methodology, its philosophical assumptions, and its practical applications found an admiring adherent and a strong voice in the French historian and literary critic Hippolyte Taine. Born in Vouziers, France, Taine was a brilliant but unorthodox student at the École Normale Supérieure in Paris. After finishing his formal education, he taught in various schools throughout France, continuing his investigations in both aesthetics and history. During the 1850s he published various philosophical and aesthetic treatises, but his chief contribution to literary criticism and history is *The History of English Literature*, published in 1863. In this work, Taine crystallizes what is now known as the historical approach to literary analysis.

In the introduction to *History of English Literature*, Taine uses a scientific simile to explain his approach to literary criticism:

> What is your first remark on turning over the great, stiff leaves of a folio, the yellow sheets of a manuscript,—a poem, a code of laws, a declaration of faith? This, you say, was not created alone. It is but a mould, like a fossil shell, an imprint, like one of those shapes embossed in stone by an animal which lived and perished. Under the shell there was an animal, and behind the document there was a man. Why do you study the shell, except to represent to yourself the animal? So do you study the document only in order to know the man.

For Taine, then, a text is like a fossil shell that naturally contains the likeness of its inhabiter, who in this case is the author. To study only the text (discovering its date of composition or the accuracy of its historical references or allusions, for example) without considering the author and his or her inner psyche would therefore result in an incomplete analysis. An investigation of both the text and the author, Taine believed, would result in an accurate understanding of the literary work.

To understand any literary text, Taine asserts that we must examine the environmental causes that joined in its creation. He divides such influences into three main categories: race, milieu, and moment. By race, Taine posits that authors of the same race, or those born and raised in the same country, share particular intellectual beliefs, emotions, and ways of understanding. By examining each author's inherited and learned personal characteristics, Taine believes we will then be able to understand more fully the author's text. In addition, we must also examine the author's milieu or surroundings. English citizens, he believed, respond differently to life than do French or Irish citizens. Accordingly, by examining the culture of the author, Taine asserts that we can understand more fully the intellectual and cultural concerns that inevitably surface in an author's text. And lastly, Taine maintains that we must investigate an author's epoch or moment—that is, the time period in which the text was written. Such information will reveal the dominant ideas or worldview held by people at that particular time and will therefore help us identify and understand the characters' actions, motivations, and concerns more fully than if we did not have such information.

Ultimately, for Taine the text becomes a literary object that can be dissected to discover its meaning. By examining the actual text itself, the circumstances of place and race, and the historical times in which the text was written, we will realize that no text is written in a vacuum, but each is instead the result of its history.

Matthew Arnold (1822–1888)

In the "Preface to *Lyrical Ballads*," Wordsworth asserts that "poetry is the breath and finer spirit of all knowledge; it is the impassioned expression which is the countenance of all science." Such a lofty statement concerning the nature and role of poetry finds an advocate in Matthew Arnold, the self-appointed voice for English Victorianism, the literary epoch immediately following Wordsworth's romanticism.

Born during the romantic era, Matthew Arnold was the son of an English educator. Following in his family's tradition, Arnold attended Oxford, and upon graduation accepted a teaching position at Oriel College. He spent most of his professional life (nearly 35 years), however, as an inspector of schools. By age 35, he had already written most of his poetry, among his most famous poems being "Dover Beach," "The Scholar-Gipsy," and "Sohrab and Rustum."

During Arnold's early career, reactions against Wordsworth's romanticism and its adherents began to occur. Writers, philosophers, and scientists began to give more credence to empirical and rationalistic methods for discovering the nature of their world than to the Wordsworthian concepts of emotion, individualism, and intuition as pathways to truth. With the publication of Charles Darwin's *The Origin of Species* in 1859 and the writings of Herbert Spencer and the philosopher David Friedrich Strauss, science seemingly usurped the place of Wordsworth's religion of nature and the beliefs of most other traditional religions, while philosophy became too esoteric and therefore less relevant as a possible vehicle for understanding reality for the average Victorian. Into this void steps Arnold, proclaiming that poetry can provide the necessary truths, values, and guidelines for society.

Fundamental to Arnold's literary theory and criticism is his reapplication of classical criteria to literature. Quotes and borrowing of ideas from Plato, Aristotle, Longinus and other classical writers pepper his criticism. From Aristotle's *Poetics,* for example, Arnold adapts his idea that the best poetry is of a "higher truth and seriousness" than history or for that matter any other human subject or activity. Like Plato, Arnold believes that literature reflects the society in which it is written and thereby heralds its values and concerns. Like Longinus, he attempts to define a classic, and decrees that such a work belongs to the "highest" or "best class." And in attempting to support many of his other ideas, he also cites the later "classical" writers such as Dante, Shakespeare, and Milton.

For Arnold, poetry—not religion, science or philosophy—is humankind's crowning activity. He notes, "More and more [human]kind will discover that we have to turn to poetry to interpret life for us, to console us, to sustain us. Without poetry, our science will appear incomplete; and most of what now passes with us for religion and philosophy will be replaced by poetry." And in the best of this poetry, he declares, we find "in the eminent degree, truth and seriousness." Equating "seriousness" with moral excellence, Arnold asserts that the best poetry can and does provide standards of excellence—a yardstick by which both Arnold and his society should judge themselves.

In his pivotal essays "The Study of Poetry" and "The Function of Criticism at the Present Time," Arnold crystallizes his critical position. Like Plato's critic, Arnold reaffirms but slightly amends the social role of criticism: creating "a current of true and fresh ideas." To accomplish this goal, the critic must avoid becoming embroiled in politics or any other activity that would lead to a form of bias, for the critic must view society "disinterestedly," keeping aloof from the world's mundane affairs. In turn, such aloofness will benefit all of society, for the critic will be able to pave the way for high culture—a prerequisite for the poet and for the writing of the best poetry.

But how may the best poetry be achieved or discovered? By establishing objective criteria whereby we can judge whether any poem contains or achieves, in Aristotelian terms, "higher truth or seriousness." The critic's task is "to have always in one's mind lines and expressions of the great masters, and to apply them as a touchstone to other poetry." By comparing the newly written lines to those classical poems that contain elements of the "sublime," the critic will instantly know whether a new poem is good or bad.

In practice, such apparent objectivity in criticism becomes quite subjective. Whose judgments, for example, shall we follow? Shall lines written by Homer and Dante be considered excellent? How about Sidney's, or even Aristophanes'? Need the critic rank all past poets in an attempt to discover who is great and who is not in order to create a basis for such comparisons and value judgments? And whose moral values shall become the yardstick whereby we judge poetry? Arnold's only?

Such "objective" touchstone theory redefines the task of the literary critic and introduces a subjective approach in literary criticism. No longer the interpreter of a literary work, the critic now functions as an authority on values, culture, and tastes. This new literary watchdog must guard and defend high culture and its literature while simultaneously defining what high culture and literature really are.

Decreeing the critic to be the preserver of society's values and poetry to be its most important activity, Arnold became the recognized spokesperson for Victorian England and its literature. By taking Wordsworth's concept of the poet one step further, Arnold separated both the critic and the poet from their society in order to create a type of poetry and criticism that could supposedly rescue society from its baser elements and preserve its most noble characteristics.

Henry James (1843–1916)

While Arnold was decreeing how poetry would rescue humanity from its baser elements and would lead us all to truth, literary works were also being written in other genres, particularly that of the novel. Throughout both the Romantic and Victorian eras, for example, people in England and America were reading such works as *Wuthering Heights, Vanity Fair, The House of the Seven Gables,* and *Great Expectations.* Few critics, however, were providing for either the writers or the readers of this genre a body of theory or criticism like the one being formulated for poetry. As Henry James notes in his critical essay "The Art of Fiction" in 1884, the English novel "had no air of having a theory, a conviction, a consciousness of itself behind it—of being the expression of an artistic faith, the result of choice and comparison." James himself provides us with such a theory.

Born in New York City in 1843, Henry James enjoyed the privileges of education, travel, and money. Throughout his early life, he and his family (including his brother William, who is considered the father of American pragmatic philosophy) traveled to the capitals of Europe, visiting the major sites and meeting the leading writers and scholars of the day. Having all things European injected early into his life and thoughts, James decided he wanted to be a lawyer and enrolled in Harvard Law School. He quickly discovered that writing, not law, captivated him, and he abandoned law school for a career in writing. By 1875, the early call of Europe on his life had to be answered, and James, a bachelor for life, settled permanently in Europe and began his writing career in earnest.

Noted for his short stores—"The Real Thing," "The Beast in the Jungle," and "The Jolly Corner"—and his novels—*The American, The Portrait of a Lady, The Bostonians,* and *The Turn of the Screw,* among others—James's favorite theme is the conflict he perceives between Europe and America. The seasoned aristocracy with its refined manners and tastes is often infiltrated in his stories by the naive American who seemingly lacks refined culture and discernment. In addition to being a practicing writer, James is also concerned with developing a theory of writing, particularly for the novel. And in his critical essay "The Art of Fiction" he provides us with the first well-articulated theory of the novel in English literature.

In "The Art of Fiction," James states that "a novel is in its broadest definition a personal, a direct impression of life: that, to begin with, constitutes its value, which is greater or less according to the intensity of the impression"; and that "the only obligation to which in advance we may hold a novel, without incurring the accusation of being arbitrary, is that it be interesting. The ways in which it is at liberty to accomplish this result [are] innumerable." From the start, James's theory rejects the romantic notion of either Wordsworth or Coleridge that the reader suspend disbelief while reading a text. For James, a text must first be realistic, a representation of life as it is and one that is recognizable to its readers. Bad novels, declares James, are either romantic or scientific; good novels show us life in action and, above all else, are interesting.

Bad novels, James continues, are written by bad authors, whereas good novels are written by good authors. Unlike weak authors, good writers are good thinkers who can select, evaluate, and imaginatively utilize the "stuff of life" (the facts or pictures of reality) in their work. These writers also recognize that a work of art is organic. The work itself is not simply an amassing of realistic data from real-life experiences, but has a life of its own that grows according to its own principles or themes. The writer must acknowledge this fact and distance himself or herself from directly telling the story. Shunning the omniscient narrator as the point of view for relating the story, James asserts that a more indirect point of view is essential so that the author *shows* characters, actions, and emotions to the reader rather than telling us about them. By showing rather than telling us about his characters and their actions, James believes that he creates a greater illusion of reality than if he presents his story through one point of view or one character. Ultimately, however, the reader must decide the worth of the text, and "nothing of course, will ever take the place of the good old fashion of 'liking' a work of art or not liking it: the most improved criticism will not abolish that primitive, that ultimate test."

Thanks to Henry James, the genre of the novel became a respectable topic for literary critics. With his emphasis on realism and "the stuff of life," James formulates a theory of fiction that is still discussed and debated today.

Modern Literary Criticism

Matthew Arnold's death in 1888 (and to a lesser degree Henry James's death in 1916) marks a transitional period in literary criticism. Like Dryden, Pope, and Wordsworth before him, Arnold was the recognized authority and leading literary critic of his day, and it is his theories and criticism that embody the major ideas of his era. The passing of Arnold ends the predominance of any one person or set of ideas representing a broad time period or literary movement. After Arnold, literary theory and criticism become splintered and more diversified, with no one theory or idea dominating for any one great period of time. At the end of the nineteenth century, most critics emphasized either a biographical or a historical approach to the text. Utilizing Taine's historical interests in a text and Henry James's newly articulated theory of the novel, many critics investigated a text as if it were the embodiment of its author or a historical artifact. No single, universally recognized voice, however, dominates literary theory in the years that follow Arnold or James. Instead, many distinctive literary voices give rise to a host of differing and exciting ways to examine a text.

What follows in the twentieth century is a variety of "schools of criticism," with each school asking legitimate, relevant but different questions concerning a text. Most of these schools abandon the **holistic approach** to literary study, which investigates, analyzes, and interprets all elements of the artistic situation, in favor of concentrating on one or more specific aspects. For example, modernism (and in particular New Criticism, the first critical movement of the twentieth century) wishes to break from the past and seemingly disavow the cultural influences on a work of literature. The text, these critics declare, will interpret the text. On the other hand, New Historicism, the newest school of thought to appear, argues that most critics' historical consciousness must be reawakened, for in reality the fictional text and its historical and cultural milieu are amazingly similar. For these critics, a reader can never fully discern the truth about either a historical or a literary text, for truth itself is perceived differently from one era to another. The text-only criticism of the early twentieth century therefore appears biased and incomplete to these New Historicists.

In the remaining chapters of this book we will examine eight of the most prominent schools of twentieth-century interpretation. For each of these diverse schools we will note the philosophical tenets that underlie their literary theory. Most, if not all, have borrowed ideas, principles, and concerns from the literary critics and theories already discussed. We will examine closely what they borrow from these past schools of criticism, what they amend, and what concepts they choose to add. We will also note each school's historical development, examining how new schools of criticism often appear as a reaction to a previously existing one.

After explaining each school's historical development, its working assumptions, and its methodology, we will then examine a student-written essay that interprets one of the literary works included at the back of this text from the point of view of the particular school of criticism under discussion. A close examination of such an essay will allow us to see how the theories of the various schools of criticism can be applied directly to a text, while simultaneously highlighting the various emphases of each critical school.

By becoming acquainted with the various schools of criticism, we can begin to examine our own theory of interpretation and to articulate our own principles of criticism. We will then realize that there is no such thing as an innocent reading of a text, for all readings presuppose either a conscious or unconscious, an articulated and well-informed or a piecemeal and uninformed reading of a literary work. An informed and intelligent reading is the better option.

Further Reading

Con Davis, Robert, and Laurie Finke, eds. *Literary Criticism and Theory: The Greeks to the Present*. New York: Longman, 1989.

Crane, R. S., et al. *Critics and Criticism: Ancient and Modern*. Chicago: University of Chicago Press, 1952.

Schorer, Mark, et al. *Criticism: The Foundations of Modern Literary Judgment*. New York: Harcourt, 1958.

Selden, Raman, ed. *The Theory of Criticism: From Plato to the Present*. New York: Longman, 1988.

Watson, George. *The Literary Critics*. London: Woburn Press, 1973.

Wimsatt, William K., and Cleanth Brooks. *Literary Criticism: A Short History*. New York: Knopf, 1964.

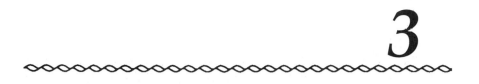

New Criticism

Introduction

Dominating American literary criticism from the early 1930s to the 1960s, **New Criticism** can no longer be considered new. Its theoretical ideas, its terminology, and its critical methods are, more frequently than not, disparaged by present-day critics who themselves are introducing new ideas concerning literary theory. Despite its current unpopularity among critics, New Criticism dominated literary theory and practice throughout much of the twentieth century and stands as one of the most important English-speaking contributions to literary critical analysis.

The name New Criticism came into popular use to describe this approach to understanding literature with the 1941 publication of John Crowe Ransom's *The New Criticism,* which contained Ransom's personal analysis of several of his contemporaries among theorists and critics. Ransom himself was a Southern poet, a critic, and one of the leading advocates of this evolving movement. In *The New Criticism* he calls for an **ontological critic,** one who will recognize that a **poem** (used in New Criticism as a synonym for any literary work) is a concrete entity like Leonardo da Vinci's "Mona Lisa" or the score of Handel's *Messiah* or even any chemical element such as iron or gold. Like these concrete objects, a poem can be analyzed to discover its true or correct meaning independent of its author's intention or emotional state, or the values and beliefs of either its author or its reader. Since this belief concerning the nature of a poem rests at the center of this movement's critical ideas, it is not surprising that the title of Ransom's book quickly became the official calling card for this approach to literary analysis.

Called modernism, formalism, aesthetic criticism, textual criticism, or ontological criticism throughout its long and successful history, New Criticism does not represent a coherent body of critical theory and methodology espoused by all its followers. At best, New Criticism and its adherents (called New Critics) are an eclectic group, challenging, borrowing, and changing terminology, theory, and practices from one another while simultaneously asserting a common core of basic ideas. Their ultimate unity stems from their opposition to the methods of literary analysis prevailing in academia in the first part of the twentieth century.

Historical Development

At the beginning of the twentieth century (often dubbed the start of the Modernist period, or **Modernism**), historical and biographical research dominated literary scholarship. Criticism's function, many believed, was to discover the historical context of the text and to ascertain how the authors' lives influenced their writings. Such **extrinsic analysis** (examining elements outside the text to uncover the text's meaning) became the norm in the English departments of many American universities and colleges. Other forms of criticism and interpretation were often intermingled with this emphasis on history and biography. Some critics, for example, believed we should appreciate the text for its beauty. For these **impressionistic critics,** how we feel and what we personally see in a work of art is what really matters. Others were more philosophical, arguing a *naturalistic* view of life that emphasizes the importance of scientific thought in literary analysis. For advocates of **naturalism,** human beings are simply animals who are caught in a world that operates on definable scientific principles and who respond somewhat instinctively to their environment and to their internal drives. Still other critics, the **New Humanists,** valued the moral qualities of art. Declaring that human experience is basically ethical, these critics demand that literary analysis be based on the moral values exhibited in a text. Finally, remnants of nineteenth-century **romanticism** asserted themselves. For the romantic scholar, literary study concerns itself with artists' feelings and attitudes exhibited in their work. Known as the **expressive school,** this romantic view values the individual artist's experiences as evidenced in the text.

Along with impressionism, the New Humanism, and naturalism, this romantic view of life and art was rejected by the New Critics. In declaring the objective existence of the poem, the New Critics assert that only the poem itself can be objectively evaluated, not the feelings, attitudes, values, and beliefs of either the author or the reader. Because they concern themselves primarily with an examination of the work itself and not its historical context or biographical elements, the New Critics belong to a broad classification of literary criticism called **formalism.** Being formalists, the New Critics espouse what many call "the text and text alone" approach to literary analysis.

Such an approach to textual criticism automatically leads to many divergent views concerning the elements that constitute what the New Critics call the poem. Since many of the practitioners of this formalistic criticism disagree with one another concerning the various elements that make up the poem and hold differing approaches to textual analysis, it is difficult to cite a definitive list of critics who consider themselves New Critics. We can, however, group together those critics who hold to some of the same New Critical assumptions concerning poetic analysis. Among this group are John Crowe Ransom, René Wellek, W. K. Wimsatt, R. P. Blackmur, I. A. Richards, Robert Penn Warren, and Cleanth Brooks. Thanks to the publication of the 1938 college text *Understanding Poetry* by Brooks and Warren, New Criticism emerged in American universities as the leading form of textual analysis from the late 1930s until the early 1960s.

Although New Criticism emerged as a powerful force in the 1940s, its roots go back to the early 1900s. Two British critics and authors, T. S. Eliot and I. A. Richards, helped lay the foundation for this form of formalistic analysis. From Eliot, New Criticism borrows its insistence that criticism be directed toward the poem, not the poet. The poet, declares Eliot, does not infuse the poem with his or her personality and emotions, but uses language in such a way as to incorporate within the poem the impersonal feelings and emotions common to all humankind. Poetry is not, then, the freeing of the poet's emotions, but an escape from them. Since the poem is an impersonal formulation of common feelings and emotions, the poem unites the poet's impressions and ideas in some mystical or unseen way, producing a text that is not a mere reflection of the poet's personal feelings.

The New Critics also borrow Eliot's belief that the reader of poetry must be instructed concerning literary technique. A good reader, maintains Eliot, perceives the poem structurally, resulting in good criticism. Such a reader must necessarily be trained in reading good poetry (especially the poetry of the Elizabethans, John Donne, and other metaphysical poets), and be well acquainted with established poetic traditions. A poor reader, on the other hand, simply expresses his or her personal reactions and emotions concerning a text. Such a reader is untrained in literary technique and craftsmanship. Following Eliot's lead, the New Critics declare that there are both good and bad readers and good and bad criticism. A poor reader and poor criticism, for example, may argue that a poem can mean anything its reader or its author wishes it to mean. On the other hand, a good critic and good criticism would assert that only through a detailed structural analysis of a poem can the correct interpretation arise.

Eliot also lends New Criticism some of its technical vocabulary. Thanks to Eliot, for example, the term *objective correlative* has become a staple in poetic jargon. According to Eliot, the only way of expressing emotion through art is by finding an **objective correlative:** a set of objects, a situation, a chain of events or reactions that can effectively serve to awaken in the reader the emotional response which the author desires without being a direct statement of that emotion. When the external facts are thus presented in the poem, they somehow come together and immediately evoke an emotion. The New Critics readily adopted and advanced such an impersonal theory concerning the arousing of emotions in poetry.

From Eliot's British contemporary, I. A. Richards, a psychologist and literary critic, New Criticism borrows a term that has become synonymous with its methods of analysis: **practical criticism.** In an experiment at Cambridge University, Richards distributed to his students copies of poems minus such information as the authors, dates, and oddities of spelling and punctuation, and asked them to record their responses. From this data he identified the difficulties that poetry presents to its readers: matters of interpretation, poetic techniques, and specific meanings. From this analysis Richards devised an intricate system for arriving at a poem's meaning, including a minute scrutiny of the text. It is this close scrutiny or "close reading" of a text that has become synonymous with New Criticism.

From Eliot, Richards, and other critics, then, New Criticism borrows, amends, and adds its own ideas and concerns. Although few of its advocates would agree upon many tenets, definitions, and techniques, there exists a core of assumptions that allows us to identify adherents of this critical approach to texts.

Assumptions

New Criticism begins by assuming that the study of imaginative literature is valuable; to study poetry or any literary work is to engage oneself in an **aesthetic experience** (the effects produced upon an individual when contemplating a work of art) that can lead to truth. The truth discoverable through an aesthetic experience, however, is distinguishable from the truth that science provides us. Science speaks propositionally, telling us whether a statement is demonstrably either true or false. Pure water, says science, freezes at 32 degrees Fahrenheit, not 30 or 31. Poetic truth, on the other hand, involves the use of the imagination and intuition, a form of mystical truth that according to the New Critics is discernible only in poetry. In the aesthetic experience alone we are cut off from mundane or practical concerns, from mere rhetorical, doctrinal or propositional statements. Through an examination of the poem itself we can ascertain truths that cannot be perceived through the language and logic of science. Science and poetry, then, provide different but equally valid sources of knowledge.

Like many other critical theories, New Criticism's theory begins by defining its object of concern, in this case a poem. New Critics assert that a poem has **ontological** status; that is, it possesses its own being and exists like any other object. In effect, a poem becomes an artifact, an objective, self-contained, autonomous entity with its own structure.

Having declared a poem an object in its own right, the New Critics then develop their **objective theory of art.** For them, the meaning of a poem must not be equated with its author's feelings or stated or implied intentions. To believe that a poem's meaning is nothing more than an expression of the private experiences or intentions of its author is to affirm what the New Critics call the **Intentional Fallacy.** Because they believe that the poem is an object, they claim that every poem must also be a public text that can be understood by applying the standards of public discourse, not simply the private experience, concerns, and vocabulary of its author.

That the poem is somehow related to its author cannot be denied. In his essay "Tradition and the Individual Talent," T. S. Eliot states the New Critical position concerning this relationship between the author and his or her work. The basis of Eliot's argument is an analogy. We all know, he says, that certain chemical reactions occur in the presence of a **catalyst,** an element that causes but is not affected by the reaction. For example, if we place hydrogen peroxide, a common household disinfectant, in a clear bottle and expose it to the sun's rays, we will no longer have hydrogen peroxide. Acting as a catalyst, the sun's rays will cause a chemical reaction to occur, breaking down the hydrogen peroxide into its various parts while the sun's rays remain unaffected.

Similarly, the poet's mind serves as a catalyst for the reaction that yields the poem. During the creative process, the poet's mind, serving as the catalyst, brings together the experiences of the author's personality (not the author's personality traits or attributes), into an external object and a new creation: the poem. It is not, then, the personality traits of the author that coalesce to form the poem, but the experiences of the author's personality. In apparently distinguishing between the personality and the mind of the poet, Eliot asserts that the created entity, the poem, is about the experiences of the author that are similar to all of our experiences. By structuring these experiences, the poem allows us to examine them objectively.

Dismissing the poet's stated or supposed intentions as a means of discovering the text's meaning, the New Critics give little credence to the biographical or contextual history of a poem. If the Intentional Fallacy is correct, then unearthing biographical data will not help us ascertain a poem's meaning. Likewise, trying to place a poem in its social or political context will tell us much social or political history concerning the time when the poem was written; while such information may indeed help in understanding the poem, its real meaning cannot reside in this extrinsic or outside-the-text information.

Of particular importance to the New Critics are individual words' etymology. Since the words of a poem sometimes change meaning from one time period to another, the critic often needs to be involved in historical research, discovering what individual words meant at the time the poem was written. The *Oxford English Dictionary* (a dictionary that cites a word's various historical meanings chronologically) then becomes one of the critic's best friends.

Placing little emphasis on the author, the social context, or a text's historical situation as a source for discovering a poem's meaning, the New Critics also assert that a reader's emotional response to the text is neither important nor equivalent to its interpretation. Such an error in judgment, called the **Affective Fallacy,** confuses what a poem is (its meaning) with what it does. If we derive our standard of criticism, say the New Critics, from the psychological effects of the poem, we are then left with impressionism or, worse yet, relativism, believing that a poem has innumerable valid interpretations.

Where, then, can we find the poem's meaning? According to the New Critics, it does not reside in the author, the historical or social context of the poem, or even in the reader. Since the poem itself is an artifact or objective entity, its meaning must reside within its own structure. Like all other objects, a poem and its structure can be scientifically analyzed. Accordingly, careful scrutiny reveals that a poem's structure operates according to a complex series of laws. By closely analyzing this structure, the New Critics believe that they have devised a methodology and a standard of excellence that we can apply to all poems to discover their correct meanings. It is the critic's job, they conclude, to ascertain the structure of the poem, to see how it operates to achieve its unity, and to discover how meaning evolves directly from the poem itself.

According to New Criticism, the poet is an organizer of the content of human experience. Structuring the poem around the often confusing and sometimes contradictory experiences of life, the poet crafts the poem in such a way that the text stirs its readers' emotions and causes readers to reflect upon the poem's contents. Being an artisan, the poet is most concerned with effectively developing the poem's structure, for the artist realizes that the meaning of a text emerges chiefly from its structure. The poet's chief concern, maintain the New Critics, is how meaning is achieved through the various and sometimes conflicting elements operating in the poem itself.

The chief characteristic of the poem and therefore its structure is co-herence or interrelatedness. Perhaps borrowing their ideas from the writings of Samuel Taylor Coleridge, the New Critics posit the **organic unity** of a poem—that is, the concept that all parts of a poem are interrelated and interconnected, with each part reflecting and helping to support the poem's central idea. Such organic unity allows for the harmonization of conflicting ideas, feelings, and attitudes, and results in the poem's oneness.

Since the poem's chief characteristic is its oneness, New Critics believe that form and content are inseparable. In other words, *form,* or the technique used to craft the poem, is indivisible from the poem's *content.* Put another way, a poem's beauty (form) and its truth (content) cannot be separated. It is inconceivable, then, say the New Critics, to believe that a poem can be equated with paraphrased prose. Declaring such erroneous belief the **Heresy of Paraphrase,** New Critics maintain that a poem is not simply a statement that is either true or false, but a bundle of harmonized tensions and resolved stresses, more like a ballet or musical composition than a statement of prose. No simple paraphrase can equal the meaning of the poem, for the poem itself resists through its inner tensions any prose statement that attempts to encapsulate its meaning. Paraphrases may help readers in their initial understanding of the poem, but such prose statements must be considered working hypotheses that may or may not lead to a true understanding of the poem's meaning. In no way should paraphrased statements about a poem, insist the New Critics, be considered equivalent to the poem's structure.

Methodology

Believing in the thematic and structural unity of a poem, New Critics begin their search for meaning within the text's structure by finding the tensions and conflicts that are eventually resolved into a harmonious whole. Such a search leads them directly to the poem's diction or word choice. Unlike scientific discourse, with its precise terminology, poetic diction often has multiple meanings and can immediately set up a series of tensions within the poem. Many words, for example, have both a **denotation** (dictionary meaning) and a **connotation** (implied meaning). A word's denotation may be in direct conflict with its connotative meaning determined by the context of the poem. In addition, it may be difficult to differentiate among the various denotations of a word. For example, if someone writes that "a *fat* head enjoys the *fat* of the land," the reader must note the various denotative and connotative differences in the word *fat*. At the start of poetic analysis, then, conflicts or tensions exist by the very nature of poetic diction. This tension New Critics call **ambiguity.** At the end of a close reading of the text, however, all such ambiguities will and must be resolved.

Even on a surface level of reading, a poem is thus a reconciliation of conflicts, of opposing meanings and tensions. Its form and content being indivisible, it is the critic's job to analyze the poetic diction to ascertain such tensions. Although various New Critics give a variety of names to the poetic elements that govern a poem's structure, all agree that the poem's meaning is derived from the oscillating tensions and conflicts that are brought to the surface through the poetic diction. Cleanth Brooks, for example, claims that the chief elements in a poem are **paradox** and **irony,** two closely related terms that imply that a word or phrase is qualified or even undercut by its context. Other critics use the word **tension** to describe the opposition or conflicts operating within the text. For these critics, tension implies the conflicts between a word's denotation and its connotation, between a literal detail and a figurative one, and between an abstract and a concrete detail.

Since conflict, ambiguity, or tension controls the poem's structure, the meaning of the poem can be discovered only by analyzing contextually the poetic elements and diction. Because context governs meaning, meanings of individual words or phrases are therefore context-related and unique to the specific poem in which they occur. It is the job of the critic, then, to unravel the various apparent conflicts and tensions within each poem and to show that ultimately the poem is an **organic unity**—that is, that all parts of a poem are interrelated and support the poem's chief paradox. This paradox can usually be expressed in one sentence that contains the main tension and the resolution of that tension. It is this key idea to which all other elements of the poem must relate. By searching out the text's use of irony, paradox, ambiguity, denotations, connotations, figures of speech, literal and figurative language, tone, theme, and meter, the critic can discover the poem's central paradox and therefore its interpretation by using only the text itself.

According to the principles of New Criticism, a *good* critic examines a poem's structure by scrutinizing its poetic elements, rooting out and showing its inner tensions, and demonstrating how the poem supports its overall meaning by reconciling these tensions into a unified whole. By implication, *bad* critics are those who insist upon imposing extrinsic evidence such as historical or biographical information upon a text to discover its meaning. These critics fail to realize that the text itself elicits its own meaning. They flounder in their analysis, often believing that a text can have multiple meanings.

Although New Critics may first approach the text through paraphrase (realizing, of course, that a paraphrase does not equal the poem's meaning), generally they begin their analysis by examining the language of the poem itself. Such analysis immediately highlights some of the poem's tensions, revealing ambiguities and paradoxes. For example, in the essay that follows at the end of this chapter, the student (a New Critic) demonstrates the ambiguity that arises when Browning's duke uses the word *last* to refer to his duchess. Does *last* mean the duke's former wife? Were there any others before this *last* one? Will he also refer to the new duchess he is presently seeking as his *last* duchess sometime in the future? Answers to these questions, insist New Critics, must be found within the structure of the text itself by examining the poem's diction and other structural elements.

While investigating a poem's diction, New Critics will often simultaneously seek out any figurative element evidenced in the text, such as **simile** (the comparison of two unlike objects using *like* or *as*), **metaphor** (the direct comparison of two unlike objects in which the qualities of one are taken on by the other), **personification** (attributing human qualities to animals, ideas, or an inanimate object), and a host of other terms describing the use of figurative language in poetic diction. At first, an examination of the text's figurative language may lead to seemingly contradictory interpretations. Upon further analysis, however, a New Critic will show how these apparent contradictions all coalesce to support the poem's chief paradox and the text's organic unity.

Having revealed through such an analysis the various tensions existing in the poem, New Critics may then turn their attention to the poem's rhyme scheme, its meter, and other technical aspects of **prosody.** Through this analysis the critic will show how the technical elements of the text aid in formulating the contextual meaning of the poem's language.

Finally, the New Critic may examine the text for tone (another word for the mood created by the text) or any imagery, paradox, or irony that seems to unite the entire poem, thereby giving it its organic unity and meaning.

This close reading of a text, claim the New Critics, allows alert readers to discover and understand the meaning of a poem. It also provides readers with a set of norms that will assist them in formulating their interpretation. Such an objective scrutiny of the text, they maintain, will aid readers in finding the correct interpretation of the poem (one that evidences the text's organic unity), rather than involving readers in an unguided and undisciplined search for the poem's meaning. By declaring a poem to have ontological status, the New Critics assert that the poem itself will reveal its own meaning.

In the sample essay that follows, note how the student uses the tenets of New Criticism to arrive at an interpretation of Robert Browning's poem "My Last Duchess" (found at the back of this book). By analyzing the poem's poetic diction, the student uncovers ambiguities and tensions within the poem. Such tensions, however, are resolved by the end of the analysis by discovering the poem's organic unity and seeing how the various elements of the text support and enhance the poem's central paradox.

Further Reading

Brooks, Cleanth. "My Credo: Formalist Critics." *Kenyon Review* 13 (1951): 72–81.
Brooks, Cleanth, and Robert Penn Warren, eds. *Understanding Poetry.* New York: Holt, 1938.
Ransom, John Crowe. *The New Criticism.* New York: New Directions, 1941.
Wellek, René, and Austin Warren. *Theory of Literature.* Revised. New York: Harcourt, 1977.
Wimsatt, W. K. *The Verbal Icon.* Lexington: University of Kentucky Press, 1954.
Winters, Yvor. *In Defense of Reason.* Denver: Swallow Press, 1947.

Student Essay

Browning's Self-Revealing Duke

In 1842, Robert Browning's "My Last Duchess" and its companion poem "Count Gismond" appeared in a collection of poems entitled *Dramatic Lyrics.* Entitled "Italy" and "France" respectively, the two poems deal with the love of husband and wife while simultaneously complementing and contrasting with one another. While Browning writes "Count Gismond" from the perspective of a woman who loved her husband, "My Last Duchess," the more famous of the two, is a dramatic monologue of an animalistic Duke who murders his young wife because he cannot love her.

Upon a close reading of "My Last Duchess," it is evident that irony and paradox rule every aspect of the poem. While showing an envoy of the Count of Tyrol around his extensive art galleries, the Italian Duke of Ferrara bargains for the hand of the Count's daughter in marriage. In the process, he unintentionally reveals his evil nature both to his silent visitor and to the reader through paradoxical meanings in his speech. Unaware of the significance of his speech, the Duke demonstrates that he is a jealous and arrogant man who wishes to control people and indulges in his power to do so. "My Last Duchess," then, is a poem about an egocentric Duke and not, as the title might suggest, about the Duke's last wife.

Through dramatic irony the poem develops its central paradox and its meaning. The Duke, not perceiving the meaning of his own words in the same way the reader does, gives the reader insight into his personality, ignorantly furnishing the damning evidence himself. Pointing toward the painting on the wall, he intends to speak about his "last Duchess," but both the emissary and the reader realize the irony contained in the adjective *last*. Although the Duke's *last* Duchess was his previous Duchess, she was obviously neither his first nor will she be his last wife. The persona thus immediately brings attention to himself, for the reader wonders what happened to the painted Duchess and why the Duke speaks of her so intently.

Just as he owns the painting on the wall, the Duke demonstrates his belief that he owned the Duchess. Noting that the painting is of "*my* last Duchess," he acts as if she, too, had been one of his numerous belongings. He invites the emissary to "sit and look at her," illustrating that the painting is one of his prized possessions and that he intends to speak of it at length. To him it is more than a good painting; it is a "wonder" painted in only one day by Fra Pandolf. The Duke's choice of a monk to paint the portrait reveals his jealous and possessive nature. Forbidden from sexual relations, a monk was the only person whom the Duke could trust to spend a day alone with his wife painting her portrait. Yet a day is a remarkably short time for any artist to create such a good portrait.

The Duke's calling the portrait a "wonder," then, also gives insight into his psychology. Completed in only one day by a monk, the painting is surely not a work of genius, yet the Duke acts as if it were. At this point the listener and the reader realize that not only is the painting a "wonder" to the Duke, but the Duke must also think himself to be a "wonder" as he attempts through his dramatic speech to portray himself as a cultured individual in the eyes of the emissary. Noting the irony in the Duke's words, the reader perceives him to be a different kind of a wonder than he sees himself. It is this irony from whence the greatest paradox of the poem emerges.

Describing the painting with words that personify it, the Duke appears at first to be a connoisseur of art, an aesthete. The Duchess looks "as if she were alive," he says, speaking of the "countenance," "The depth and passion of its earnest glance," and the "spot of joy" in the cheek of the woman pictured there. On the surface he appears to be an art expert, but, paradoxically, he seems unable to appreciate the painting as would a true lover of art. Rather than appreciating art for its own sake, the Duke wonders what caused the "spot of joy" to appear in his Duchess' cheek and thereby disregards the aesthetic value of the portrait.

Unlike the Duke, the reader understands that the Duke's knowledge of art is not as genuine as it first appears, for the Duke feels it necessary to couple the name of the artist of the painting with his sculpture of Neptune taming a sea-horse located in close proximity to his portrait. "[T]hought a rarity" by others, the statue must be valuable, assumes the Duke, but he must depend on the judgment of others because his knowledge of art is limited. By bringing the statue to the envoy's attention, the Duke compares himself to the god Neptune and likens his treatment of the Duchess to Neptune's treatment of the sea-horse. Neptune, a symbol of power and might in the sea, symbolizes the Duke and his power in his duchy. Just as Neptune overpowers a sea-horse, the Duke overpowered his wife, who might as well have been an animal, an object lacking the worth of a human being. By killing his wife and framing her likeness, the Duke turns her into a thing, a painting only representing the human being she used to be. This surprise ending throws light on the whole poem by symbolically reinforcing the paradox of the animalistic Duke who pretends to be an aristocratic and cultured individual.

Through her death, the Duke reduces his wife to something he can control. To him, the painting is a "wonder, *now*" because it represents his accomplished feat of murdering his wife and indulging in his power to control others. Keeping her portrait behind a closed curtain who "none puts by" but he, the Duke controls even the things she can now see. He brags about his power over others, too. At his command, his subjects will even kill: "I gave commands; / Then all smiles stopped together." Instead of admiring the persona's greatness, the reader realizes this "cultured" Duke is a monster who has no regard for human life other than his own.

The Duke's condemnation of the Duchess's warm and cheerful personality develops another aspect of paradox in the poem. By using the word *countenance,* the Duke implies that it is his Duchess's inward state of mind only represented by her outward appearance about which he is concerned. Words like *earnest glance* connote a quick and fleeting look here and there without any real sincerity to that upon which the eyes fall. Even the attention he gave her, the Duke believes, was no more pleasing to her than the "courtesy" paid to her by the artist painting her portrait. He complains that "She thanked men . . . as if she ranked / My gift of a nine-hundred-years-old name / With anybody's gift." Just as he mentions the names of the artists to increase his importance in the envoy's eyes, the Duke reminds the listener that his own name is "nine-hundred-years-old," a fact about which he feels he should be able to boast. He does not feel, however, that his Duchess recognized that he was a personage. Clearly, the Duke believes that his name gives him more importance than his last Duchess ascribed to him.

Unlike the Duchess, whom the Duke believes is ungrateful for the privilege of wearing his name, the Duke is proud and believes he radiates the dignity and sophistication that she lacks. His aristocratic arrogance and vanity blind him to his wife's unconditional kindness to all and he assumes she was being unfaithful to him. Proud of his name, the Duke believes she should have placed him above all else. Instead, he thinks she was "Too easily impressed; she liked whate'er / She looked on, and her looks went everywhere." Perceiving her to be flirtatious, he becomes jealous and crushed, unwilling to believe his wife had even-tempered amiability to all. Paradoxically, it was the Duchess's warm and outgoing personality, her entire essence, for which the Duke killed her. Her personality, it seems, was at the same time her greatest asset and, at least to the Duke, her greatest fault.

Because the Duke believes his Duchess lacked a discriminating taste, he murders her. He was ashamed to have her for his wife because he considered her to be flippant and immature, and he was sure no proper Duchess would lack seriousness. He believes his wife, being a Duchess, should have acted as a Duchess would, with all the aristocratic sophistication the title embraces. In his imagined grandeur, he chooses "Never to stoop," and was therefore unable to ask his wife to practice any amount of discrimination and to devote her attentions to him. Such a request would surely be condescending.

As much as he may like the portrait on the wall, the Duke did not like the personality of his "last Duchess." To him, the painting and the Duchess are one and the same, her only positive quality he saw being her outward appearance. Apparently, her indiscreet emotions and personality were not worthy of being those of his Duchess and therefore justify his murdering her.

Near the end of the poem appears yet another paradox. The Duke comments on the "known munificence" of the Count and assures the emissary that it is the Count's daughter in whom he is interested, not her dowry. Both the emissary and the reader know, however, that this statement is not true. For a selfish man who is proud of his possessions to say that he is not interested in the dowry of a wealthy individual is absurd. Being too proud to admit this fact, he would never stoop to bargain for the dowry. He again unknowingly admits that he is a greedy individual in search of possessions, though he puts on the facade of an educated aesthete.

Even the prosody of the poem adds to the Duke's character. Though written in the nineteenth century, the physical structure of the poem contains Neoclassic elements such as the heroic couplet. These couplets of rhymed iambic pentameter represent the high culture of the Italian Renaissance. It is appropriate that Browning's Duke should speak in the language of the educated elite. While the couplets of the Renaissance were end-stopped, the form of Browning's couplets is altered. Instead of each couplet containing its own unit of thought, enjambment characterizes the couplets in "My Last Duchess." Freely flowing ideas without the restriction of convention produce a smooth reading of the poem almost as if the Duke were whispering to himself. Browning thereby extends into the structure of the poem the central paradox of the Duke, who appears to be both calm and cultured but who is in reality an animalistic murderer who refuses to be restrained by society. The Duke of Ferrara becomes all the more horrible because he tries to cover up his evil nature with quiet words and hushed conversations.

In his dramatic monologue the Duke of Ferrara reveals more about himself than he intends. Meaning to speak about his "last Duchess" instead of himself, he speaks ironically, unintentionally cluing the listener that he is a boastful, arrogant, and dominating individual who will even sacrifice a human life in order to achieve absolute control of people and things and "never to stoop."

DWAYNE PIPER

Reader-Response Criticism

Introduction

In a college-level introductory literature course, several class members are voicing their interpretations of chapter 31 of Mark Twain's *Adventures of Huckleberry Finn* (part of which is quoted at the beginning of Chapter 1 in this text). Student A declares that Huck Finn's struggle is obvious; he is simply debating whether he should listen to his feelings and keep Jim's whereabouts a secret, or listen to his conscience, which dictates that he must report the slave's location to Miss Watson, Jim's lawful owner. This chapter, asserts Student A, illustrates the novel's unifying theme: Huck's struggle to obey his innately good feelings versus his obeying the abstract commandments of an institutionalized system, his society. What unites all the chapters in the text and is now highlighted and climaxed in this chapter, maintains Student A, is Huck's realization that his inner feelings are correct and his society-dominated conscience is wrong. He accordingly opts for declaring Jim's humanity and thus tears up the letter he has written to Miss Watson.

Student B objects, declaring that Student A's interpretation is not relevant for the 1990s. Student A is correct, claims Student B, when she notes that Huck chooses to obey his conscience and disavow his allegiance to society's dictates. This is indeed Twain's chief purpose in his novel. But the novel's significance rests in how it can be applied today. Prejudice, she contends, still exists in our college town. We, like Huck, must see the humanness in all our citizens.

Student C observes that Students A and B have both made valid criticisms. What they overlook, however, is the change that now takes place in Huck himself. No longer will we see, maintains Student C, a Huck who will play dirty tricks on Jim or even consider hurting him in any way. We now have a Huck who has positioned himself against his society and will not retreat. In the rest of the novel, declares Student C, we will observe this more mature and directed Huck as he responds to Jim's personal needs.

With a quiver in his voice, Student D remarks that Huck reminds him of his friend George. One day when he and George were walking down the hall of their high school on their way to eleventh-grade biology class, they passed a group of students who began cursing and throwing milk cartons at them. "Go home, Jap," "USA all the way," and other derogatory comments came their way. Then George retorted, "Cut it out, guys. Pete has feelings too. Should we call some of you towheads, carrot tops, or other names because of how you look and because of your ancestors?" Like George, says Student D, Huck hates prejudice no matter where he finds it. Being on the side of the oppressed, he chooses to guard his friend's dignity and sense of self-worth. He therefore destroys the letter to Miss Watson and will eventually help Jim obtain his freedom.

Each of the four students sees something slightly different in Twain's passage. Consciously or unconsciously, each of their interpretations rests upon different theoretical assumptions and their corresponding interpretative methodologies. Of the four interpretations, Student A's is the most theoretically distinct approach to the passage. Seeing an overall textual unity, Student A presupposes that the text is autonomous; it must interpret itself with little or no help from historical, societal, or any other extrinsic factors, with all its parts relating back to its central theme. Utilizing the tenets of New Criticism, Student A posits the organic unity of the text. For this student, learning and applying literary terminology and searching for the correct interpretation are of utmost importance.

Unlike Student A, who applies a given set of criteria to the text in an attempt to discover its meaning, Students B, C, and D become participants in the interpretive process, actively bringing their own experiences to bear upon the text's meaning. Student B's interpretation, for example, highlights the theoretical difference between a text's meaning (the author's intentions) and its significance or relevance to present-day readers. Student C's approach begins filling in the gaps in the text, hypothesizing how Huck Finn will act in the pages yet unread based upon Huck's decision not to write to Jim's owner. Whether Student C is correct or not, and whether she will have to alter some of her presently held ideas concerning Jim, remains open. And Student D's theoretical framework objectifies the text and its meaning based on the reader's personal experiences with prejudice.

Although Students B, C, and D differ in their various approaches, none view the text as an objective entity that contains its own meaning (as does Student A). For these students, the text does not and cannot interpret itself. To determine meaning, these students believe they must become active readers and participants in the interpretive process. Their various theoretical assumptions and methodologies used to discover a text's meaning exemplify **reader-response criticism.**

Historical Development

Although reader-response criticism rose to prominence in literary analysis in the early 1970s and still influences much contemporary criticism, its historical roots can be traced to the 1920s and 1930s. Such precise dating, however, is artificial, for readers have obviously been responding to what they have read and experienced since the dawn of literature itself. Even the classical writers Plato and Aristotle were aware of and concerned about the reader's (or viewer's) reactions. Plato, for example, asserts that watching a play could so inflame the passions of the audience that the viewers would forget that they were rational beings and allow passion, not reason, to rule their actions. Similarly, in the *Poetics* Aristotle voices concern about the effects a play will have on the audience's emotions. Will it arouse the spectators' pity or fear? Will these emotions purge the viewer? Will they cleanse a spectator of all emotions by the play's end? Such interest in audience response to the artistic creation dominates much literary criticism.

Underlying both Plato's and Aristotle's concern about audience response, and the concern of many critics who follow in their paths, is the assumption that the audience (or the reader) is passive. As if watching a play or reading a book were a spectator sport, readers sit passively, absorbing the contents of the artistic creation and allowing it to dominate their thoughts and actions. From this point of view, the reader brings little to the play or text. The text provides all that is needed to interpret itself.

From Plato's time until the being of the romantic movement in British literature at the beginning of the 1800s, such a passive view of the reader existed. Although many critics recognized that a text did indeed have an effect upon its readers, criticism concerned itself primarily with the text. With the advent of romanticism, emphasis shifted from the text to the author. The author now became the genius who could assimilate truths that were unacknowledged or unseen by the general populace. And as the nineteenth century progressed, concern for the author continued, with literary criticism stressing the importance of the author's life, times, and social context as chief aids in textual analysis.

But by the 1920s, emphasis in textual analysis once again shifted to the text. With the advent of the New Criticism, the text became autonomous—an objective entity that could be analyzed and dissected. If studied thoroughly, the New Critics believed, the text would reveal its own meaning. Extrinsic factors such as historical or social context mattered little. The text itself contains what we need to discover its meaning. We need only master the technical jargon and techniques to unlock its meaning.

While positing the autonomy of the text, the New Critics did acknowledge the effects a text could have on its readers. Studying the effects of a literary work, they decreed, was not the same as studying the text itself, however. This emphasis on the objective nature of the text once again created a passive reader who did not bring personal experiences, private emotions, and past literary experiences to bear upon textual analysis.

In the midst of New Criticism's rise to dominance in textual analysis, which would last for more than 30 years, one of its founding fathers, I. A. Richards, became interested in the reading process itself. Distributing to classes copies of poems without their authors and titles and with various editorial changes that updated spelling and pronunciation, Richards asked his students to record their free responses to the texts. After collecting and analyzing these responses, Richards was amazed at the many contradictory responses to the same texts, and realized the part context plays in the interpretative process. He proposed that his students brought to the text many interests, philosophies, and contexts that were simply wrong. Being a New Critic, he wanted to direct them toward the "correct" assumptions and contexts. Nevertheless, he did recognize the contextual nature of reading poems; that is, the reader brings to the text a vast array of ideas amassed through life's experiences, including previous literary experiences, and applies such information to the text. In so doing, the reader is no longer the passive receiver of knowledge but becomes an active participant in the creation of a text's meaning.

In the 1930s, Louise Rosenblatt further developed Richards' earlier assumptions concerning the contextual nature of the reading process. In her text *Literature as Exploration*, published in 1938, Rosenblatt asserts that the reader and the text must work together to produce meaning. Unlike the New Critics, she shifts the emphasis of textual analysis away from the text alone and views the reader and the text as partners in the interpretative process.

In the late 1930s, however, Rosenblatt's ideas seemed revolutionary, too abstract, and simply off the beaten critical path. Although New Criticism dominated literary practice for the next 30 years or so, Rosenblatt continued to develop her ideas, culminating her critical work with the publication of *The Reader, the Text, the Poem* in 1978. In this work, she clarifies her earlier ideas and presents what has become one of the main critical positions held by many theorists and practical critics today.

According to Rosenblatt, the reading process involves a reader and a text. The reader and the text interact or share a **transactional** experience: the text acts as a stimulus for eliciting various past experiences, thoughts, and ideas from the reader, those found both in real life and in past reading experiences. Simultaneously, the text shapes the reader's experiences, selecting, limiting, and ordering those ideas that best conform to the text. Through this transactional experience, the reader and the text produce a new creation, a poem. For Rosenblatt and many other reader-response critics, a **poem** now becomes an event that takes place during the reading process or what Rosenblatt calls the aesthetic transaction. No longer synonymous with the word *text*, a poem is created each time a reader interacts with a text, be that interaction a first reading or any of countless rereadings of the same text.

For Rosenblatt, readers can and do read in one of two ways: efferently or aesthetically. When we read for information—for example, when we read the directions on how to heat a can of soup—we are engaging in **efferent reading**. During this process we are interested only in newly gained information, not in the actual words themselves. When we engage in **aesthetic reading**, we experience the text. We note its every word, its sounds, its patterns, and so on. In essence, we live through the transactional experience of creating the poem.

When reading aesthetically, we involve ourselves in an elaborate encounter of give-and-take with the text. While the text may allow for many interpretations by eliciting and highlighting different past experiences of the reader, it simultaneously limits the valid meanings the poem can acquire. For Rosenblatt, a poem's meaning is not therefore a smorgasbord of endless interpretations, but a transactional experience in which several different yet probable meanings emerge and thereby create a variety of "poems."

What differentiates Rosenblatt's and all reader-response approaches from other critical approaches (especially formalism and/or New Criticism) is their diverting the emphasis away from the text as the sole determiner of meaning to the significance of the reader as an essential participant in the reading process and in the creation of meaning. Such a shift negates the formalists' assumption that the text is autonomous and can therefore be scientifically analyzed to discover its meaning. No longer, then, is the reader passive, merely applying a long list of learned poetic devices to a text in the hope of discovering its intricate patterns of paradox and irony, which, in turn, will lead to a supposed correct interpretation. For reader-response critics, the reader now becomes an active participant along with the text in creating meaning. It is from the **literacy experience** (an event that occurs when reader and print interact), they believe, that meaning evolves.

Assumptions

Like most approaches to literary analysis, reader-response criticism does not provide us with a unified body of theory or a single methodological approach for textual analysis. What those who call themselves reader-response critics, reader-critics, or audience-oriented critics share is a concern for the reader. Believing that a literary work's interpretation is created when a reader and a text interact and/or transact, these critics assert that the proper study of textual analysis must consider both the reader and the text, not simply the text in isolation. For these critics, the reader + the text = meaning. Only in context with a reader actively involved in the reading process with the text, they decree, can meaning emerge.

Meaning, declare reader-response critics, is context-dependent and intricately associated with the reading process. Like literary theory, several theoretical models and their practical applications exist to explain the reading process, or how we make sense of printed material. Using these various models, reader-response critics have devised three approaches to the literacy experience. Each approach emphasizes different philosophies, assumptions, and methodologies to explain what these various critics believe happens when a reader interacts with printed material.

Although each model espouses a different approach to textual analysis, all share some of the same presuppositions and concerns and ask similar questions. All, for example, focus directly on the reading process. What happens, they ask, when a person picks up printed material and reads it? Put another way, their chief interest lies in what occurs when a text and a reader interact. During this interaction, reader-response critics investigate and theorize whether the reader, the text, or some combination finally determine the text's interpretation. Is it the reader who manipulates the text, they ponder, or does the text manipulate the reader to produce meaning? Does some word, phrase, or image trigger in the reader's mind a specific interpretation, or does the reader approach the text with a conscious or unconscious collection of learned reading strategies that systematically impose an interpretation on the text?

Such questions then lead reader-response critics to a further narrowing and developing of terminology. They ask, for example, what is a text? Is it simply the words or symbols on a page? How, they ask, can we differentiate between what is actually in the text and what is in the mind of the reader? And who is this reader, anyway? Are there various kinds of readers? Is it possible that different texts presuppose different kinds of readers?

And what about a reader's response to a text? Are the responses equivalent to the text's meaning? Can one reader's response, they speculate, be more correct than some other reader's, or are all responses of equal validity? Although readers respond to the same text in a variety of ways, why is it, they ask, that oftentimes different readers individually arrive at the same conclusions or interpretations of the same text?

Reader-response critics also ask questions about another person, the author. What part, if any, does the author play in a work's interpretation? Can the author's attitudes toward the reader, they wonder, actually influence a work's meaning? And if a reader knows the author's clearly stated intentions for a text, does this information have any part in creating the text's meaning, or should an author's intentions for a work simply be ignored?

The concerns, then, of reader-response critics can best be summarized in one question: What is the reading process? Overall, these critics concern themselves with the entire process of the literacy experience. Their approaches to this reading experience or event, however, are many.

Methodology

Most reader-response critics can be divided into three distinct groups. Although members within each group may differ slightly, each group espouses similar theoretical and methodological concerns. Student B's interpretation at the beginning of this chapter represents the focus of the first group. Like all reader-response critics, this group believes that the reader must be an active participant in the creation of meaning. but for these critics, the text has more control over the interpretative process than does the reader. Some of these critics lean toward New Critical theory, asserting that some interpretations are more valid than others. Others, like Student B at the beginning of this chapter, differentiate between a text's meaning and its significance. For them, the text's meaning can be synonymous with its author's intention, while its significance can change from one context or historical period to another.

But the majority of critics in this first group belong to the school known as **structuralism**. Some scholars would argue (and perhaps successfully so) that the structuralists should not be placed in this group, for ultimately meaning for them does not reside in the text. But since these critics begin with the text and because the next chapter will be devoted solely to their theories and practices, as a matter of convenience we will place them midway between text-oriented critics and those who claim that meaning basically resides in the reader's mind.

Basing their ideas on the writings of Ferdinand de Saussure, the father of modern linguistics, these critics often approach textual analysis as if it were a science. Their proponents—Roland Barthes, Gerard Genette, Roman Jakobson, Claude Lévi-Strauss, Gerald Prince, and Jonathan Culler in his early works—look for specific codes within the text that allow meaning to occur. These codes or signs embedded in the text are part of a larger system that allows meaning to occur in all facets of society, including literature. For example, when we are driving a car and we see a red light hanging above an intersection, we have learned that we must stop our car. And if we hear a fire engine or an ambulance siren, we have learned that we must drive our car to the side of the road. Both the red light and the sirens are signs or codes in our society that provide us with ways of interpreting and ordering our world.

According to structuralist critics, a reader brings to the text a predetermined system of ascertaining meaning (a complex system of signs or codes like the sirens and the red light) and applies this sign system directly to the text. The text becomes important because it contains signs or signals to the reader that have established and acceptable interpretations. Many structuralists are therefore more concerned with the overall system of meaning a given society has developed than with textual analysis itself, and concentrate their efforts on what a reader needs to know about interpreting any sign (such as a road sign or a word) in the context of acceptable societal standards. Because of this emphasis, structuralists seem to push both the text and the reader to the background and highlight a linguistic theory of communication and interpretation. Since structuralism has become a springboard for many other modern theories of literary criticism, its significance to literary theory and practical criticism will be explored at length in the next chapter.

Student C represents the second group of reader-response critics. For the most part, these follow Rosenblatt's assumption that the reader is involved in a transactional experience when interpreting a text. The text and the reader, they declare, play somewhat equal parts in the interpretative process. For these critics, reading is an event that culminates in the creation of the poem.

Many adherents of this approach—George Poulet, Wolfgang Iser, Hans Robert Jauss, and Louise Rosenblatt—are associated with phenomenology. **Phenomenology** is a modern philosophical tendency that emphasizes the perceiver. Objects can have meaning, phenomenologists maintain, only if an active consciousness (a perceiver) absorbs or notes their existence. In other words, objects exist if and only if we register them on our consciousness. Rosenblatt's definition of a poem directly applies this theory to literary study. The true poem can exist only in the reader's consciousness, not on the printed page. When reader and text interact, the poem and therefore meaning are created; they exist only in the consciousness of the reader. Reading and textual analysis now become an aesthetic experience whereby the reader and the text combine in the consciousness of the reader and create the poem. Like Student C's interpretation at the beginning of the chapter, the reader's imagination must work, filling in the gaps in the text and conjecturing about characters' actions, personality traits, and motives.

Student D represents the third group of reader-response critics, who place the greatest emphasis on the reader in the interpretative process. For these psychological or subjective critics, the reader's thoughts, beliefs, and experiences play a greater part in shaping a work's meaning than the actual text. Led by Norman Holland and David Bleich, these critics assert that we shape and find our self-identities in the reading process. We impose upon the text, they believe, our ideas, seeing ourselves within the text. By merging our dreams and fantasies with elements within the text, we produce an interpretation that could be accepted by members of our culture.

Acceptance by our social group is the key. Subjective critics assert that when reading a text a reader may respond to something in the text in a bizarre and personal way. These private responses will, through discussion, be pruned away by members of their social group. Finally, the group will decide what is the acceptable interpretation of the text. Like Student D's interpretation, cited at the beginning of this chapter, the reader responds personally to some specific element in the text and then seeks to objectify this personal response and declares it to be an interpretation of the text itself.

Although reader-response critics all believe the reader plays a part in discovering a text's meaning, just how small or large a part is debatable. Espousing various theoretical assumptions, these critics must necessarily have different methodologies with regard to textual analysis. According to the contemporary critic Steven Mailloux, however, they all share a two-step procedure which they then adapt to their own theories. All show (1) that a work gives a reader a task or something to do a and (2) the reader's response or answer to that task. For example, Student D, cited at the beginning of this chapter, obviously saw something in the text that triggered his memories of his friend George. He moves, then, from the text to his own thoughts, memories, and past experiences. These personal experiences temporarily overshadow the text, but he realizes that his personal reactions must in some way become acceptable to his peers. He therefore compares George to Huck and himself to Jim and thereby objectifies his personal feelings while at the same time having his interpretation deemed socially respectable in his "interpretative community" or social setting.

Because the term reader-response criticism allows for so much diversity in theory and methods, many twentieth-century schools of criticism, such as deconstruction, feminism, Marxism, and New Historicism, declare their membership in this broad classification. Each of these approaches to textual analysis provides its own ideological basis to reader-response theory and develops its unique methods of practical criticism. Such an eclectic membership, however, denotes the continued growth and ongoing development of reader-response criticism.

In the student essay that follows, note carefully how the student demonstrates the two basic moves or reading strategies described by Mailloux. To which group of reader-response criticism does this essay belong? Is the text, the reader + text, or the reader being stressed the most? Can you point out the various personal strategies or moves the author uses to arrive at her interpretation of the text?

Further Reading

Bleich, David. *Subjective Criticism*. Baltimore: Johns Hopkins University Press, 1978.

Fish, Stanley. *Is There a Text in This Class? The Authority of Interpretive Communities*. Cambridge, MA: Harvard University Press, 1980.

Mailloux, Steven. "Learning to Read: Interpretation and Reader-Response Criticism." *Studies in the Literary Imagination* 12 (1979): 93–108.

Rosenblatt, Louise M. "Towards a Transactional Theory of Reading." *Journal of Reading Behavior* 1 (1969): 31–47.

Suleiman, Susan R. and Inge Crosman, eds. *The Reader in the Text: Essays on Audience and Interpretation*. Princeton: Princeton University Press, 1980.

Tompkins, Jane, ed. *Reader-Response Criticism: From Formalism to Post-Structuralism*. Baltimore: Johns Hopkins University Press, 1980.

Student Essay

"Young Goodman Brown" and Me

Nathaniel Hawthorne's "Young Goodman Brown" evoked strong, negative emotions from me. Finding a basis for my reactions in my past experiences with my father, I dislike the harsh depiction of "religious" people and, by implication, God; and I identify with the character Goodman Brown, but by story's end reject that identification.

Hawthorne's story denounces a viewpoint that I thoroughly dislike: the stereotypical Puritan mind-set that condemns everyone except the elect to hell. Because my Christian theistic outlook posits a loving and merciful God, it both hurts and angers me to see God portrayed as—well, puritanical, hanging sinners "by a slender thread, with the flames of divine wrath flashing about it and ready every moment to singe it and burn it asunder" (Jonathan Edwards's "Sinners in the Hands of an Angry God"). As I read "Young Goodman Brown," I reacted against this attitude, which I found both in the characters themselves and in the author.

I believe my emotional reaction to the story and to the harsh Puritan God derives from my relationship with my father. My father and I love each other, and beyond that, we are friends. But during my youth, my father disciplined my sister and me more than my mother did, and I came to see Dad as "justice" while Mom was "mercy." In the insecurities of my teenage years I hesitated to approach Dad, and this uncertainty coupled with his infrequent communication of his feelings made me feel I had to prove myself to him in everything I did. Only lately have I seen the latent anger and frustration in me, and how I often projected my concept of my father's characteristics onto God. I felt a need to prove myself to God, too. Frequently I pictured God punishing me for my behavior by withholding or giving me things that I wanted. Even now, to envision a loving God is difficult for me.

Because I struggle against conceptualizing a judgmental God, I react against anything that reinforces this view. "Young Goodman Brown" presents a frightening picture of an individual who fears that at any moment "the roof should thunder down" upon his church in judgment. Brown's God, a divine lightening bolt, repulses me. A loving and accepting God is what I seek.

God seems at best indifferent in this story. Satan has the power and the fun: he breaks into "irrepressible mirth" during his conversation with Goodman Brown. In fact, I see a parallel between Satan's educating the reader about the same thing. Goodman Brown, like the reader, initially doubts that such holy persons as the minister and Goody Cloyse (she taught Brown his catechism) could be agents of evil. Goodman Brown protests as the devil reveals these hypocrisies to him: "We are a people of prayer, and good works to boot, and abide no such wickedness." I like this sentence because it reveals Brown's shallow faith not only in God but also in the "righteous" citizens of Salem village.

But in the end Satan educates Goodman Brown too well. Disillusioned at the prevalence of Satan's power, Brown despairs and rejects his race. Hawthorne conveys the same hopeless conclusion to the reader: sin prevails on earth, and a malevolent or disinterested God remains detached. As the reader, I dislike Hawthorne's "education" because of my personal struggle against this desolate view of life.

I feel that Hawthorne overemphasized the evil in his characters. Pessimism overwhelms the final paragraph; Goodman Brown escapes damnation, but lives the rest of his life (including "his dying hour") in gloom. Can this dark ending be the final word? Like Brown himself and most people, I vacillate between pessimism and optimism, realism and idealism, despair and joy. In my more desperate moments I would end "Young Goodman Brown" as Hawthorne did; but beauty and truth do exist, and, as in J. R. R. Tolkien's Middle Earth, one cannot often predict which side will triumph.

My dislike of the ending relates to my identification with Goodman Brown himself. Brown's Faith is a timid, pink-ribboned, newlywed June Cleaver, and my faith had the same naivete. Like George Herbert's "Affliction," my adolescent belief sparkled with rainbows and Care Bears. Disillusionment came in high school, when a young man upon whom I developed and all-consuming crush rejected me. It warped my image of myself. I hated my braces and my glasses and myself. God became that someone who withheld the thing I wanted most (intimacy), and I began to hate him, too, or at least fear him. My faith either had to sully her pink ribbons or else disappear altogether. Over the next few years she cast off the Cleaver image and began to look more like Barbara Bush, calloused and weathered and wrinkly.

In addition to my identification with Goodman Brown's faith, I also relate to his misuse of reason. Relying too much on his own insight, Goodman Brown reasons his way out of Faith's arms in the sixth paragraph of the story: "What a wretch am I to leave her on such an errand! . . . after this one night I'll cling to her skirts and follow her to heaven." He rationalizes his faithlessness with thoughts of his future devotion.

Goodman Brown having already elevated reason above his faith, Satan had easy prey. While walking with Brown farther into the woods, Satan says, "Let us walk on, nevertheless, reasoning as we go; and if I convince thee not thou shalt turn back." Later:

> They continued to walk onward, while the elder traveller exhorted his companion to make good speed and persevere in the path, discoursing so aptly that his arguments seemed rather to spring up in the bosom of his auditor than to be suggested by himself.

I think Hawthorne indicates that Satan led Goodman Brown astray by capitalizing on Brown's elevation of reason.

Like Brown himself, I often reason myself into despair. Again, this tendency relates to my relationship with my father. During my teenage years he recognized the adolescent impulse in me to have Mount Everest highs followed by Dead Sea lows, depending on the changing situations in my life. Hoping to anchor me near sea-level, my father communicated his observation to me. In defense I interpreted him as labeling me a person unable to control her emotions, and this label became part of my self-image. I began attributing my problems to my emotions. As I look back at those problems, I see now that I usually *reasoned* myself into a mental corner first, then responded with emotion. Believing that concentrated thought inevitably provided an answer, I elevated reason beyond its capabilities.

Although I can identify with Goodman Brown's faith and reason during the story, my identification ends before the final paragraph. Brown faces reality and becomes "a stern, a sad, a darkly meditative, a distrustful, if not a desperate man." I understand his reaction, but I could never be independent (or maybe foolhardy) enough to reject humanity and withdraw from society. Having recognized life's worst, I believe the proper response is compassion, not despair.

"Young Goodman Brown" portrays no middle ground. The title character goes from naive optimism to absolute despair, and genuine "good" neglects the entire situation. Because my perceptions of my father have influenced my image of God, I feel uncomfortable and even angry as I read of Goodman Brown's desperate response to the hypocrisy he correctly sees in the people around him. Complicating my negative response, but still relating to my father's influence, I identify with Goodman Brown's immature faith and exalted reason.

KATHLEEN STOCKIN

5

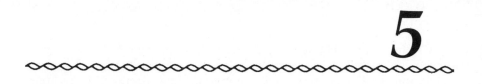

Structuralism

Introduction

Having narrowed her list of job candidates to two, the personnel director of a large computer company instructed her secretary to invite each applicant in for a job interview. Both seemed equally qualified for the position. Applicant A had graduated from an Ivy League university, earning a B.S. in accounting and business, while applicant B, also a graduate of an Ivy League institution, earned a B.S. in business administration. Each had received outstanding references from his professors and business mentors. And each scored in the 95th percentile on the Graduate Record Examination. The personnel director's choice, no doubt, would be difficult.

On the day of the interview, applicant A arrived wearing a gray suit, a white cotton shirt, a subdued but somewhat bright yellow tie, a pair of highly polished black oxfords, and an appropriate smile and short haircut. Applicant B arrived a few minutes after applicant A's interview had begun. Wearing a green pullover sweater with a yellow shirt collar protruding around the neck, a pair of brown plush corduroys, and neatly polished topsiders, applicant B brushed back his long hair and wondered why the first applicant's interview was lasting more than an hour. After another 15 minutes had passed, applicant A finally exited through the main doors, and the secretary ushered applicant B into the director's office. Eighteen minutes later applicant B passed by the secretary's desk and left the building, his interview apparently over.

Shortly thereafter, the personnel director buzzed for her secretary to come to her office. When he entered, the director instructed him, "Please send applicant A the contract. He will represent our business well. Also, mail applicant B an "I'm sorry, but . . ." letter. Evidently he doesn't understand our image, our values, and our standards. Corduroys, no tie, and long hair, in this office and for this company! Never!"

Applicant A's ability to grasp what his future employer valued earned him his job. Through the language of fashion (**language** being used in a broad sense to mean any system of signs or codes that convey meaning), applicant A demonstrated to the personnel director his understanding of the company's image and its concern for appropriate dress and physical appearance. Applicant B, on the other hand, silently signaled his lack of understanding of the company's values and public image through his tieless and seemingly inappropriate attire. While applicant B seemingly failed to master those fashion codes that represented his understanding of the company's standards (or perhaps he didn't really want the job unless he could be his long-haired tieless self), applicant A demonstrated his command of the language of fashion and his potential to learn other similar intricate systems or languages used in such areas as economics, education, the sciences, and social life in general. Through his mastery of these codes and his ability (either consciously or unconsciously) to analyze and employ them correctly in a given situation, applicant A demonstrated his knowledge of structuralism.

Flourishing in the 1960s, **structuralism** is an approach to literary analysis grounded in **structural linguistics**, the science of language. By utilizing the techniques, methodologies, and vocabulary of linguistics, structuralism offers a scientific view of how we achieve meaning not only in literary works but in all forms of communication and social behavior.

To understand structuralism, we must trace its historical roots to the linguistic writings and theories of Ferdinand de Saussure, a Swiss professor and linguist of the late nineteenth and early twentieth century. It is his scientific investigations of language and language theory that provide the basis for structuralism's unique approach to literary analysis.

Historical Development

Throughout the nineteenth and early twentieth centuries, **philology**, not linguistics, was the science of language. Its practitioners, **philologists**, described, compared, and analyzed the languages of the world to discover similarities and relationships. Their approach to language study was **diachronic**; that is, they traced language change through long expanses of time, investigating, for example, how a particular phenomenon in one language had changed through several centuries and whether a similar change could be noted in other languages. Using a cause-and-effect relationship as the basis for their research, the philologists' main emphasis was the historical development of all languages.

Such an emphasis reflected the nineteenth-century philologists' theoretical assumptions about the nature of language. Language, they believed, mirrored the structure of the world it imitated and therefore had no structure of its own. Known as the **mimetic theory** of language, this hypothesis asserts that words are symbols for things in the world, each word having its own **referent**—the object, concept, or idea that represents and/or symbolizes a word. According to this theory, the symbol (the word) equals a thing.

In the first decade of the 1900s, a Swiss philologist and teacher, Ferdinand de Saussure (1857–1913), began questioning these long-held ideas and, by so doing, triggered a reformation in language study. Through his research and his innovative theories, Saussure changed the direction and subject matter of linguistic studies. His *Course in General Linguistics*, a compilation of his 1906–11 lecture notes published posthumously by his students, is one of the seminal works of modern linguistics and forms the basis for much twentieth-century literary theory and practical criticism. Through the efforts of this father of modern linguistics, nineteenth-century philology evolved into the more multifaceted science of twentieth-century linguistics.

While affirming the validity and necessity of the diachronic approach to language study utilized by nineteenth-century philologists, Saussure introduced the **synchronic** approach, focusing attention on studying a language at one particular time in its evolution and emphasizing how the language functions, not its historical development. By highlighting the activity of language and how it operates, rather than its evolution, Saussure drew attention to the nature and composition of language and its constituent parts. This new concern necessitated a rethinking of language theory and a reevaluation of the aims of language research, and finally resulted in Saussure's articulating the basic principles of modern linguistics.

Unlike many other linguists of his time, Saussure rejected the mimetic theory of language structure. In its place, he asserted that language is primarily determined by its own internally structured and highly systematized rules. These rules govern all aspects of a language, including the sounds its speakers will identify as meaningful, various combinations of these sounds into words, and how these words may be arranged to produce meaningful communication within a given language.

By age five or six, native speakers of a language have consciously and unconsciously mastered their language's system of rules—the rules that enable them to participate in language communication. Although they may not have obviously mastered the advanced elements of their language's grammar, native speakers of English, for instance, would immediately know that the utterance *Alice looked up into the sky* was an acceptable English sentence, but the word combination *Alice up the book* is somehow incorrect or violates English sentence structure. What this speaker has learned Saussure dubs **langue**, the structure of the language that is mastered and shared by all its speakers.

While langue emphasizes the social aspect of language, an individual's actual speech utterances Saussure calls **parole**. A speaker can generate countless examples of individual utterances, but these will all be governed by the language's system, its langue. It is the task of the linguist, Saussure believes, to infer a language's langue from the analysis of many instances of parole. In other words, for Saussure, the proper study of linguistics is the system (langue), not the individual utterances of its speakers (parole).

Having established that languages are systems that operate according to verifiable rules and that they need to be investigated both diachronically and synchronically, Saussure then reexamined philology's definition of a word. Rejecting the long-held belief that a word is a symbol that equals a thing (its referent), Saussure proposed that words are **signs** made up of two parts: the **signifier** (a written or spoken mark) and a signified (a concept). For example, when we hear the sound combination *ball*, the sound is the signifier and the concept of a ball that comes to our minds is the signified. Like the two sides of a sheet of paper, the linguistic sign is the union of these two elements. As oxygen combines with hydrogen to form water, Saussure says, so the signifier joins with the signified to form a sign that has properties unlike those of its parts. Accordingly, a word does not represent a referent in the objective world for Saussure, but a concept in our minds.

Furthermore, the linguistic sign, declares Saussure, is arbitrary: the relationship between the signifier (*ball*) and the signified (the concept of *ball*) is a matter of convention. The speakers of a language have simply agreed that the written or spoken sounds or marks represented by *ball* will equal the concept *ball*. With few exceptions, proclaims Saussure, there is no natural link between the signifier and the signified, nor is there any natural relationship between the linguistic sign and what it represents.

If, as Saussure maintains, there is no natural link between the linguistic sign and the reality it represents, how do we know the difference between one sign and another? In other words, how does language create meaning? We know what a sign means, says Saussure, because it differs from all other signs. By comparing and contrasting one sign to other signs, we learn to distinguish each individual sign.

For Saussure, meaning is therefore relational and a matter of difference. Within the system of sound markers that comprise our language, we know *ball*, for instance, because we differentiate it from *hall*, *tail*, and *pipe*.

Likewise, we know the concept "bug" because it differs from the concepts "truck," grass," and "kite." As Saussure declares, "in language there are only differences."

Since signs are arbitrary, conventional, and differential, Saussure concludes that the proper study of language is not an examination of isolated entities but of the system of relationships among them. He asserts , for example, that individual words cannot have meaning by themselves. Because language is a system of rules governing sounds, words, and other components, individual words obtain their meaning only within that system. To know language and how it functions, he declares, we must study the system (langue), not individual utterances (parole) that operate according to the rules of langue.

For Saussure, language is the primary sign system whereby we structure our world. Language's structure, he believes, is not unlike that of any other sign system of social behavior such as fashion and table manners. Like language, all such expressions of social behavior generate meaning through a system of signs. Saussure proposed a new science called **semiology** that would study how we create meaning through these signs in all our social behavioral systems. Since language was the chief and most characteristic of all these systems, Saussure declared, it was to be the main branch of semiology. The investigation of all other sign systems would be patterned after language, for like language's signs, the meaning of all signs was arbitrary, conventional, and differential.

Although semiology never became an important new science as Saussure envisioned, a similar science was being proposed in America almost simultaneously by philosopher and teacher Charles Sanders Peirce. Called **semiotics**, this science borrowed linguistic methods utilized by Saussure and applied them to all meaningful cultural phenomena. Meaning in society, this science of signs declares, can be systematically studied, both in terms of how this meaning occurs and in terms of the structures that allow it to operate. Distinguishing among the various kinds of signs, semiotics as a particular field of study continues to develop today. Because it uses structuralist methods borrowed from Saussure, semiotics and structuralism are terms often used interchangeably, although the former denotes a particular field of study while the latter is more an approach and method of analysis.

Assumptions

Borrowing their linguistic vocabulary, theory, and methods from Saussure and to a smaller degree from Peirce, structuralists—their studies being variously called structuralism, semiotics, stylistics, or narratology—believe that codes, signs, and rules govern all human social and cultural practices, including communication. Whether that communication is the language of fashion as exhibited in the story at the beginning of this chapter, or the language of sports, education, friendship, or literature, each is a systematized combination of codes (signs) governed by rules. Structuralists wish to discover these codes, which they believe give meaning to all our social and cultural customs and behavior. The proper study of meaning and therefore reality, they assert, is an investigation of the system behind these practices, not the individual practices themselves. To discover how all the parts fit together and function is their aim.

Structuralists find meaning, then, in the relationships among the various components of a system. When applied to literature, this principle becomes revolutionary. The proper study of literature, for the structuralists, now involves an inquiry into the conditions surrounding the act of interpretation itself (how literature conveys meaning), not an in-depth investigation of an individual work. Since an individual work can express only those values and beliefs of the system of which it is a part, structuralists emphasize the system (langue) whereby texts relate to each other, not an examination of an isolated text (parole). They believe that a study of the **grammar**, or the system of rules that govern literary interpretation, becomes the critic's primary task.

Such a belief presupposes that the structure of literature is similar to the structure of language. Like language, say the structuralists, literature is a self-enclosed system of rules that is composed of language. And also like language, literature needs no outside referent but its own rule-governed, but socially constrained system.

In addition to emphasizing the system of literature and not individual texts, structuralism also claims it demystifies literature. By explaining literature as a system of signs encased in a cultural frame that allows that system to operate, no longer, says structuralism, can a literary work be considered to represent a mystical or magical relationship between the author and the reader, the place where author and reader share emotions, ideas, and truth. An objective analysis of how readers interpret texts, not a transcendental or intuitive response to any one text, leads to meaning. Similarly, an author's intentions can no longer be equated with the text's overall meaning, for meaning is determined by the system that governs the writer, not by an individual author's own quirks. And no longer can the text be autonomous, an object whose meaning is contained solely within itself. All texts, declare structuralists, are part of a shared system of meaning that is intertextual, not text specific; that is, all texts refer readers to other texts. Meaning, claim the structuralists, can therefore be expressed only through this shared system of relations.

Declaring both isolated text and author to be of little importance, structuralism attempts to strip literature of its magical powers or so-called hidden meanings that can only be discovered by a small, elite group of highly trained specialists. Meaning can be found, it declares, by analyzing the system of rules that comprise literature itself.

Methodology

Like all other approaches to textual analysis, structuralism follows neither one methodological strategy nor one set of ideological assumptions. Although most structuralists use many of Saussure's ideas in formulating their theoretical assumptions and the foundations for their literary theories, how these assumptions are employed when applied to textual analysis varies greatly.

One of the first scholar/researchers to apply Saussure's principles of linguistics to narrative discourse was the anthropologist Claude Lévi-Strauss. Attracted to the rich symbols in myths, Lévi-Strauss spent years studying many of the world's myths. Myth, he assumed, possessed a structure like language. Each individual myth was therefore an example of parole. What he wanted to discover was myth's langue, or the overall structure that allows individual examples (parole) to function and have meaning.

After reading countless myths, Lévi-Strauss identified recurrent themes running through all of them. These basic structures, which he called **mythemes**, were similar to the primary building blocks of language, the individual, meaningful sounds of a language called **phonemes**. Like phonemes, these mythemes find meaning in and through their relationships within the mythic structure. The rules that govern how these mythemes may be combined constitute myth's structure or grammar. The meaning of any individual myth, then, depends on the interaction and order of the mythemes within the story. Out of this structural pattern will come the myth's meaning.

Like our unconscious mastery of our language's langue, we also master myth's structure. Our ability to grasp this structure, says Lévi-Strauss, is innate. Like language, myths are simply another way we classify and organize our world.

Expanding Lévi-Strauss's linguistic model of oral myths to cover a variety of written stories, a group of structuralists called *narratologists* began another kind of structuralism: **narratology** or **structuralist narratology**, the science of narrative. Like Saussure and Lévi-Strauss, these structuralists illustrate how a story's meaning develops from its overall structure, its langue, rather than from each individual story's isolated theme. The Russian linguist Vladimir Propp, for example, investigated fairy tales and decoded their langue. According to his analysis, all folk or fairy tales are based on 31 fixed elements that will occur in sequence. Any story may use any number of these elements, but each element will occur in its proper sequence.

Another narratologist, the Bulgarian Tzvetan Todorov, declares that all stories are composed of grammatical units. For Todorov, the syntax of narrative—how the various grammatical elements of a story combine—is essential. By applying a grammatical model to narrative, Todorov believes he can discover the narrative's langue. Establishing a grammar of narrative, Todorov decrees that the grammatical clause, and, in turn, the subject and verb, is the basic interpretative unit of each sentence and can be linguistically analyzed and further dissected into a variety of grammatical categories to show how all narratives are structured.

Other narratologists, such as Roland Barthes and Gerard Genette, have also developed methods of analyzing a story's structure to unearth its meaning, each building on the previous work of another narratologist and adding an additional element or two of his own. Genette, for example, believes that **tropes** or figures of speech require a reader's special attention. Barthes, on the other hand, points us back to Todorov and provides us with more linguistic terminology to dissect a story. While additional narratologists appear on the scene, each believes that his or her linguistic model when applied to a text will finally allow us to discover the meaning of the story.

By the mid-1970s, Jonathan Culler became the voice of structuralism in America and took structuralism in another direction. In his work *Structuralist Poetics*, Culler declared that abstract linguistic models used by narratologists tended to focus on parole, spending too much time analyzing individual stories, poems, and novels. What was needed, he believed, was a return to an investigation of langue, Saussure's main premise.

According to Culler, readers, when given a chance, will somehow make sense out of even the most bizarre text. Somehow, readers possess literary competence. They have, says Culler, internalized a set of rules that govern their acts of interpretation. Instead of analyzing individual interpretations of a work, we must spend our time, Culler insists, on analyzing the act of interpretation itself. We must, then, shift the focus from the text to the reader. How, asks Culler, does interpretation take place in the first place? What system underlies the very act of reading that allows any other system to operate?

Unlike other structuralists, Culler presents a theory of reading. What, he asks, is the internalized system of literary competence readers use to interpret a work? In other words, how do they read? What system guides them through the process of interpreting the work, of making sense of the spoken or printed word?

In *Structuralist Poetics*, Culler asserts that three elements undergird any reading, for instance, of a poem: (1) that a poem should be unified, (2) that it should be thematically significant, and (3) that this significance can take the form of reflection in poetry. Accordingly, Culler then seeks to establish the system, the langue, that undergirds the reading process. By focusing on the act of interpretation itself to discover literature's langue, Culler believes he is returning structuralism to its Saussurean roots.

Like Culler's approach to a text, all structuralist methodologies attempt to reveal the signifying systems that operate in a text. Whereas some structuralists attempt to map out the themes, events, or grammatical structures that they believe will reveal this underlying signifying system, others, like Culler, endeavor to find this system in the act of interpretation itself and not in the text.

Still others believe that the primary signifying system is best found as a series of binary oppositions that the reader organizes, values, and then uses to interpret the text. Each binary operation can be pictured as a fraction, the top half (the numerator) being what is more valued than its related bottom half (the denominator). Accordingly, in the binary operation "light/dark" the reader has learned to value light over dark, and in the binary operation "good/evil" the reader has similarly valued good over evil. How the reader organizes the various binary operations found within the text but already existing in the mind of the reader will determine for that particular reader the text's interpretation.

A structuralist interpretation may, for example, contrast a narrator's reordering of events within the story to the chronological, cause-and-effect order of events present within the story itself. Or it may map out the series of binary operations that the structuralist believes control the story's meanings. It may, for instance, equate one character with goodness and another character with evil. Light may represent good while darkness represents evil. Anything green in the story may be equated with safety while any red object means danger. By mapping out these binary oppositions throughout the text, structuralists would be able, they maintain, to chart how the story's meaning evolves.

No matter what its methodology, structuralism emphasizes form and structure, not actual content of a text. Although individual texts must be analyzed, structuralists are more interested in the rule-governed system that underlies texts rather than in the texts themselves. *How* texts mean, not *what* texts mean, is their chief interest.

In the student essay that follows, note how the interpretation of Susan Glaspell's play *Trifles* revolves around three major binary oppositions or tensions. While the writer specifically mentions these oppositions, she also uses an intricate web of secondary or minor oppositions that become the structural bases of her interpretation. What are the secondary or minor oppositions in relationship to the major binary oppositions? How are the major and secondary oppositions linked? Can you map out a listing of these binary oppositions on which the interpretation is based?

Further Reading

Barthes, Roland. *S/Z*. Trans. R. Miller. New York: Hill and Wang, 1975.

Berman, Art. *From the New Criticism to Deconstruction*. Chicago: University of Illinois Press, 1988.

Culler, Jonathan. *Structuralist Poetics: Structuralism, Linguistics and the Study of Literature*. London: Routledge & Kegan Paul, 1975.

Eagleton, Terry. *Literary Theory: An Introduction*. Minneapolis: University of Minnesota Press, 1983.

Lentricchia, Frank. *After the New Criticism*. Chicago: University of Chicago Press, 1980.

Scholes, Robert. *Structuralism in Literature: An Introduction*. New Haven: Yale University Press, 1974.

Selden, Raman. *A Reader's Guide to Comtemporary Literary Theory*. Lexington: University Press of Kentucky, 1985.

Student Essay

A Structuralist Look at Glaspell's Trifles

Susan Glaspell's *Trifles* centers around the investigation of John Wright's murder and takes place entirely within the walls of his farmhouse kitchen. Only five characters command the stage. Three are men, consisting of George Henderson, the county attorney; Henry Peters, the sheriff; and Lewis Hale, a neighboring farmer. The men have come to Wright's house to look for evidence incriminating to Minnie Wright, held in jail for the murder of her husband. Along with them come two of their wives, Mrs. Peters and Mrs. Hale, to collect everyday items needed by Minnie during her imprisonment. Ironically, the women, through noticing the "trifles" of Mrs. Wright's life common to their own, stumble onto the material searched for by their husbands. A dead canary with a twisted neck found in a pretty box awaiting burial tells them that John Wright killed the only thing of joy in his wife's life. His cruel action spurs Mrs. Wright to kill him, and the knotting on a quilt shows them the method she employed.

Scoffing at the women's interest in minor details such as the quilt, the men overlook the canary and the knotting, and Mrs. Hale and Mrs. Peters keep their discoveries to themselves. They protect Minnie because they empathize with her, sharing the bond of oppression placed over them by their husbands. Though they are horrified at Mrs. Wright's gross act, they respect the woman who put an end to her oppressor, something they do not have the courage to do themselves.

Such an analysis of the play reveals three complex binary oppositions upon which the above interpretation is built, with each binary opposition being connected to and interwoven with the others. The most obvious of the three centers on the relationship between women and men—in this case, how Mrs. Peters and Mrs. Hale interact with each other as opposed to how they do so with their husbands. Part of the way they relate rests heavily on the second binary opposition, the concept of freedom vs. oppression that provides a motive both for Mr. Wright's murder and for the protection the two ladies lend his wife at the expense of the destruction of evidence. The evidence falls into the women's hands because male and female opinion differ in what each gender deems as noteworthy, thus revealing the third binary opposition. The men, for example, consider their wives' interest in fruit preserves and quilts as merely "trifles." Yet it is by paying attention to these small things that Mrs. Hale and Mrs. Peters stumble across the material sought by the men.

The opening stage directions establish the first tension between male and female by the men's entering first instead of demonstrating respect by following the "ladies first" rule of that era. The nonchalant manner of the men seems to reflect that they take their wives for granted, and Mr. Hale attests to this fact when he speaks of the late Mr. Wright: "I didn't know as what his wife wanted made much difference to John." The implication is that the husband has command in what goes on in his household.

Shortly thereafter, the sheriff, Mr. Peters, verbally acknowledges a difference between genders, though he does not articulate the thought completely. "Well, can you beat the women!" he exclaims, referring to one woman but using the plural form, "Held for murder and worryin' about her preserves." Obviously, Mr. Peters thinks that if a man were incarcerated for such a crime, he would not worry about mundane matters but would concern himself with the logistics of his imprisonment. In association with Mrs. Wright's worrying over her preserves, women in general, according to Mr. Hale, "are used to worrying over trifles." Such a statement degrades female concerns and is an insult to Mrs. Hale and Mrs. Peters, whether or not Mr. Hale meant it as one.

Also introduced as a characteristic of women is loyalty to their gender, as observed somewhat condescendingly by the county attorney when Mrs. Hale defends Mrs. Wright's seeming lack of housekeeping. Stage directions reinforce this idea; the two women stand physically close together until the men exit to go upstairs. After they have gone, Mrs. Hale says that she'd "hate to have men coming into my kitchen, snooping around and criticizing." Mrs. Peters, though understanding, merely labels the invasion of privacy as "their duty," but both women imply that their husbands are insensitive to Mrs. Wright's plight. They sympathize with her because they know the physical labor it takes to keep up a farmhouse and because she did not have time to clean up before she was trundled off to jail.

Other tensions between genders are revealed through the characters' interaction. Every time the men enter the stage, for example, they dominate the conversation, moving boldly and decisively from one place to another. Conversely, the women speak sparingly in the presence of their husbands, timid in their movements and speech until left alone when they can relax once more.

Many of these characteristics arise from the second major binary opposition of freedom over oppression. The best support of this tension develops from the description of Minnie Foster 30 years ago as opposed to the present-day Mrs. Wright. Seeing the drabness of Mrs. Wright's clothes, Mrs. Hale says, "She used to wear pretty clothes and be lively, when she was Minnie Foster, one of the town girls singing in the choir," and later, "She was kind of like a bird herself—real sweet and pretty. . . . How—she—did—change." This description depicts Miss Foster as a cheerful, pretty woman who loved to sing and be among people. Both women know, however, that 30 years has greatly changed her. Her clothes are "shabby," her home "weren't cheerful," and she no longer sings. Mrs. Hale and Mrs. Peters attribute the change to John Wright. "Wright was close," Mrs. Hale says and continues later, "But he was a hard man, Mrs. Peters. . . . Like a raw wind that gets to the bone." She has no doubt that Wright killed the joy and life out of Minnie Foster, just as she believes he strangled the canary.

Interrelated to the tension of oppression is the women's empathy with Minnie. Mrs. Hale demonstrates this tension early in the play by defending Minnie from the attorney's criticism of her housekeeping. She understands the work involved in maintaining a farm as well as the injustice of having men search through her house when she is not there. Mrs. Peters, though "married to the law," similarly empathizes with Minnie. The dead canary reminds her of her violent reaction to a boy who axed a kitten she owned in her youth, and she remembers the stillness and isolation of her homestead in Dakota after she lost her first child.

The empathy both women feel gives them a common bond with Minnie Wright, causing them first to notice the household details with which she would have been concerned, and second, to hide the "trifles" that would condemn her. Their attention to detail encompasses simple things such as the fruit preserves and the tidiness of the house, but the more significant finds are the dead canary and the quilt, both discovered by accident, both overlooked by the men who fail to recognize the importance of examining her personal belongings. Had the men taken more of an interest in the "trifles," they would have discovered the method of strangulation. Mrs. Wright seemingly "knotted" her husband, following the technique used in quilting. Mrs. Hale and Mrs. Peters recognize the knotting method, but the men overlook it, even ridiculing it: "They wonder if she was going to quilt it or just knot it!" At this point in the play the stage directions order

the men to laugh and the women look abashed. The men's superior attitude causes them to miss the evidence which would link Mrs. Wright to
the crime, even though it is right in front of them.

Seemingly, the dead bird provides the motive for the murder. Mrs.
Hale and Mrs. Peters must believe that Mr. Wright broke the canary's neck
or else they would never lie about a cat that does not exist nor would they
hide the burial box in the pocket of Mrs. Hale's overcoat. Trifles, then, discovered accidentally by the women, explain motive and method, even
though the men have searched the entire house and barnyard, going about
what even Mrs. Peters calls "important things."

That Mrs. Hale and Mrs. Peters do not turn in their evidence shows
that they understand the oppression John Wright placed on his wife and
why she chose to liberate herself the way she did. Her freedom is something they will protect, perhaps because they empathize with her or perhaps because they wish for the kind of freedom she now has, even while
sitting in the jail cell. The oppression the men place on their women, from
their insensitive comments about keeping house to the ridicule expressed
for interest in simple things, explains why the women do not relinquish
the bird and the knotted quilt. Mrs. Hale and Mrs. Peters have the satisfac-
tion of knowing they have solved a crime their husbands could not while
still protecting a friend. Their secret is their bid for freedom, something the
men cannot dominate or quash.

JULIE CLAYPOOL

6

Deconstruction

Introduction

Emerging in the late 1960s as a new strategy for textual analysis and an alternative approach to interpreting literature, **poststructuralism** captured the attention of American critical theorists. Like structuralism, its immediate predecessor, this new movement is best characterized as an activity or reading strategy, not a philosophy. Unlike other schools of criticism, poststructuralism possesses neither an accepted body of doctrines nor methodologies. Rather than providing answers about the meaning of texts, this critical activity asks questions, endeavoring to show that what a text claims it says and what it actually says are discernibly different. By casting doubt on most previously held theories, poststructuralism declares that a text has an infinite number of possible interpretations. And the interpretations themselves, the poststructuralists posit, are just as creative and important as the text being interpreted.

Although the term poststructuralism presently refers to a variety of theories (New Historicism, for example) that have developed *after* structuralism, today the terms poststructuralism and **deconstruction** are often used interchangeably. Coined by its founding father, Jacques Derrida, deconstruction first emerged on the American literary stage in 1966 when Derrida, a French philosopher and teacher, read his paper "Structure, Sign, and Play" at a Johns Hopkins University symposium. By questioning and disputing in this paper the metaphysical assumptions held to be true by Western philosophy since the time of Plato, Derrida inaugurated what many critics believe to be the most intricate and challenging method of textual analysis yet to appear.

Derrida himself, however, would not want deconstruction dubbed a critical theory, a school of criticism, a mode or method of literary criticism, or a philosophy. Nowhere in Derrida's writings does he state the encompassing tenets of his critical approach, nor does he ever present a codified body of deconstructive theory or methodology. Although he gives his views in bits and pieces throughout his works, he believes that he cannot develop a formalized statement of his "rules for reading, interpretation, and writing." Unlike a unified treatise, Derrida claims, his approach to reading (and literary analysis) is more a "strategic device" than a methodology, more a strategy or approach to literature than a school or theory of criticism. Such theories of criticism, he believes, must identify with a body of knowledge that they decree to be true or to contain truth. It is this assertion (that truth or a core of metaphysical ideals can be definitely believed, articulated, and supported) that Derrida and deconstruction wish to dispute and "deconstruct."

Because deconstruction utilizes previously formulated theories from other schools of criticism, coins many words for its newly established ideas, and challenges beliefs long held by Western culture, many students, teachers, and even critics avoid studying deconstruction, fearing its supposed complexity. But by dividing deconstruction and its assumptions into three smaller areas of study rather than plunging directly into some of its complex terminology, we can begin to grasp this approach to textual analysis. In order to understand deconstruction and its "strategic" approach to a text, then, we must first gain a working knowledge of the historical and philosophical roots of structuralism, a linguistic approach to textual analysis that gained critical attention and popularity in the 1950s and 1960s (see Chapter 5 for a detailed analysis of structuralism). From this school of criticism Derrida borrows the basis of and the starting point for his deconstructive strategy. After examining structuralism, we must then investigate the proposed radical changes Derrida makes in Western philosophy and metaphysics. Such changes, Derrida readily admits, literally turn Western metaphysics on its head. And finally, we must master some new terminology coupled with new philosophical assumptions and their corresponding methodological approaches to textual analysis if we wish to understand and utilize deconstruction's approach to interpreting a text.

Historical Development

Derrida begins formulating his "strategy of reading" by critiquing Ferdinand de Saussure's *Course in General Linguistics*. Saussure, the father of modern linguistics, dramatically shifted the focus of linguistic science in the early part of the twentieth century. It is his ideas concerning language that form the core of structuralism, the critical body of literary theory from which Derrida borrows one of the major philosophical building blocks of deconstruction.

According to Saussure, structural linguistics (and structuralism itself) rests on a few basic principles. First, language is a system of rules, and these rules govern its every aspect, including individual sounds that comprise a word (the *t* in *cat*, for example), small units that join together to form a word (*garden* + *er* = *gardener*), grammatical relationships between words (such as the rule that a singular subject must combine with a singular verb—for example, in *John eats ice cream*), and the relationships among all words in a sentence (such as the relationship between the phrase *under a tree* and all remaining words in the sentence *Mary sits under a tree to eat her lunch*). Every speaker of a language both consciously and unconsciously learns these rules and knows when they are broken. Speakers of English know, for example, that the sentence *Simon grew up to be a brilliant doctor* seems correct or follows the rules of the English language but that the sentence *Simon up grew a brilliant doctor* is somehow incorrect or violates the rules of English. These rules that comprise a language Saussure dubs **langue**. Saussure recognizes that individual speakers of a language evidence langue in their individual speech utterances, which he calls **parole**. It is the task of the linguist, Saussure believes, to infer a language's langue from the analysis of many instances of parole.

Emphasizing the systematized nature of language, Saussure then asserts that all languages are composed of basic units or **emes**. Identifying these paradigms (models) or relationships between the symbols (the letters of the alphabet, for example) in a given language is the job of a linguist. This task becomes especially difficult when the emes in the linguist's native language and those in an unfamiliar language under investigation differ. Generally, linguists must first recognize and understand the various emes in their native language. For example, one eme in all languages is the individual sounds that comprise words. The number of distinct and significant sounds (or **phonemes**) that comprise a language ranges from the low teens to 60 and above. English, for instance, has approximately 45 phonemes. When, however, is a sound a phoneme that can change the meaning of a group of phonemes (i.e., a word) or simply a variation of a phoneme that is linguistically insignificant? For example, in English the letter *t* represents the sound /t/. But is there one distinct pronunciation for this sound whenever and wherever it appears in an English word? Is the *t* in the word *tip*, for instance, pronounced the same as the *t* in *stop*? Obviously no, for the first *t* is **aspirated** or pronounced with a greater force of air than the *t* in *stop*. In either word, however, a speaker of English could still identify the /t/ as a phoneme, or a distinct sound. If we then replace the *t* in *tip* with a *d*, we now have *dip*, the difference between the two words being the sounds /t/ and /d/. Upon analysis, we find that these sounds are pronounced in the same location in the mouth but with one difference: /d/ is **voiced** or pronounced with the vocal cords vibrating, whereas /t/ is **unvoiced**, with the vocal cords remaining basically still. It is this difference between the sounds /t/ and /d/ that allows us to say that /t/ and /d/ are phonemes or distinct sounds in English. Whether the eme (any linguistic category such as phoneme) is a sound, a minimal unit of grammar such as the adding of an -*s* in English to form the plural, or any other distinct category of a language, Saussure's basic premise operates: within each eme, distinctions depend on differences.

That distinctions or meaning in language depend on differences within each eme radically changes some fundamental concepts long held by linguists preceding Saussure. Before Saussure, linguists believed that the structure of language was *mimetic*, merely mimicking the outside world; language, then, had no structure of its own. It simply copied its structure from the reality exhibited in the world in which it was utilized. Saussure denies that language is intrinsically mimetic and demonstrates that it is primarily determined by its own internal rules, such as phonology (individual sounds), grammar (the principles and rules of a language), and syntax (how words combine within an utterance to form meaning). Furthermore, these rules are highly systematized and structured. But most importantly, Saussure argues that the **linguistic sign** (the sounds of words and their representations in a language) that comprises language itself is both arbitrary and conventional. For example, most languages have different words for the same concept. For instance, the English word *man* is *homme* in French. And in English we know that the meaning or function of the word *pit* exists not because it possesses some innate acoustic quality but because it differs from *hit*, *wit*, and *lit*. In other words, the linguistic sign is composed of two parts: the **signifier**, or the spoken or written constituent such as the sound /t/ and the orthographic (written) symbol *t*, and the **signified**, the concept that is signaled by the signifier. It is this relationship between the signifier (the word *dog*, for example) and the signified (the concept or the reality behind the word *dog*) that Saussure maintains is arbitrary and conventional. The linguistic sign, then, is defined by differences that distinguish it from other signs, not by any innate properties.

Believing that our knowledge of the world is shaped by the language that represents it, Saussure insists upon the arbitrary relationship between the signifier and the signified. By so doing, he undermines the long-held belief that there is some natural link between the word and the thing it represents. For Saussure, meaning in language, then, resides in a systematized combination of sounds that chiefly rely on the differences among these signs, not any innate properties within the signs themselves. It is this concept that meaning in language is determined by the differences among the language signs that Derrida borrows from Saussure as a key building block in the formulation of deconstruction.

Derridean deconstruction begins with and emphatically affirms Saussure's decree that language is a system based on differences. Derrida agrees with Saussure that we can know the meaning of signifiers through and because of their relationships and their differences among themselves. Unlike Saussure, Derrida also applies this reasoning to the signified. Like the signifier, the signified (or concept) can also be known only through its relationships and its differences from other signifieds. Furthermore, declares Derrida, the signified cannot orient or make permanent the meaning of the signifier, for the relationship between the signifier and the signified is both arbitrary and conventional. And, accordingly, signifieds often function as signifiers. For example, in the sentence *I filled the glass with milk*, the spoken or written word *glass* is a signifier; its signified is the concept of a container that can be filled. But in the sentence *The container was filled with glass*, the spoken or written word *container*, a signified in the previous sentence, is now a signifier, its signified being the concept of an object that can be filled.

Assumptions

Believing that **signification** (how we arrive at meaning from the linguistic signs in language) is both arbitrary and conventional, Derrida now begins his process of turning Western philosophy on its head: he boldly asserts that the entire history of Western metaphysics from Plato to the present is founded upon a classic, fundamental error: the searching for a **transcendental signified**, an external point of reference upon which one may build a concept or philosophy. Once found, this transcendental signified would provide ultimate meaning, being the origin of origins, reflecting itself, and as Derrida says, providing a "reassuring end to the reference from sign to sign." It would, in essence, guarantee to those who believe in it that they do exist and have meaning. For example, if we posit that *I* or *self* is a transcendental signified, then the concept of *self* becomes the unifying principle upon which I structure my world. Objects, concepts, ideas or even people only take on meaning in my world if I filter them through my unifying, ultimate signified: *self*.

Unlike other signifieds, the transcendental signified would have to be understood without comparing it to other signifieds or signifiers. In other words, its meaning would originate directly with itself, not differentially or relationally as does the meaning of all other signifieds or signifiers. These transcendental signifieds would then provide the "center" of meaning, allowing those who believed in them to structure their ideas of reality around these "centers" of truth. Such a center of meaning could not subject itself to structural analysis, for by so doing it would lose its place as a transcendental signified to another center. For example, if I declare the concept *self* to be my transcendental signified and then learn that my mind or self is composed of the id, the ego, and the superego, I could no longer hold the *self* or *I* to be my transcendental signified. In the process of discovering the three parts of my conscious and unconscious mind, I have both structurally analyzed and "decentered" *self*, thus negating it as a transcendental signified.

According to Derrida, Western metaphysics has invented a variety of terms that function as centers: God, reason, origin, being, essence, truth, humanity, beginning, end, and self, to name a few. Each operates as a concept or term that is self-sufficient and self-originating and serves as a transcendental signified. This Western proclivity for desiring a center Derrida names **logocentrism**: the belief that there is an ultimate reality or center of truth that can serve as the basis for all our thoughts and actions.

That we can never totally free ourselves from our logocentric habit of thinking and our inherited concept of the universe Derrida readily admits. To "decenter" any transcendental signified is to be caught up automatically in the terminology that allows that centering concept to operate. For example, if the concept *self* functions as my center and I then "discover" my unconscious *self*, I automatically place in motion a binary operation or two opposing concepts: the *self* and the *unconscious self*. By decentering and questioning the *self*, I may cause the *unconscious self* to become the new center. By questioning the old center, I may establish a new one.

Since the establishing of one center of unity automatically means that another is decentered, Derrida concludes that Western metaphysics is based on a system of binary operations or conceptual oppositions. For each center, there exists an opposing center (God/humankind, for example). In addition, Western philosophy decrees that in each of these binary operations or two opposing centers, one concept is superior and defines itself by its opposite or inferior center. We know *truth*, for instance, because we know *deception*; we know *good* because we know *bad*. It is the creating of these hierarchal binaries as the basis for Western metaphysics to which Derrida objects.

Such a fragile basis for believing what is really real Derrida wishes to dismantle. In the binary oppositions upon which Western metaphysics has built itself from the time of Plato, Derrida declares that one element will always be in a superior position, or **privileged**, while the other becomes inferior, or **unprivileged**. According to this way of thinking, the first or top elements in the following list of binary oppositions are privileged, for example: man/woman, human/animal, soul/body, good/bad. Most importantly, Derrida decrees that Western thought has long privileged speech over writing. This privileging of speech over writing Derrida calls **phonocentrism**.

In placing speech in the privileged position, phonocentrism treats writing as inferior. We value, says Derrida, a speaker's words more than the speaker's writing, for words imply presence. Through the vehicle of spoken words, we supposedly learn directly what a speaker is trying to say. From this point of view, writing becomes a mere copy of speech, an attempt to capture the idea that was once spoken. Whereas speech implies presence, writing signifies absence, thereby placing into action another binary opposition: presence/absence.

Since phonocentrism is based on the assumption that speech conveys the meaning or direct ideas of a speaker better than writing (a mere copy of speech), phonocentrism assumes a logocentric way of thinking, that the "self" is the center of meaning and can best ascertain ideas directly from other "selves" through spoken words. Through speaking, the self declares its presence, its significance, and its being (or existence).

Accordingly, Derrida coins the phrase **metaphysics of presence** to encompass ideas such as logocentrism, phonocentrism, the operation of binary oppositions, and other notions that Western thought holds concerning language and metaphysics. His objective is to demonstrate the shaky foundations upon which such beliefs have been established. By deconstructing the basic premises of metaphysics of presence, Derrida believes he gives us a strategy for reading that opens up a variety of new interpretations heretofore unseen by those who are bound by the restraints of Western thought.

Methodology

The first stage in a deconstructive reading is to recognize the existence and the operation of binary oppositions in our thinking. One of the most "violent hierarchies" derived from Platonic and Aristotelian thought is speech/writing, with speech being privileged. Consequently, speech is awarded presence, and writing is equated with absence. Being the inferior of the two, writing becomes simply the symbols of speech, a second-hand representation of ideas.

Once the speech/writing hierarchy or any other hierarchy is recognized and acknowledged, Derrida asserts, we can readily reverse its elements. Such a reversal is possible since truth is ever-elusive, for we can always decenter the center if any is found. By reversing the hierarchy, Derrida does not wish merely to substitute one hierarchy for another and to involve himself in a negative mode. When the hierarchy is reversed, says Derrida, we can examine those values and beliefs that give rise to both the original hierarchy and the newly created one. Such an examination will reveal how the meaning of terms arises from the differences between them.

In *Of Grammatology*, Derrida spends much time explaining why the speech/writing hierarchy can and must be reversed. In short, he argues that spoken language is a kind of writing which he calls **archi-écriture** or **arche-writing**. Both spoken language and writing, he declares, share common characteristics. Both, for example, involve an encoding or inscription. In writing, this coding is obvious, for the written symbols represent various sounds. And in language or speech, a similar encoding exists. As Saussure has already shown, there exists an arbitrary relationship between the signifier and the signified (between the spoken word *cat* and the concept of cat itself). There is, then, no innate relationship between the spoken word and the concept, object, or idea it represents. Nevertheless, a relationship now exists in English between the spoken word *cat* and its concept, thereby implying that some kind of inscription or encoding has taken place.

In Derrida's arche-writing, then, writing becomes privileged while speech becomes unprivileged, for speech is a kind of writing. This being so, Derrida then challenges Western philosophy's concept that human consciousness gives birth to language. Without language (or arche-writing), argues Derrida, there can be no consciousness, for consciousness presupposes language. Through arche-writing, we impose human consciousness upon the world.

The relationship between any binary hierarchy, however, is always unstable and problematic. It is not Derrida's purpose simply to reverse all binary oppositions that exist in Western thought but rather to show the fragile basis for the establishment of such hierarchies and the possibility of inverting these hierarchies to gain new insights into language and life. Derrida uses the term **supplement** to refer to the unstable relationship between elements in a binary operation. For example, in the speech/writing opposition, writing supplements speech and in actuality takes the place of speech (arche-writing). In all binary oppositions such supplementation exists. In the truth/deception hierarchy, for example, Western thought would assert the supremacy of truth over deception, attributing to deception a mere supplementary role. Such a logocentric way of thinking asserts the purity of truth over deception. Upon examination, deception more frequently than not contains at least some truth. And who is to say, asks Derrida, when truth has been spoken, achieved, or even conceived. The purity of truth may simply not exist. In all human activity, then, supplementation operates.

By realizing that supplementation operates in all of Western metaphysics' binary operations, and by inverting the privileged and unprivileged elements, Derrida begins to develop his reading strategy of deconstruction. Once he "turns Western metaphysics on its head," he asserts his answer to logocentrism and other Western elements by coining a new word and concept: **différance**. The word itself is derived from the

French word *différer*, meaning (1) to defer, postpone, or delay, and (2) to differ, to be different from. Derrida deliberately coins his word to be ambiguous, taking on both meanings simultaneously. And in French, the word is a pun, for it exists only in writing; in speech there is no way to tell the difference between the French word *différence* and Derrida's coined word *différance*.

Understanding what Derrida means by *différance* is one of the primary keys to understanding deconstruction. Basically, *différance* is Derrida's "What if?" question. What if no transcendental signified exists? What if there is no presence in which we can find ultimate truth? What if all our knowledge does not arise from self-identity? What if there is no essence, being, or inherently unifying element in the universe? What then?

The presence of such a transcendental signified would immediately establish the binary operation presence/absence. Since Western metaphysics holds that presence is supreme or privileged and absence unprivileged, Derrida suggests that we temporarily reverse this hierarchy, its now becoming absence/presence. By such a reversal, no longer can we posit a transcendental signified. No longer is there some absolute standard or coherent unity from which all knowledge proceeds and develops. All human knowledge and all self-identity must now spring from difference, not sameness, from absence, not presence.

When such a reversal of Western metaphysics' pivotal binary operation occurs, two dramatic results follow. First: All human knowledge becomes referential; that is, we can only know something because it differs from some other bit of knowledge, not because we can compare this knowledge to any absolute or coherent unity (a transcendental signified). Human knowledge, then, must now be based on *difference*. We know something because it differs from something else to which it is related. Nothing can now be studied or learned in isolation, for all knowledge becomes context-related. Second: We must also forgo closure; that is, since no transcendental signified exists, all interpretations concerning life, self-identity, and knowledge are possible, probable, and legitimate.

But what is the significance of *différance* when reading texts? If we, like Derrida, assert that *différance* operates in language and therefore also in writing (Derrida sometimes equates *différance* and arche-writing), what are the implications for textual analysis? The most obvious answer is that texts lack presence. Once we do away with the transcendental signified and reverse the presence/absence binary operation, texts can no longer have presence; that is, in isolation, texts cannot possess meaning. Since all meaning and knowledge is now based on differences, no text can simply mean one thing. Texts become intertextual. Meaning evolves from the interrelatedness of one text to many other texts. Like language itself, texts are caught in a dynamic, context-related interchange. Never can we state a text's definitive meaning, for it has none. No longer can we declare one interpretation to be right and another wrong, for meaning in a text is always elusive, always dynamic, always transitory.

The search, then, for the text's correct meaning or the author's so-called intentions becomes meaningless. Since meaning is derived from differences in a dynamic, context-related, ongoing process, all texts have multiple meanings or interpretations. If we assert, as does Derrida, that no transcendental signified exists, then there can exist no absolute or pure meaning supposedly conveyed by authorial intent or professorial dictates. Meaning evolves as we, the readers, interact with the text, with both the readers and the text providing social and cultural context.

A deconstructor would thus begin textual analysis assuming that a text has multiple interpretations and that it allows itself to be reread and thus reinterpreted countless times. Since no one correct interpretation of a text exists, the joy of textual analysis resides in discovering new interpretations each time a text is read or reread. Ultimately, a text's meaning is undecidable, for each reading or rereading can elicit different interpretations.

When beginning the interpretative process, deconstructors seek to overrule their own logocentric and inherited ways of viewing a text. Such revolutionary thinking decrees that they find the binary oppositions at work in the text itself. These binary oppositions, they believe, represent established and accepted ideologies that more frequently than not posit the existence of transcendental signifieds. These binary operations, then, restrict meaning, for they already assume a fixed interpretation of reality or of the universe. They assume, for instance, the existence of truth and falsehood, reason and insanity, good and bad. Realizing that these hierarchies presuppose a fixed and biased way of viewing the world, deconstructors seek out the binary oppositions operating in the text and reverse them. By reversing these hierarchies, deconstructors wish to challenge the fixed views assumed by such hierarchies and the values associated with such rigid beliefs.

By identifying the binary operations that exist in the text, deconstructors can then show the preconceived assumptions upon which most of us base our interpretations. We all, for example, declare some activity, being, or object to be good or bad, valuable or worthless, significant or insignificant. Such values or ideas automatically operate when we write or read a text. By reversing the hierarchies upon which we base our interpretations, deconstructors wish to free us from the constraints of our prejudiced beliefs. Such freedom, they hope, will allow us to see a text from exciting new perspectives or levels that we have never before recognized.

These various levels of a text are not simultaneously perceived by the reader or even the writer of a text. In Nathaniel Hawthorne's "Young Goodman Brown," for example, many readers believe that the 50 year-old character who shepherds Goodman Brown through his night's visit in the forest is Satan and therefore necessarily an evil character. Brown's own interpretation of this character seems to support this view. According to deconstructionist ideas, as least two binary operations are at work here: good/evil and God/Satan. But what if we reverse these hierarchies? Then the sceptered figure may not be Satan and therefore may not be evil! such a new perspective may dramatically change our interpretation of the text.

According to deconstructors, we cannot simultaneously see both of these views or levels in the story. To discover where the new hierarchy Satan/God or evil/good will lead us in our interpretation, we must suspend our first level of interpretation. We do not, however, forget it, its being locked in our minds. We simply shift our allegiance to another level.

Such oscillating between interpretations, levels, or meanings allows us to see the impossibility of ever choosing a correct interpretation, for meaning is an ongoing activity that is always in progress, always based upon *différance*. By asking what will happen if we reverse the hierarchies that frame our preconceived ways of thinking, we open ourselves to a never-ending process of interpretation that decrees that no hierarchy or binary operation is right and no other is wrong.

Deconstructors do not wish, then, to set up a new philosophy, a new literary theory of analysis, or a new school of literary criticism. Instead, they present a reading strategy that allows us to make choices concerning the various levels of interpretation we see operating in a text. All levels, they maintain, have validity. They furthermore believe that their approach to reading frees them and us from ideological allegiances that restrict our finding meaning in a text.

Since meaning, they believe, emerges through interpretation, even the author does not control a text's interpretation. Although writers may have clearly stated intentions concerning their texts, such statements should and must be given little credence. Like language itself, texts have no outside referents (or transcendental signifieds). What an author thinks he or she says or means in a text may be quite different from what is actually written. Deconstructors therefore look for places in the text where the author loses control of language and says what was supposedly not meant to be said. These "slips of language" often occur in questions, figurative language, and strong declarations. By examining these slips and the binary operations that govern them, deconstructors show the undecidability of a text's meaning.

On first glance, a deconstructionist reading strategy may appear to be linear—that is, having a clearly delineated beginning, middle, and end. If this is so, then to apply this strategy to a text, we must (1) discover the binary operations that govern a text, (2) comment on the values, concepts, and ideas behind these operations, (3) reverse these present binary operations, (4) dismantle previously held worldviews, (5) accept the possibility of various levels of a text based on the new binary inversions, and (6) allow the meaning of the text to be undecidable. Although all the above elements do operate in a deconstructionist reading, they may not always operate in this exact sequence. Since we all tend toward logocentrism when reading, for example, we may not note some logocentric binary operations functioning in the text until we have reversed some obvious binary oppositions and are interpreting the text on several levels. In addition, we may never declare such a reading to be complete or finished, for the process of meaning is ongoing, never allowing us to pledge allegiance to any one view.

Such a reading strategy disturbs most readers and critics, for it is not a neat, completed package whereby if we follow step A through to step Z we arrive at "the" reading of the text. Since texts have no external referents, their meanings depend on the close interaction of the text, the reader, and social and cultural elements, as does every reading or interpretative process. Denying the organic unity of a text, deconstructors declare the free play of language in a text. Since language itself is reflexive, not mimetic, we can never stop finding meaning in a text, whether we have read it once or a hundred times.

Overall, deconstruction aims at an ongoing relationship between the interpreter (the critic) and the text. By examining the text alone, deconstructors hope to ask a set of questions that continually challenges the ideological positions of power and authority that dominate literary criticism. And in the process of discovering meaning in a text, they declare that the criticism itself is just as valuable as the creative writing that is being read, thus inverting the creative writing/criticism hierarchy.

The following essay demonstrates many aspects of deconstruction. Note carefully the stating of the binary oppositions and their effects that govern an interpretation of the text, the inversion of these operations, and the various levels of readings that evolve once these binary oppositions are reversed. Also note how the writer tries to divorce himself from logocentric thinking and the metaphysics of presence as he seeks to find meaning in the text.

Further Reading

Atkins, G. Douglas. *Reading Deconstruction: Deconstructive Reading*. Lexington: University Press of Kentucky, 1983.

Culler, Jonathan D. *On Deconstruction: Theory and Criticism After Structuralism*. Ithaca, NY: Cornell University Press, 1982.

Ellis, John M. *Against Deconstruction*. Princeton: Princeton University Press, 1989.

Gasche, Rodolphe. "Deconstruction as Criticism." *Glyph Textual Studies* 6 (1979): 177–215.

Jefferson, Ann. "Structuralism and Post Structuralism." *Modern Literary Theory: A Comparative Introduction*. Totowa, NJ: Barnes, 1982. 84–112.

Norris, Christopher. *Deconstruction: Theory and Practice*. London: Methuen, 1982.
Rajnath, ed. *Deconstruction: A Critique*. New York: Macmillan, 1989.

Student Essay

A Deconstructor's View
of "Young Goodman Brown"

In the text of "Young Goodman Brown," we find about nine pages of written words, most of them having several definitions. How is it that we read the work and perhaps assume a definite message behind each word every time we read the text? We do so because we privilege some ideas while devaluing others. By utilizing a deconstructive reading process, we will discover the conventions and prejudices of our own thinking which prescribe meaning to the words of the story. After we acknowledge and recognize some of our prejudices through the use of binary oppositions, we will explore what the text allows the words to mean outside of our own assumptions. But we will not stop there, for we bring to the text a previously formed system of interrelated, privileged ideas. Light, for instance, not only symbolizes truth but also civilization, God, heaven, and possibly faith. Our first analysis and reading of Hawthorne's story, then, comes as no surprise if we associate Goodman Brown's journey with our unprivileged network of ideas, i.e., darkness, the forest, Satan, hell, and doubt. Using deconstructive methods, we will challenge our world view and provide a fresh interpretation of Hawthorne's tale.

Most probably middle-class, white readers like me privilege light over darkness. We have learned that "God is Light." As a result, the white, Anglo-Saxon interpretation of "Young Goodman Brown" may assume that Brown's nighttime journey, occurring between dusk and sunrise, strays from God and truth, ideas we associate with light. When Brown leaves Faith, his wife (her name having obvious figurative meaning), he also leaves his faith in that "Light in which there is no darkness." According to this interpretation, we might assume, then, that his journey is an evil deception, one of Satan's lies.

Perhaps we have also learned to value reason as opposed to illogical or irrational thinking. At the onset of the tale, before Brown has left the light of day, the text suggests only Brown's ignorance. First, we see that he is a newlywed, and thus inexperienced. Even his name, Young Goodman Brown, implies that he is too young and naive to possess the wisdom that might accompany age. Before entering darkness, Brown hopes that he will return to his wife after his trip and "cling to her skirts and follow her to heaven," suggesting that he himself lacks the initiative to reason on his own journey to heaven; instead he will depend upon his "sweet, pretty wife" for moral guidance.

But after Brown walks into the darkness, his companion suggests to him that they should "reason as we go." Brown's companion soon realizes that "his arguments seemed rather to spring up in the bosom of his auditor than to be suggested by himself." This quotation might serve as evidence of Satan's deception, that "his arguments" are in human nature and consequently surface in Brown's reasoning. Privileging both light and reason, we assume that this is perverse, devil-imposed reasoning which takes place in the night. The quotation might also suggest that in the discourse between Brown and the alleged devil, Brown was merely deceived into believing that the arguments were his own and not Satan's. I suggest, however, that the text misspeaks at this point. If the arguments were indeed Satan's, then the arguments would have to be suggested by Satan. But the text allows us to believe that the arguments could have been Brown's. These arguments, then, could not be Satan's fallen influence on human nature, but merely human reasoning. For the first time we see that Brown has left his naivete behind and reasons for himself as the arguments "spring up" from his own bosom. We now see conflict in privileging both light and reason, for it is the night that brings about Brown's first reasoning. Perhaps Brown leaves the "light" (in both the biblical and literal senses of the word) to discover that knowledge of truth resides in opposition to his Puritanical "Light." In this case, Brown's Puritan God represents the icon of Brown's unreasoned faith, for his faith in God consists of blindly following his wife to heaven, but his doubt begins with reason. Truth, then, might reside in Satan who provokes Brown to reason on his own, the antithesis of the Puritan God. In this case, Satan would represent the God of truth and reason.

Not only does Brown leave light upon his departure, but he also leaves the city and enters the forest, a "darkened, " "gloomy," and threatening forest. After leaving Faith, Brown soon meets a man, thought to be Satan, in the forest. We can assume that this man is Satan by acknowledging several figurative cues in the text. First, he resides in the dark of the forest, and because we privilege the concept of city over forest, or civilization over crude uncivilized existence, we will be suspicious of people or things appearing in the forest. As Brown walks away from the city, at first alone, he suspects the presence of a"a devilish Indian behind every tree." This "devilish Indian" represents the opposite of city and civility; such a figure is the essence of savage, uncivilized existence.

Immediately after Brown's suspicions are announced, the Satan figure appears. Our associations with the aforementioned unprivileged ideas lead us to assign this character an evil status. Several more figurative clues affirm his role as Satan; he carries a staff, he encourages Brown to doubt Faith, and so on. We realize, though, that the text itself does not insist on the identity of the alleged devil; instead, the text remains ambiguous leaving it to our own assumptions to devise a definite identity. From the start of the story we conjecture that Brown's relation to the alleged Devil will lead him into darkness or evil. But to condemn this devil figure who asks Brown only to reason along the forest path would be to condemn reason itself.

We find, however, that the text allows us to privilege the forest and solitude as opposed to civilization and the city. As we privilege the darkness in which Brown first reasons for himself, we may also privilege the forest as opposed to the city, for it was in the dark forest where Brown gained his own power to reason. The forest frees him from his city-bound naivete. In this case, Brown first "sees the light" upon leaving the city.

Another binary opposition affecting our interpretation is that of reality versus the dream. This binary possesses an elusive dilemma, for we are not even sure if Brown's journey is more than a dream. If we privilege the notion of dream, then we will readily accept Faith's warning at the beginning of the story when she requests that Brown postpone his journey because she "is troubled with such dreams and thoughts." But if we allow her dream-inspired warning to take precedence, then we must also privilege the dream at the end of the story when the text states that "it was a dream of evil omen for Young Goodman Brown." In accepting Faith's warning as a valid one, we recognize its source as valid, which is an innocent and faithful Puritan woman. On the other hand, if we accept Brown's experience in the forest as a valid dream, we are forced to accept the fraudulence of the Puritan culture to which Faith belongs. We realize, then, that in consistently privileging the notion of dream over reality, we are forced to see faith as both fraudulent and innocent. In such a case we will say that the text "unravels" itself. If we were to privilege the notion of reality over the dream, we will not value Faith's dream-inspired warning. At the same time we will not accept Brown's entire experience which the text literally states to be a dream. Why, then, would we value the message of the work at all if we did not first value the concept of dream?

In either case, to state that Brown's nighttime excursion was, in fact, a dream is to literally accept the claim that "it was a dream of evil omen for Young Goodman Brown." But even this literal acceptance contradicts our privileging of the figurative over the literal. We assume that the claim is only figurative. In fact, we so obviously privilege figurative over literal language that without considering the alternative, we assume that Faith symbolized more than Brown's wife. Through figurative thinking we assumed that Brown met Satan in the forest. And if it were not for such figurative assumptions, Brown's entire experience in the forest would be no more than a dream. If we were to privilege literal language over figurative language, we would be confined to reading a simple story about a man who dreams about a walk in the woods and as a result despises his own wife and his entire community. In privileging the literal, we will not reach for a moral but instead simply enjoy the plot.

As we see in the relationship between several binary oppositions in the text, each binary is connected to a contingent web of binaries. All of the binaries in the text rely upon one another for interpretation. We therefore find that we cannot discard the figurative/literal binary when considering the relationship between dream and reality, for if we privilege the figurative reading, we will have ruled out the consideration of the story as a dream. Because each binary is contingent upon one or more of the other binaries, we find that if, at one point, the text misspeaks, several binaries in the contingent web will be affected. As a result, we see that it is nearly impossible to detach faith/doubt from God/Devil or city/forest or dark/light from good/evil. But once we decenter any, several, or all of these binary operations, we can begin to enjoy the multiple meanings of Hawthorne's tale.

KEVIN A. EATON

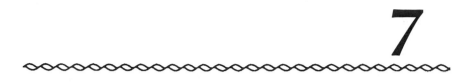

7

Psychoanalytic Criticism

Introduction

While Miss Skeets was placing the day's English assignment on the chalk-board, Fred exclaimed to a group of students seated around him, "Boy, did I have a wild dream last night."

"About what?" asked Karen.

"Well, I was the star of a soap opera, and I had just broken my six-month engagement with this pretty yet conceited bank president. While leaving the bank for what I thought was my final time, I spotted this beautiful bank teller; our eyes connected, and then I knew I was in love. But, but. . . . "

"But what?" insisted Peter.

"But the bank teller looked exactly like Miss Skeets!"

After the whistles, laughs, and exclamations, Karen quipped, "Now the truth comes out. You and Miss Skeets. That's why you've been completing all your English assignments."

Like Karen, most of us at one time or another have attempted to interpret either our own dreams or those of others. We are seemingly fascinated by the bizarre twists of fate, wild exploits, and often highly sexual content of our dreams. And like Karen, many of us wonder if our true feelings, concerns, and actions really surface in such dream experiences. Do dreams, we wonder, contain any degree of truth or serve any useful function?

The chemist Friedrich August Kekule answers in the affirmative. For years, Kekule was investigating the molecular structure of benzene. One night he dreamed of a string of atoms in the shape of a snake swallowing its tail. Upon awakening, he drew this figure in his notebook and soon realized it was the graphic structure of the benzene ring he had been struggling to decipher. When reporting his findings at a scientific meeting in 1890, he stated, "Let us learn to dream, gentlemen, and then we may perhaps find the truth."

Giuseppe Tartini, an Italian violinist of the eighteenth century, similarly discovered the value of dreams. One night he dreamed that the devil came to his bedside and offered to help him finish a rather difficult sonata in exchange for his soul. Tartini agreed, whereupon the devil picked up Tartini's violin and completed the unfinished work. Upon awakening, Tartini jotted down from memory what he had just heard. Known as *The Devil's Trill Sonata*, this piece is Tartini's best-known composition.

Like numerous scientists and composers, many authors have claimed that they too have received some of their best ideas from their dreams. Robert Louis Stevenson, for instance, declared that many of the ideas for *Dr. Jekyll and Mr. Hyde* came directly from his nightmares. Similarly, Dante, Goethe, Blake, Bunyan, and a host of others owed much of their writings, they asserted, to their world of dreams. And others, like Poe, De Quincey, and Coleridge, borrowed from their drug-induced dreams the content of some of their most famous works.

That our dreams and those of others fascinate us cannot be denied. Whether it be their bizarre and often erotic content or even their seemingly prophetic powers, dreams cause us to question and explore that part of our minds over which we have seemingly little control—the unconscious.

One of the foremost investigators of the unconscious and its activities was the Viennese neurologist and psychologist Sigmund Freud. Beginning with the publication of *The Interpretation of Dreams* in 1900, Freud laid the foundation for a new model of how our minds work. Hidden from the workings of the conscious mind, the unconscious, he believed, plays a large part in how we act, think, and feel. The best avenue for discovering some of the content and activity of the unconscious, he declared, is through our dreams. But according to Freud, it is the interaction of the conscious and the unconscious, and not either one working in isolation, by which we shape ourselves and our world.

Developing both a body of theory and a practical method for his science of the mind, Freud became the founding father of psychoanalysis, a method of treating emotional and psychological disorders by having the patient talk freely in a patient–analyst setting about early childhood experiences and his or her dreams. When we apply these same methods to our interpretations of works of literature, we engage in **psychoanalytic criticism**.

Unlike some other schools of criticism, psychoanalytic criticism can exist side by side with any other critical method of interpretation. Because this approach attempts to explain the hows and whys of human actions without developing an aesthetic theory (a systematic, philosophical body of beliefs concerning how meaning occurs in literature), Marxists, feminists, and New Historicists, for example, can utilize psychoanalytic methods in their interpretations without violating their own **hermeneutics**. Psychoanalytic criticism, then, may best be called an approach to literary interpretation rather than a particular school of criticism.

Although Freud is unquestionably the father of this approach to literary analysis, psychoanalytic criticism has continued to develop and expand throughout the twentieth century both in theory and practice. Carl Jung, Freud's rebellious student, for example, borrowed some of Freud's ideas while rejecting many others, and branched out into new theories and concerns, establishing the field of analytical psychology. Utilizing some of Jung's ideas, Northrop Frye, an English professor and literary theorist, developed symbolic or archetypal criticism in the mid-1950s, helping to change the direction of twentieth-century literary analysis. And in the 1960s, the French neo-Freudian psychoanalyst Jacques Lacan revised and expanded Freud's theories in the light of new linguistic and literary theories, thereby revitalizing psychoanalytic criticism and ensuring its continued influence on literary theory and practice.

Historical Development

The theories and practice of Sigmund Freud provide the foundation for psychoanalytic criticism. While working with his patients diagnosed as hysterics, Freud theorized that the root of their problems was psychological, not physical. These patients, he believed, had suppressed incestuous desires with which they had unconsciously refused to deal.

Freud was the first to suggest that the storehouse for these desires was the **unconscious**—his name for that part of the psyche or mind that receives and stores our hidden desires, ambitions, fears, passions, and irrational thoughts. Unaware of the presence of the unconscious, we operate *consciously*, Freud asserted, believing that our reasoning and analytical skills are solely responsible for our behavior. But it is the unconscious, Freud believed, that evidences itself through slips of the tongue, dreams, art, and irrational behavior that motivates most of our actions.

At first, Freud declared that our minds were a dichotomy consisting of the conscious (the rational) and the unconscious (the irrational). He later revised this theory, believing that no thought was either totally conscious or totally unconscious, and he spoke rather of modes of consciousness or unconsciousness. The irrational, instinctual, unknown and unconscious part of the psyche Freud calls the **id**, and the rational, logical, waking part the **ego.** A third part, the **superego,** acts like an internal censor, causing us to make moral judgments in the light of social pressures. The ego's job is to mediate between the instinctual (especially sexual) desires of the id and the demands of social pressure issued by the superego. What the ego (consciousness) deems unacceptable it suppresses and deposits in the unconscious. And what it has most frequently repressed in all of us is the sexual desires of our early childhood.

According to Freud, in our early childhood all of us go through three overlapping phases: the oral, anal, and phallic stages. As infants, we experience the **oral phase**: by sucking our mother's breast to be fed, our sexuality (or **libido**) is activated. Our mouths become an erotogenic zone that will later cause us to enjoy sucking our tongues and, still later, kissing. In the second phase, or **anal stage**, the anus becomes the object of pleasure when the child learns the delights of defecation. During this stage the anus becomes an erotogenic zone, for the child becomes sadistic, expelling and destroying through defecation. By withholding faeces, the child also learns that he or she can control or manipulate others. In the last phase, the **phallic stage**, the child's sexual desires or libido is directed toward the genitals.

At this point in our development, Freud posited, the pleasure principle basically controls the child. Being self-centered, sadistic, and assertive, the child cares for nothing but his or her own pleasure and recognizes neither male nor female. If the child, however, is to grow up as a "normal" adult, he or she must develop a sense of sexuality, a sense of his maleness or her femaleness. This awareness, Freud asserted, is expressed through the Oedipus complex.

During the late infantile stage (somewhere between the ages of 3 and 6), both the male and female child wish to possess their mother. Unconsciously, the male child desires to engage in sexual union with his mother, while the female child, Freud asserts, develops homosexual desires toward her mother. But each child now recognizes a rival for his or her mother's affection: the father. Already in the phallic stage and therefore sexually aware of his or her own erogenous organs, the child interprets the father's attention given to the mother as sexual.

If the child's sexual development is to proceed normally, Freud maintained, each must pass through the **castration complex**. From observing themselves, their mothers, and perhaps their sisters, little boys know they have a penis like their fathers while their mothers and sisters do not. What prevents the male child from continuing to have incestuous desires for his mother is fear of castration by his father. The child therefore represses his sexual desire, identifies with his father, and hopes someday to possess a woman as his father now possesses his mother. Unconsciously, the boy has then successfully made the transition to manhood. On the other hand, the little girl unconsciously realizes that she is already castrated as is her mother. Since she knows her father possesses that which she desires, a penis, she turns her desires to him and away from her mother. After the seduction of her father fails, she turns back toward the mother and identifies with her. Her transition into womanhood complete, the girl realizes that one day she, too, like her mother, will possess a man. Through her relationship with a man, her unfulfilled desire for a penis (penis envy) will be mitigated and her sense of lacking can be somewhat appeased.

The process of becoming a man or a woman, Freud maintained, may be long and difficult, but necessary. For within this process, the child passes from basing his or her life on the pleasure principle (wherein all decisions are based on the immediate gratification of pleasure) to the reality principle (wherein societal needs and the operation of the superego occur). During this stage, Freud believed that a child's moral development and conscience appear for the first time.

Although the passage into manhood or womanhood may be successful, according to Freud the child has stored many painful memories of repressed sexual desires, anger/rage, and guilt in his or her unconscious. Since the conscious and the unconscious are part of the same psyche, the unconscious with its hidden desires and repressed wishes continues to affect the conscious in the form of inferiority feelings, guilt, irrational thoughts and feelings, and dreams and nightmares.

In dreams, Freud asserted, the unconscious expresses its suppressed wishes and desires. Since such wishes may be too hard for the conscious psyche to handle without producing feelings of self-hatred or rage, the unconscious will present our concealed wishes through symbols, softening our desires. Through the process of **displacement**, for example, the unconscious may switch a person's hatred of another (named Mr. Appleby, for instance), onto a rotting apple in a dream, or through **condensation**, it may consolidate one's anger to a variety of people and objects into a simple sentence. Whatever the case, through symbols and usually not directly, the unconscious continually asserts its influence over our motivations and behavior.

When certain repressed feelings or ideas cannot be adequately released through dreams, jokes, or other mechanisms such as slips of tongue, the ego must act and block any outward response. In so doing, the ego and id become involved in an internal battle that Freud called neurosis. From a fear of heights to a pounding headache, neurosis shows itself in many physical and psychological abnormalities. According to Freud, it is the job of the psychoanalyst to identify those unresolved conflicts that give rise to a patient's neurosis and through psychoanalytic therapy, which includes dream analysis, return the patient to a state of well-being.

For Freud, the unresolved conflicts that give rise to any neurosis constitute the stuff of literature. A work of literature, he believed, was the external expression of the author's unconscious mind. Accordingly, the literary work must then be treated like a dream, applying psychoanalytic techniques to the text to uncover the author's hidden motivations, repressed desires, and wishes.

But Freud's most famous student, the Swiss psychologist, physician, and psychiatrist Carl Gustav Jung, disagreed. Although Jung accepted Freud's assumption that the unconscious exists and plays a major role in our conscious decisions, he rejected Freud's analysis of the contents of the unconscious, and he formulated a new approach to the understanding of a literary work.

According to Jung, the human psyche consists of three parts: the conscious, the personal unconscious, and the collective unconscious. The **conscious** or waking state is directly affected by the unconscious. In turn, the unconscious is divided into two parts. The first part, or the **personal unconscious**, exists directly below the surface of the conscious and contains elements of all those private affairs that occur daily in each of our lives. What may be in one person's personal unconscious may not, then, appear in someone else's.

But in the depths of the psyche and blocked off from human consciousness lies the **collective unconscious**, which houses the cumulative knowledge, experiences, and images of the entire human race. According to Jung, people from all over the world respond to certain myths or stories in the same way not because everyone knows and appreciates the same story, but because lying deep in our collective unconscious are the racial memories of humanity's past. These memories exist in the form of **archetypes**: patterns or images of repeated human experiences (such as birth, death, rebirth, the four seasons, and motherhood, to name a few) that express themselves in our stories, our dreams, our religions, and our fantasies. Occurring in literature in the form of recurrent plot patterns, images, or character types, these archetypes stir profound emotions in the reader because they awaken images stored in the collective unconscious, and thereby produce feelings or emotions over which the reader initially has little control.

Jung was the first to suggest that such archetypes directly affect the way we respond to external elements. When we see or read about an infant in diapers surrounded by a litter of puppies licking the child's face, for example, feelings of contentment, warmth, and love seemingly pop up in most of us. These somewhat uncontrollable emotions, Jung would claim, are the result of the stirring of an archetype via one of our senses in our collective unconscious.

Throughout the 1920s and until his death in 1961, Jung continued developing his methods of analytical psychology. When we apply his theories and methods to literature, we engage in **archetypal criticism**. Unquestionably, the foremost archetypal critic of the twentieth century is Northrop Frye.

With the publication of his work *Anatomy of Criticism* in 1957, Frye became the primary advocate of the principles of archetypal criticism in literary theory. Although he never declares allegiance to Jung's concept of the collective unconscious, Frye borrows Jung's schematic of symbols and how they may operate in a literary text.

Frye believes that all of literature comprises one complete and whole story called the **monomyth**. This monomyth can best be diagrammed as a circle containing four separate phases, with each phase corresponding to a season of the year and to peculiar cycles of human experience. The romance phase, located at the top of the circle, is our summer story. In this kind of story, all our wishes are fulfilled and we can achieve total happiness. At the bottom of the circle is winter or the anti-romance phase. Being the opposite of summer, this phase tells the story of bondage, imprisonment, frustration, and fear. Midway between romance and anti-romance and to the right of the circle is spring, or comedy. This phase relates the story of our rise from anti-romance and frustration to freedom and happiness. Correspondingly, across the circle is tragedy or fall, narrating our fall from the romance phase and from happiness and freedom to disaster. According to Frye, all stories can be placed somewhere on this diagram.

What Frye provides for us is a schematic of all possible kinds of stories. Such a structural framework furnishes the context whereby we can identify stories according to their particular genre, kinds of symbolization, themes, points of view, and other literary elements. In addition, Frye's schematic supplies the background and context for his form of literary criticism and allows us to compare and contrast stories on the basis of their relationship among themselves.

With the advent of archetypal criticism and Frye's schematics in the 1950s, few critics utilized Freudian analysis in their practical criticism. But in the 1960s, the French psychoanalyst and neo-Freudian Jacques Lacan helped revive Freudian criticism and position it as one of the leading psychanalytic approaches to literature today.

Like his fellow structuralist and poststructuralist critics, Lacan borrows from, while simultaneously challenging, some of the theories of the father of modern linguistics, Ferdinand de Saussure. Unlike Freud, who declared the unconscious to be chaotic and unstructured, Lacan decrees that "the unconscious is structured like a language." And it is to Saussure that Lacan turns to find the structure of language. Through a chain of linguistic reasoning, Lacan disagrees with Saussure's foundational principle that language is stable; that is , that a word or symbol represents one entity. For Lacan, language becomes chiefly figurative and the sole means by which a person defines himself or herself. In Lacan's view, there are no absolutes outside language itself.

Like Freud, Lacan also focuses on dreams, but declares that dreams, like language itself, are structured on linguistic principles and can therefore be scientifically analyzed.

Lacan's theories have been quickly adopted by many poststructural critics, who assert that Freud's theories grossly neglect the female and fail to explain the female psyche's development. His theories have also revitalized psychoanalytic criticism and have served as the catalyst for a renewed interest in Freudian criticism.

Assumptions

Unquestionably, the foundation for all forms of psychoanalytic criticism is Freud's theories and the techniques he developed during his psychiatric practice. Whether any practicing psychoanalytic critic utilizes the ideas of Jung, Frye, or Lacan, all must acknowledge Freud as the intellectual founding father of this form of criticism.

Central to psychoanalytic criticism is Freud's assumption that all artists, including authors, are neurotic. Unlike most other neurotics, however, the artist escapes many of the outward manifestations and end results of neurosis (such as madness or self-destruction) by finding in the act of creating his or her art a pathway back to saneness and wholeness.

According to Freud, an author's chief motivation for writing any story is to gratify some secret desire, some forbidden wish that probably developed during the author's infancy and was immediately suppressed and dumped in the unconscious. The outward manifestation of this suppressed wish becomes the literary work itself. In actuality, Freud declares that the literary work is therefore the author's dream or fantasy. By employing Freud's psychoanalytic techniques used in dream therapy, psychanalytic critics believe we can unlock the hidden meanings housed in symbols throughout the story and arrive at an accurate interpretation of the text.

Since Freud believes that the literary text is really an artist's dream or fantasy, the text can and must be analyzed like a dream. For Freud, this means that we must assume that the dream is a disguised wish. All of our present wishes, Freud believed, originated in some way during infancy. As infants, we longed to be both sensually and emotionally satisfied. It is the memory of these satisfied infantile desires or wishes that provides the fertile ground in which our present wishes can occur. All present wishes are therefore re-creations of a past infantile memory (especially elements of the Oedipal phase) brought to the surface of our unconscious and conscious states through sensations, emotions, and other present-day situations.

But the actual wish is often too strong and too forbidden to be acknowledged by the mind's censor, the ego. Accordingly, the ego distorts and hides the wish or **latent content** of the dream, allowing the dreamer to remember a somewhat changed and often radically different dream. It is this changed dream or **manifest content** of the dream that the dreamer tells the dream analyst. In turn, the dream analyst must strip back conversation and carefully analyze the various layers of the dream, much in the way an archaeologist uncovers a valued historical site layer by layer. Like the archaeologist, the analyst must peel back the various layers of a dream until the true wish is uncovered.

Like the dream analyst, the psychoanalytic critic believes that any author's story is a dream that on the surface reveals only the manifest content of the tale. Hidden and censored throughout the story on various levels lies the latent content of the story, its real meaning or interpretation. More frequently than not, this latent content directly relates to some element and memory of the Oedipal phase of our development—that stage in child development (between the ages of three and six) when a child develops a sexual desire for the parent of the opposite sex (See **Oedipus complex**). By directly applying the techniques employed in Freudian dream analysis, the psychoanalytic critic believes the actual, uncensored wish can be brought to the surface, thereby revealing the story's true meaning.

Methodology

First introduced to literary studies in the 1920s and 1930s, Freud's psychoanalytic criticism survives today. Although its methods have been challenged, revised, and supplemented by sympathetic but somewhat rebellious followers such as Jung, Frye, and Lacan, psychoanalytic criticism provides a stimulating approach to literary analysis that decrees that we humans are complex yet somewhat understandable creatures who often fail to note the influence of the unconscious on both our motivations and our everyday actions.

For several decades after its introduction, psychoanalytic criticism focused mainly on the author. By amassing biographical data on an author through biographies, personal letters, lectures, and any other written documents, coupled with the author's canon, psychoanalytic critics believed they could theoretically construct the author's personality with all its idiosyncrasies, internal and external conflicts, and, most importantly, its neuroses. In turn, such a devised theory, they believed, could illuminate an author's individual works, exposing the hidden meanings or latent content in the author's various texts. By gaining an in-depth understanding of the author, these critics assumed they could better interpret the author's canon.

In the 1950s, psychoanalytic critics turned their attention away from developing a theory based on the author's personality to an exploration of the minds of the characters found in an author's canon. Such a view gave rise to a more complex understanding and analysis of a literary work. Individual characters within a text now became the focus. Realizing that the author obviously had in mind a particular personality for his or her characters, critics also noted that readers develop their own conceptions of each character's personality. Analyzing a character's motivations and actions, then, becomes more complex than simply attributing them to the author's ideas. How readers interpret the various characters now becomes an integral part of the text's interpretation. Whereas the author creates a character, a reader re-creates the same character, bringing to the text and the individual character all the reader's past experiences and knowledge. The character simultaneously, then, becomes partly the creation of the author and partly that of the reader. To interpret the story, a psychoanalytic analysis of the author and the reader are thus needed.

This approach leads to the most comprehensive psychoanalytic analysis of a work. Most psychoanalytic critics realize that the reader plays a major role in interpreting a work. Understanding ourselves from a Freudian point of view and the context in which we live is therefore essential if we are to interpret the works of another.

Overall, psychoanalytic criticism still relies heavily on Freud's theories and declarations concerning the development of human personality and the underlying motivations concerning our actions. By directly applying Freud's psychoanalytic techniques of dream analysis, personality development, and psychological theories, psychoanalytic critics decree that they can dive beneath the surface level of a text and ascertain its true meaning. Although this process requires a critic to master Freudian theory, or Jungian principles, or even the linguistically based approach of Lacan, such a procedure, they assert, can help us discover the truth that lies within each of us.

In the essay that follows, note carefully how the author applies Freudian psychoanalytic terminology and methodology to arrive at his interpretation. Is the author concentrating his analysis more on the author or on the characters in the drama? Can you find any evidence where the author interacts with the text and imposes his own personality traits upon his interpretation of the play? In your opinion, is this psychoanalytic essay a valid and legitimate interpretation of the text? Be able to defend your response.

Further Reading

Crews, Frederick C. *Out of My System*. New York: Oxford University Press, 1975.
Feldman, Shoshana, ed. *Literature and Psychoanalysis: The Question of Reading: Otherwise*. Baltimore: Johns Hopkins University Press, 1981.

Freud, Sigmund. *Introductory Lectures on Psycho-Analysis.* Trans. Joan Riviere. London: Allen, 1922.

Holland, Norman N. *The Dynamics of Literary Response.* New York: Oxford University Press, 1968.

———. "The 'Unconscious' of Literature." *Contemporary Criticism.* Ed. Norman Bradbury and David Palmer. Stratford-upon-Avon Series, vol. 12. New York: St. Martin's, 1970.

Meisel, Perry, ed. *Freud: Twentieth Century Views.* Englewood Cliffs, NJ: Prentice Hall, 1981.

Scott, Wilbur. *Five Approaches to Literary Criticism.* London: Collier-Macmillan, 1962.

Student Essay

A Psychoanalytic View of Glaspell's Trifles

Susan Glaspell's *Trifles* attempts to promote her feminist philosophy by demonstrating that women can be as competent or even more competent than men. Telling a story of allegedly helpless women solving a murder mystery while the male characters impotently overlook any relevant evidence, Glaspell writes her female-dominated fantasy. But after analyzing the imagery of the play, we can see that although her characters seem to rise above their secondary roles as women, it is penis envy that drives Mrs. Wright to murder her husband. As a result, we will question Glaspell's fantasy of female dominance, for the females in the play do not, in fact, escape their dependency upon phallus.

Being a feminist playwright in the early twentieth century, Glaspell will first present the conflict that exists in her own life as well as in the play. From the start of the play, she describes a male-dominated community to set the stage for the females to domineer later in the drama. From the first lines we see the male characters exert obvious dominance over the females, beginning with the county attorney giving instructions to the women, "Come up to the fire, ladies." Mrs. Peters follows with unquestioned obedience. After obeying the command and taking a step closer to the fire, she says, "I'm not cold," thus showing her valuing obedience to men over her own ability to decide if she should be warmed by the fire. Later, Mr. Hale recognizes about John Wright that "I didn't know as what his wife wanted made much difference to John." The entire lives of the women, then, as the title and several quotations will suggest, are reduced to "trifles," inconsequential concerns. As Hale states, "Women are used to worrying over trifles." And when the county attorney turns from speaking to Mr. Hale to the women, he, likewise, is "as one turning from serious things to little pleasantries." We find, then, that the men assume their primary domineering roles while expecting the women to fulfill the function of the pleasant supplement.

Bitter at the idea of being a supplemental creature, Glaspell will present her fantasy of female dominance. She will suggest that women do, in fact, possess the capacity to reason independently but struggle with the expectations of their roles as women. Mrs. Peters and Mrs. Hale repeatedly discover their own ability to think and to reason independently from men, although the two women will not know how to handle this newly found capacity. After Mrs. Hale discovers, for example, the half clean table and the dropped bread (primary evidence for the unknown motive of the murder), she refuses initiative and claims to take "up our time with little things while we're waiting for them [the men] to get the evidence." Later, after further discoveries the women "sit there not looking at one another, but as if peering into something and at the same time holding back." What they peer into is the solution of the crime, but they feel they should hold back as their subordinate role would demand. "When they talk now it is in the manner of feeling their way over strange ground, as if afraid of what they are saying, but as if they cannot help saying it." This strange ground is that of assertiveness, competence, and autonomy. On their own, they have discovered the evidence that the men cannot find. But never before have they been allowed such initiative and independence, for they are but pleasantries to their male counterparts. According to the men, Mrs. Peters is only "married to the law," but could not, herself, enact the law.

But in Glaspell's fantasy, Mrs. Peters will become more than the sheriff's wife. She will, in fact, assume the power of the sheriff as law enforcer without his consent, thus dominating him. She and Mrs. Hale become both the law enforcers and the jury when they decide to hide the evidence from the men, thereby acquitting Mrs. Wright for the murder of her husband. We see here part of Glaspell's fantasy. The women have become the objects of power and of primary importance, reducing the men to helpless secondary figures.

Though we perceive Glaspell's intent for the female characters to overcome male dominance, we find, interwoven in the evidence found by Mrs. Hale and Mrs. Peters, that the motive for the crime is penis envy. Mrs. Wright cannot be whole because her husband does not allow her to complement him. John Wright was a "hard" man, and he thought that "folks talk too much." Mrs. Wright, then, was denied her need to nurture in her "lonesome" home. She could not become the Great Mother figure with no children and a husband who would not be loved. She was even denied a role as supplement, so her need to nurture a male counterpart could only be hoped for in a male child who could, then, fulfill her lack by supplying her need for phallus. Though she desires a child, this too has been denied by her husband.

When viewed from this psychoanalytic perspective, the bird in the drama represents much more than Mrs. Wright's violated treasure. Having obvious phallic shape, this canary symbolizes the male child that Mrs. Wright desires to make her whole. Glaspell repeatedly suggests that the bird is actually much more than just a bird. Mrs. Hale, for instance, notes about Mrs. Wright that "she used to sing real pretty herself" and that "she was kind of like a bird herself—real sweet and pretty, but kind of timid and—fluttery." More than coincidentally, the bird has characteristics of Mrs. Wright much like a child would have of his/her mother, but Glaspell gives us more than similar attributes between mother and child.

If the bird symbolizes her wish for a male child, then the bird cage becomes an image of the womb. As the cage has a narrow opening that leads to a hollow cavity in which the bird will perch, so the womb has a narrow vaginal opening that leads to the uterus, a hollow cavity for the embryo to develop. We also find evidence of the bird's significance when Mrs. Hale and Mrs. Peters speak of the bird and children as if the two concepts were interchangeable. The cage being a womb image, Mrs. Peters says, "seems funny to think of a bird here. But she must have had one, or why would she have a cage?" as if asking, Why would a woman have a womb if she would not have a child? or What identity could she find if she did not fulfill her childbearing function? Later, Mrs. Peters says, "I wonder how it would seem never to have had any children around. No, Wright wouldn't like the bird—a thing that sang. She used to sing." In Mrs. Peters' words, we find that the bird is symbolic of a child. Empathizing with Mrs. Wright's loss, Mrs. Peters says, "When we homesteaded in Dakota, and my first baby died—after he was two years old, and me with no other then—" again comparing the bird to the male child for whom Mrs. Wright had wished.

But we not only find evidence of the bird's significance in the speculation of the women but also in Mrs. Wright's handling of the bird in such a way as to make its significance clear. After Mr. Wright has killed the bird, Mrs. Wright wraps it in silk and places it in a "fancy box," much like a child would be placed in a silk-lined coffin upon his/her death. Here, we symbolically see that Mr. Wright puts to death Mrs. Wright's hopes for a child, which she, then, takes from the cage (womb image) and places into a symbolic casket. As we will later note, he puts her hopes literally to death by denying the possibility of conception until she has approached menopause.

Instead of granting her a son, Mr. Wright refused physical affection and only gave violent attention to the cage-womb image. Only the women realize that one of the hinges on the cage door has been pulled apart; "Someone must have been rough with it." We might visualize this hinge as having two parts, the pin, being a phallic symbol that slides into the hollow cylindrical part of the hinge, represents a vaginal image. The intact hinge, then, represents sexual intercourse with the penis sliding into the vaginal image. But because the hinge was roughly pulled apart, we can assume that Mr. Wright abruptly withdrew his penis from Mrs. Wright's vagina before the act of intercourse was complete; i.e., before ejaculation. Mr. Wright had thus denied Mrs. Wright's desire for a child by refusing her the complete act of intercourse necessary for conception.

Mrs. Wright's desire to conceive intensifies as she experiences the permanent ending of her menstrual cycle. Remembering her as "one of the town girls" before she was married, Mrs. Hale reveals "that was thirty years ago." If Mrs. Wright married at a traditional age (approximately twenty), then she would now be about fifty, a common age for menopause to occur. And Mrs. Peters recalls about Mrs. Wright, "Her fruit (cherries); it did freeze. She worried about that when it turned so cold. She said the fire'd go out and her jars would break." The coldness in her marital relationship poses this threat, that the red fruit of her womb would freeze (her menstrual cycle would freeze at menopause) and she would be left with no child, the red cherries resembling the blood of menstruation. Being a symbol of the uterus containing the fruit of her womb, her jar of cherries would then break, for upon menopause her womb would, in effect, be broken and would no longer be able to fulfill its function. So while Mr. Wright would not allow conception, her menstrual cycle had ended, shattering any hope to conceive. We see, now, the root of Mrs. Wright's penis envy, for this phallus (which she lacks) has ultimate power over her.

We also know now that Mrs. Wright has far more reason to kill than the loss of a pet; her victim has denied her her purpose of nurturing and bearing children. In the words of Mrs. Hale, "She felt she couldn't do her part, and then you don't enjoy things when you feel shabby." We thus understand her resentment against phallus which has made her feel lacking of purpose and "shabby." This resentment toward phallus also explains why she refuses the gun, a phallic symbol. Instead, she will dominate, for the first time in her oppressed life, the phallus which has denied her wholeness. But she will not resort to the despised phallic gun; that would reinstate the power of the phallic symbol. Because her attempts to possess phallus vicariously through her husband or a male child have failed, she will retaliate by trying to destroy this symbol of oppression. While she is in bed with her husband, she wraps a rope around his neck, thereby surrounding the phallic neck and strangling it much like the skin of the vagina would stretch around the neck-shaped penis during intercourse.

By destroying her phallic oppressor with a symbolic vagina, Glaspell completes her fantasy. And we can now understand Mrs. Wright's reaction when confronted by Mr. Hale as she "sat there with her hands held together and looking down." Here, she forms with her hands the shape of the vulva, the narrow crease between the hands mimicking the narrow opening of the vagina, with each hand representing the folds of skin on either side. As she sits looking into this vaginal symbol, she stares also into the focal point of the power struggle between herself and her phallic oppressor.

The various images of Glaspell's play—the bird, the cage, the jar of preserves, etc.—reveal that she does not merely write of a fantasy in which females overcome their subservience to men. Instead, we find that it is the inherent lack of phallus which the women resent. Glaspell's imagery, then, reveals evidence of penis envy which is Mrs. Wright's true motive for murder. In her lack, she desires to possess phallus vicariously, but her husband will not allow this to occur either through himself or a male child. Resentfully, Mrs. Wright will then retaliate by attempting to destroy the phallus which she lacks. Accordingly, Glaspell's fantasy fails to overcome male dominance, for it is the male phallus from which Mrs. Wright fails to gain independence.

KEVIN A. EATON

8

∽∽

Feminism

> What enrages me is the way women are used as extensions of men, mirrors of men, devices for showing men off, devices for helping men get what they want. They are never there in their own right, or rarely. The world of the Western contains no women.
> Sometimes I think *the world* contains no women.
>
> JANE TOMPKINS, "Me and My Shadow"

Introduction

After placing Jane Tompkins's quote on the overhead projector, Professor Brown asked members of his twentieth-century literature class their reactions. Immediately many hands sprang up.

"How ridiculous," shouted Robert; "the world is full of women. I can't even leave my house in the morning without seeing several: my mother, for starters, then my five older sisters. And, boy, they aren't extensions of any man. My oldest sister is working on her Ph.D. in chemistry, the next two are elementary school teachers, and the last two are executive assistants for major accounting firms in the city."

"But you've just proven Tompkins's argument," quipped Karen. "I know for a fact that your mother does not work outside the home. Any financial security she has comes from your father. Second, your sister's major professor at the university is a male, and *she* is working on *his* project for *her* dissertation. Third, your other sisters are all working for men, in positions that our society has prescribed for females: elementary school teachers and secretaries. Tompkins is right. Men view women as mere extensions of themselves, as rungs in a ladder to be stepped on to reach the heights of their careers, and as mere bodies to satisfy their sexual desires, not as equals or as persons to be respected in their own right."

"What nonsense," yelled Tom. "All women have to do is work as hard as we men and they will earn the right to be professors or to be the boss instead of the employee. Can we men help it if for centuries women have chosen to stay at home and raise the kids instead of earning a living in the work force? Now they want to be the engineer, the superintendent, the professor, or the chair of the board without first being the student or the laborer."

"But that's the point," responded Karen. "You men have not allowed us the opportunity to become the student or the laborer. For centuries you have suppressed us, keeping us away from the social, political, and economic centers of power in our culture. And now, when we have just begun to assert our rights as human beings, you call us radicals, braless bubbleheads, or raving feminists. All we want is the chance to be us: women who are respected and valued as human beings in our own right, holding our own opinions, and functioning in jobs that can and will make a difference in our society. Give us the chance, and we will show you men that women are not second-class citizens, but individuals who can and must set their own goals, dream their own dreams, and help change their own world into a better place to live."

The viewpoints Professor Brown's students have espoused represent some of the points of conflict surrounding feminism and feminist criticism today. Like Robert, many men think that women are valued human beings who are not extensions of any man. Becoming doctors, teachers, and secretaries, today's women, they claim, are leading lives of their own choosing, not ones dictated by men. Other men, like Tom, believe that women have historically chosen not to work outside the home, thereby keeping themselves out of the work force. When they begin to work outside the home, declare men like Tom, these women must therefore start at the bottom rung of the employment ladder and work their way up to management positions.

But it is Karen's arguments that crystallize the center of **feminism**: the assertion that men, either unconsciously like Robert or consciously like Tom, have oppressed women, allowing them little or no voice in the political, social, and economic issues of their society. By not giving voice and value to women's opinions, responses, and writings, men have suppressed the female, defined what it means to be feminine, and thereby devoiced, devalued, and trivialized what it means to be a woman. In effect, men have made women the "nonsignificant Other."

Feminism's goal is to change this degrading view of women so that all women will realize that they are not a "nonsignificant Other," but that instead each woman is a valuable person possessing the same privileges and rights as every man. Women, feminists declare, must define themselves and assert their own voices in the arenas of politics, society, education, and the arts. By personally committing themselves to fostering such change, feminists hope to create a society in which the female voice is valued equally with the male.

Historical Development

Although many people believe present-day feminists and their accompanying literary theories and practices find their beginnings in the women's liberation movement of the 1960s, the true roots of feminist criticism lie in the early decades of the twentieth century during what has been dubbed the Progressive Era. During this time, women gained the right to vote and became prominent activists in the social issues of the day, such as health care, education, politics, and literature. But equality with men in these arenas remained outside their grasp.

In 1919, the British scholar, teacher, and early feminist Virginia Woolf laid the foundation for feminist criticism in her work *A Room of One's Own*, in which she declared that men have treated women, and continue to treat them, as inferiors. It is the male, she asserted, who defines what it means to be female and who controls the political, economic, social, and literary structures. Agreeing with Samuel Taylor Coleridge, one of the foremost nineteenth-century literary critics, that great minds possess both male and female characteristics, she believed that a female Shakespeare could achieve literary prominence in the twentieth century if women scholars, teachers, and critics would only pave the way. But the Great Depression of the 1930s and World War II in the 1940s focused humankind's attention on other matters and delayed the development of such feminist ideas.

With the 1949 publication of the French writer Simone de Beauvoir's *The Second Sex*, however, feminist interests began to surface again. Heralded as the foundational work of twentieth-century feminism, Beauvoir's text declares that both French and Western societies are **patriarchal**—that is, they are controlled by males. Like Woolf before her, Beauvoir believed that the male in these societies defines what it means to be human, including, therefore, what it means to be female. Since the female is not male, Beauvoir asserted, she becomes the Other, an object whose existence is defined and interpreted by the male, who is the dominant being in society. Always subordinate to the male, the female finds herself a secondary or nonexistent player in the major social institutions of her culture, such as the church, government, and educational systems. According to Beauvoir, a woman must break the bonds of patriarchal society and define herself if she wishes to become a significant human being in her own right and to defy male classification as the Other.

With the advent of the 1960s and its political activism and social concerns, feminist issues found new voices. Moving from the political to the literary arena throughout the 1960s and 1970s, feminist critics began examining the traditional literary canon and discovered abundant evidence of male dominance and prejudice that supported Beauvoir's assertion that males considered the female "the Other," an unnatural or deviant being. First, stereotypes of women abounded in the canon: women were sex maniacs, goddesses of beauty, mindless entities, or old spinsters. Second, while Dickens, Wordsworth, Hawthorne, Thoreau, Twain and a host of other male authors were "canonized," few female writers achieved such status. Third, for the most part, the roles of female, fictionalized characters were limited to secondary positions, more frequently than not occupying minor parts within the stories or simply conforming to the male's stereotypical images of women. And fourth, female scholars such as Virginia Woolf and Simone de Beauvoir were ignored, their writings seldom if ever referred to by the male crafters of the literary canon.

Having chosen the works that comprise the canon, these male professors, scholars, and writers assumed that all readers were males, assert feminist critics of this era. Women reading such works could unconsciously, then, be duped into reading as males. In addition, since most of the university professors were males, more frequently than not female students were trained to read literature as if they were males. But the feminists of the 1960s and 1970s now postulated the existence of a female reader who was affronted by the male prejudices abounding in the canon. Questions concerning the male or female qualities of literary form, style, voice, and theme became the rallying points for feminist criticism, and throughout the late 1970s books that defined women's writings in feminine terms proliferated.

Having highlighted the importance of gender, feminist critics then discovered a body of literary works written by females that their male counterparts had decreed inferior and therefore unworthy to be part of the canon. In America, Kate Chopin's late-nineteenth-century novel *The Awakening* served as the archetypal, rediscovered feminist text of this period, while in England Doris Lessing's *The Golden Notebook* (1962) and in France Monique Wittig's *Les Guerilleres* (1969) fulfilled these roles. Throughout the universities and in the reading populace, readers turned their attention to historical and current works by women. Simultaneously, works that attempted to define the feminine imagination, to categorize and explain female literary history, and to define the female aesthetic or concept of beauty became the focus of feminist critics.

The ongoing debate concerning definitive answers to these key feminist interests continued throughout the decade of the 1980s, as it does today. Coined by the feminist scholar Elaine Showalter, the term **gynocriticism** has now become synonymous with the study of women as writers, and provides critics with four models concerning the nature of women's writing that help answer some of the chief concerns of feminist criticism. Each of Showalter's models is sequential, subsuming and developing the preceding model(s), as follows: (1) the biological model, with its emphasis on how the female body marks itself upon the text by providing a host of literary images and a personal, intimate tone; (2) the linguistic model, concerning itself with the differences between women's and men's use of language and with the question of whether women can and do create a language peculiar to their gender and utilize such a language in their writings; (3) the psychoanalytic model, based on an analysis of the female psyche and how such an analysis affects the writing process, and (4) the cultural model, investigating how the society in which female authors work and function shapes women's goals, responses, and points of view.

Since no one critical theory of writing dominates feminist criticism, it is understandable that three distinct geographical strains of feminism have developed: American, British, and French. For the most part, American feminism emphasizes the actual text with all its textual qualities, such as theme, voice, and tone, while at the same time being suspicious of any one theory that would attempt to explain the differences between male and female writings. It has found its home in American universities, in departments of English and women's studies.

British feminism, on the other hand, declares itself to be more political than American feminism, advocating social change. Often viewed as Marxist, British feminism is more ideological and therefore seemingly more concerned with social and cultural change than its American counterpart. Finding its home outside the university in the publishing world, journalism, and politics, British feminism attempts to analyze the relationship between gender and class and to show how the dominant power structures controlled by men influence all of society and oppress women.

Unlike American or British feminism, French feminism concentrates on language, analyzing how meaning is produced through various linguistic symbols. Such an analysis usually leads these critics into other areas of study, such as metaphysics, psychology, and art. Most recently, these theorists have speculated that a style of writing peculiar to women exists. **L'écriture féminine** or "women's writing," they maintain, is fundamentally different from male writing and obtains meaning through the writing process.

No matter what they emphasize in theory, however, all feminist critics assert that they are on a journey of self-discovery that will lead them to a better understanding of themselves. And once they understand and then define themselves as women, they believe they will be able to change their world.

Assumptions

To the onlooker, feminist theory and practice appear to be a diffuse, loosely connected body of criticism that is more divided than unified, housing more internal disagreements than unity among its adherents than perhaps any other approach to literary analysis. Since it claims no ultimate spokesperson but many different voices, there exists not one but a variety of feminist theories. Behind all these seemingly contradictory voices and theories, however, is a set of principles that unites this criticism.

Although feminist critics' ideas concerning the directions of their criticism vary, feminists possess a collective identity: they are women (and some men) who are struggling to discover who they are, how they arrived at their present situation, and where they are going. In their search, they value differing opinions, thereby giving significance to the personal as opposed to a school of theorists or a codified and authoritative collection of texts. Their search, they assert, is political, for their aim is to change the world in which they live, a world that they maintain needs to be changed and must be changed if all individuals, all cultures, all subcultures, and both sexes are to be valued as creative, rational beings who can contribute to their societies and their world.

Such a revisionist, revolutionary, and ideological stance seeks to understand the place of women in society and to analyze everything that affects women as writers and their writings in what feminists believe is a male-dominated world. In this masculine world, the feminists declare that it is man who defines what it means to be human, not woman. Because a woman is not a man, she has become the "Other," the not-male. Man is the subject, the one who defines meaning; woman is the object, having her existence defined and determined by the male. The man is therefore the significant figure in the male/female relationship while the female is subordinate.

Such female insignificance did not first appear in the twentieth century, declare feminists such as Jane Tompkins and others. Long before the existence of our present-day, male-dominated world, societies have been governed, for the most part, by males. These patriarchal societies, say the feminists, have simply passed down their erroneous beliefs from generation to generation, culminating with the predominant Western assumption that women are less than, not equal to, men. Arbitrarily using the male as the standard, these societies apparently agree with Aristotle's assertion that "the female is female by virtue of a certain lack of qualities." Or they quote and support St. Thomas Aquinas's conviction that all women are simply imperfect men. And some in Western society still believe that Freud is correct when he argues that female sexuality is based upon the lack of a penis, the male sexual organ.

Feminist critics wish to show humankind the errors of such a way of thinking. Women, they declare, are people in their own right; they are not imcomplete or inferior men. Literature and society have frequently stereotyped women as angels, barmaids, bitches, whores, brainless housewives, or old maids; women must break free from such oppression and define themselves. No longer, assert these critics, can they allow male-dominated society to define and articulate their roles, their values, and their opinions.

To free themselves from such oppression, say feminist critics, women must analyze and challenge the established literary canon that has helped shape the images of female inferiority and oppression ingrained in our culture. Women themselves must create an atmosphere that is less oppressive by contesting the long-held patriarchal assumptions concerning their sex. Since no female Aristotle has articulated a philosophy or coined a battle cry for women's equality, all women must muster a variety of resources to clarify, assert, and implement their beliefs. Through reexamining the established literary canon, validating what it means to be a woman, and involving themselves in literary theory and its multiple approaches to a text, women can legitimize their responses to texts written by both males and females, their own writings, and their political, economic, and social positions in their culture.

Methodology

Just as there is no single feminist theory but many theories, so there exists not one but a variety of feminist approaches to a text. Wishing to challenge and change Western culture's assumption that males are superior to females and therefore are better thinkers, more rational, more serious, and more reflective than women, feminist critics may begin their debunking of male superiority by exposing stereotypes of women found throughout the literary canon. Women, they argue, cannot be simply depicted and classified as either angels or demons, saints or whores, brainless housewives or eccentric spinsters. Such characterizations must be identified and challenged, and such abuse of women by male authors must be acknowledged as ways men have consciously or unconsciously demeaned, devalued, and demoralized women.

Having identified the antifeminist characterizations that occur in many texts, the feminist critic may then turn to the American, the English, or a non-Western literary canon, seeking to discover works written by women. This is more frequently than not a difficult task, since males have written the majority of texts. The American literary canon, for example, is decidedly male. With the works of Hawthorne, Melville, Poe, and other male notables filling the pages of the canon, little or no room is allowed for the writings of Susan Warner, E. D. N. Southwick, and Mary E. Wilkins Freeman, three of the most widely read authors in nineteenth-century America. Feminists assert that these female authors must be rediscovered by having their works republished and reevaluated. When complete, this rediscovery will necessarily bring to the surface a valuable body of female authors who share common themes, histories, and often writing styles.

Other feminist critics suggest that we reread the canonized works of male authors from a woman's point of view. Such an analysis is possible, they maintain, by developing a uniquely female consciousness based on female experience rather than the traditional male theories of reading, writing, and critiquing. Known as gynocriticism (see the Historical Development section of this chapter for additional information), this female model of literary analysis offers four areas of investigation:

1. Images of the female body as presented in a text. Such an anatomical study, for example, would highlight how various parts of the female body, such as the uterus and breasts, often become significant images in works authored by women.

2. Female language. Such a concern centers on the differences between male and female language. Since we live in patriarchal societies, it would be fair to assume, say feminists, that our language is also male-dominated. Do women speak or write differently from men? Although there is little consensus on the answers to these questions, critics interested in this kind of investigation analyze grammatical constructions, recurring themes, and other linguistic elements.

3. The female psyche and its relationship to the writing process. Such an analysis applies the psychological works of Freud (whose theories most feminists wish to debunk) and Lacan to a text and shows how the physical and psychological development of the female evidences itself in the writing process through a variety of psychological stages.

4. Culture. By analyzing cultural forces (such as the importance and value of women's roles in a given society), critics who emphasize this area of study investigate how society shapes a woman's understanding of herself, her society, and her world.

Whatever method of feminist criticism we choose to apply to a text, we can begin textual analysis by asking some general questions: Is the author male or female? Is the text narrated by a male or a female? What types of roles do women have in the text? Are the female characters the protagonists or secondary and minor characters? Do any stereotypical characterizations of women appear? What are the attitudes toward women held by the male characters? What is the author's attitude toward women in society? How does the author's culture influence her or his attitude? Is feminine imagery used? If so, what is the significance of such imagery? Do the female characters speak differently from the male characters? By asking any or all of these questions of a text, we can begin our journey in feminist criticism while simultaneously helping ourselves to better understand the world in which we live.

In the following feminist interpretation of Susan Glaspell's *Trifles*, which of the questions posed above does the author use in her analysis? Is the critic more concerned with the author's understanding of feminist issues? the characters? the readers? According to the essay, what is the main point of the play? Has this interpretation brought to your attention any feminist issues with which you were previously unaware? If so, what are they?

Further Reading

Beauvoir, Simone de. *The Second Sex*. 1949. Ed. and trans. H. M. Parshley. New York: Modern Library, 1952.

Cohen, Ralph, ed. "Feminist Directions." *New Literary History: A Journal of Theory and Interpretation* 19 (Autumn 1987): 1–208.

Gilbert, Sandra M., and Susan Gubar. *The Madwoman in the Attic: The Woman Writer and the Nineteenth-Century Literary Imagination*. New Haven: Yale University Press, 1979.

Kolodny, Annette. "Some Notes on Defining a 'Feminist Literary Criticism.'" *Critical Inquiry* 2 (1975): 75–92.

Showalter, Elaine. *A Literature of Their Own: British Women Novelists from Brontë to Lessing*. Princeton: Princeton University Press, 1977.

——, ed. *The New Feminist Criticism: Essays on Women, Literature, Theory*. New York: Pantheon Books, 1985.

Student Essay

Feminist Criticism and Susan Glaspell's Trifles

"Are women human?" the British scholar Dorothy Sayers wondered in the 1940s; after examining the evidence of attitudes toward women and the roles of women in her society, Sayers concluded a sardonic "No." Men are human: they reason, they find pleasure in their work outside the home, and they enjoy freedom of choice. Women are not like men: they act solely on intuition, they belong in the home (whether they enjoy it or not), and they make no choices outside of whatever male influence exists in their lives. Women, therefore, are not human (Sayers, *Are Women Human?* Eerdmans, 1971).

For modern feminist literary scholars, little has changed in western society since the writings of Fanny Burney, Jane Austen, George Eliot, Gertrude Stein, Dorothy Sayers, and other notables of the female literati. Feminist writers posit that our culture continues to be economically, politically, and socially dominated by the male; men hold the majority of powerful positions in business, politics, education, and the home. Despite heightened awareness against stereotypes, our society gives authority to the reasoning and rational male, not the female who supposedly acts according to a mysterious intuition of dubious value. Even when she does succeed in her career, a woman must submit to male expectations of femininity or risk the stereotype that "women in power are masculine." In our culture women most often experience life as inferiors whose very identities depend on the men around them.

With this cultural milieu in hand, Susan Glaspell wrote her play *Trifles* in 1916. Using the setting of a small-town murder investigation, the playwright explores the larger issues of the experience of women in marriage and society. Throughout the play, Glaspell educates her audience through two distinct female experiences: that of Mrs. Hale and Mrs. Peters as they interact with their husbands and George Henderson, and that of Minnie Wright's story-within-the-story, which Mrs. Hale and Mrs. Peters develop over the course of the play.

Beginning with the first-hand interaction, Glaspell immediately presents several obvious stereotypes. She describes George Henderson, the county attorney, as a young man, with his first words (the first words in the play) setting the tone for his continuing volley of patronizing comments about "the ladies." By the play's end, Henderson, the stereotypical young gallant, will miss the truth concerning the murder because of his inability to take the women seriously.

At first, the two women seem to be additional formulaic characters. In the list of characters, for example, the women are defined solely by their husbands: Glaspell never reveals their first names, and even outside the company of men the women address each other as *Mrs.* Hale and *Mrs.* Peters. Describing Mrs. Peters as "a slight wiry woman" with "a thin nervous face," Glaspell continues the stock characterization by having Mrs. Peters' actions and comments for the most part bear out this physical description. Her nervous body, for instance, reflects her tentative mindset, and she submits to the men and defends their actions ("Of course it's no more than their duty") more readily than does Mrs. Hale. For the larger and "more comfortable looking" Mrs. Hale, who spearheads the deception of the men, a defiant attitude accompanies a robust frame. But while the men in *Trifles* remain consistent throughout the play to their stereotypes, the women gain a new independence from their expected roles. Glaspell uses these female stock characters so that they can achieve together a subversion which neither of them alone could have accomplished.

As the play begins, all five characters gather in the Wright kitchen. After a preliminary recapitulation by farmer Hale of the discovery of the murder, the county attorney discovers spilled cherry preserves on a kitchen shelf. A discussion ensues among the five characters in which all three men generalize about the nature of women. In response to Mrs. Peters' statement that the jailed Minnie Wright frets about her fruit jars, the sheriff exclaims, "Well, can you beat the women! Held for murder and worryin' about her preserves." By his saying "women" and not "woman," we learn that the sheriff assumes that not only Minnie Wright remains oblivious to her situation but also that all women think just as Minnie Wright does. Another male, Lewis Hale, explains Minnie's seemingly frivolous concern with, "Well, women are used to worrying over trifles," and Henderson caps the argument with an indulgent "And yet, for all their worries, what would we do without the ladies?" Treated not as individuals but as a mysterious subculture, the women react in defense and "move a little closer together."

The men then remark upon the untidy state of the kitchen which they assume directly reflects upon the nature of Minnie Wright. Having heard her neighbor accused of poor housekeeping as well as murder, Mrs. Hale risks condescension and defends the disorder of the kitchen ("Those towels get dirty awful quick. Men's hands aren't always as clean as they might be"). When Henderson assumes that the cheerlessness of the house stems from Minnie Wright's lack of "the homemaking instinct," Mrs. Hale holds another view: "I don't think a place'd be any cheerfuller for John Wright's being in it." Convinced that nothing that would point to any motive exists in the kitchen, the three men move upstairs to the murder scene.

Left behind, Mrs. Hale and Mrs. Peters discover a poignant motive in the disarrayed kitchen. The women reveal themselves to be keen listeners as they recount to each other the previous comments made by the men. Through a process of deduction worthy of Sherlock Holmes, they piece together their own theory from the clues in the kitchen. But as the women gradually analyze the evidence of the deserted loaf of bread, the half-wiped table, the erratic sewing, and the strangled bird, a hesitancy to believe in their conclusions develops. To illustrate visually this hesitancy, Glaspell writes in the stage directions that Mrs. Hale "Picks up loaf, then abruptly drops it. In a manner of returning to familiar things." For these women, reasoning itself seems to be foreign, and it frightens them. As they realize that the truth which they are grasping escapes the men entirely, Mrs. Hale and Mrs. Peters resort to pregnant silences and practicality ("Wonder how they are finding things upstairs." "I wonder if she was goin' to quilt it or just knot it?").

At this point the men enter and deride what they see as the women's irrelevant musings about knotting and quilting. Mrs. Hale resents their comments, and, when the men go outside, she moves beyond speculation and begins to destroy the evidence against Minnie Wright. Acting on their reasoning, the women hide the dead canary from the lawmen. When the men return from the barn, Mrs. Hale and Mrs. Peters speak of trifles and superstitions even as they realize that Minnie had revenged the years of emotional abuse and the violent death of her canary.

Educating her audience through the interaction between male and female on stage, Glaspell furthers the instruction through the background story of the relationship between Mr. and Mrs. Wright. *Trifles* asks the question of motive, a question which is answered through the deductions of Mrs. Hale and Mrs. Peters. A broken jar of preserves, a dirty towel and table, irregular stitching, and a bird with its neck "other side to" provide enough physical evidence, however trivial, for the women to empathize with their unfortunate sister. Although she merely hints at first that John

Wright was a difficult man, Mrs. Hale becomes harsher as the evidence mounts: she compares him to "a raw wind that gets to the bone," and she says of Minnie Wright, "She used to sing. [Mr. Wright] killed that, too." Remembering the carefree youth of Minnie removes any sympathy Mrs. Hale might have had for the murdered husband.

Both Mrs. Hale and Mrs. Peters recall incidents in their own lives which relate to those experiences of Minnie Wright. Mrs. Peters remembers a boy who took a hatchet to her kitten. Contemplating the loneliness of Minnie, Mrs. Hale says, "I know how things can be—for women." Mrs. Peters knew that stillness when her baby died in Dakota. A recognition of the similar elements in female life draws these women together and effects a subversion of the law, the male law to which Mrs. Peters herself is married.

Through plot and subplot Glaspell highlights the repression women encounter in their relationships with the men of our society. Because George Henderson, Henry Peters, Lewis Hale, and the deceased John Wright believe that women are irrational and preoccupied with trifles, the women come to believe it of themselves. But Glaspell educates her female characters as well as her audience; Mrs. Hale and Mrs. Peters believe in and act upon their reasoning before the curtain falls. Ultimately, all three women subvert the male hierarchy: Minnie Wright breaks the law, and Mrs. Peters and Mrs. Hale deceive it.

KATHLEEN STOCKIN

9

∿∿∿∿∿∿∿∿∿∿∿∿∿∿∿∿∿∿∿∿∿∿∿∿∿∿∿∿∿∿∿

Marxism

Introduction

"Rise up, oh proletariat, rise up. Rise up, oh common worker, and seize the moment. Rise up, you who are about to be enlightened concerning the nature of reality and the true relationships among humankind, material possessions, and philosophical ideas that affect the way we live. Listen, learn, and be free." Having successfully captured the attention of her Introduction to Marxism students on the first day of class, Professor Stone continued her opening remarks while distributing the syllabus to the remaining class members.

"Whether Marxism is considered a philosophy, a theory, a method or a movement is of little concern. Its goal and hopefully your goal by the time this semester ends is to change the world. For too long the world's peoples have been oppressed, suppressed, deluded or cajoled into believing that reality is simply the way things are. No, a thousand times no! If we can but for a moment remove the blinders placed upon our eyes, the plugs within our ears, and the walls encasing our thoughts placed there by the so-called upper classes of society, we will be free for the first time to examine how our own thoughts and allegiances have been manipulated so that many of us have actually accepted the values and beliefs of a group of people whose only goal is to keep us in our place by now and then pacifying us with a meager increase in salary."

"In this course we will discover the true nature of reality and thereby reject some, if not many, of our present beliefs. We will learn how to free ourselves from the yoke of our boss's ideology that may presently bind us and unconsciously keep us from becoming what we know we can be. We will be confronted with an understanding of ourselves and realize, perhaps for the first time, that our consciousness has been shaped by social and economic conditions, and apart from society we cannot understand ourselves. And through our study of Marxism we will learn not only how to interpret our world but also how to transform it from a place populated by the 'haves' and the 'have nots' to a classless society where economics and its accompanying social relationships no longer determine our values and sense of self-worth. By studying, learning, and applying the principles of Marxism we are about to master, we can shape our world and free it from sexism, bigotry, and prejudice for all peoples. Working and studying together, we can transform both ourselves and our world."

Although Professor Stone's introductory remarks were designed to stir her students' interest in Marxism and do not represent all Marxist positions, her statements do embody some of the core principles of Marxist thought: that reality itself can be defined and understood; that society shapes our consciousness; that social and economic conditions directly influence how and what we believe and value; and that Marxism offers us an opportunity and a plan for changing the world from a place of bigotry, hatred, and conflict resulting from class struggle to a classless society where wealth, opportunity, and education are actually accessible for all people.

Historical Development

Unlike other schools of literary criticism, **Marxism** did not begin as an alternative theoretical approach to literary analysis. Before twentieth-century writers and critics embraced the principles of Marxism and employed these ideas in their criticism, Marxism had already flourished in the nineteenth century as a pragmatic view of history that offered the working classes of society an opportunity to change their world and therefore their lifestyles. By providing both a philosophical system and a plan of action to bring about change in society, Marxism offers to humanity a social, political, economic, and cultural understanding of the nature of reality, of society, and of the individual. These and other similar ideas have become the basis of what we know today as socialism and communism.

Two German writers, philosophers, and social critics—Karl Heinrich Marx (1818–1883) and Friedrich Engels (1820–1895)—coauthored a text in 1848 that proclaimed Marxism's basic doctrines: *The Communist Manifesto*. In this work, Engels and Marx declare that the capitalists, or the **bourgeoisie**, had successfully enslaved the working class, or the **proletariat**, through economic policies and control of the production of goods. Now the proletariat, Engels and Marx assert, must revolt and strip the bourgeoisie of their economic and political power and place the ownership of all property in the hands of the government, which will then fairly distribute the people's wealth.

In addition to this work, Marx himself authored *Das Kapital* a few years later, in 1867. In this text, Marx enunciates the view of history that has become the basis for twentieth-century Marxism, socialism, and communism. According to Marx, history and therefore our understanding of people and their actions and beliefs is determined by economic conditions. Marx maintains that an intricate web of social relationships emerges when any group of people engage in the production of goods. A few, for example, will be the employers, but many more will be the employees. It is the employers (the bourgeoisie) who have the economic power and who will readily gain social and political control of their society. Eventually this "upper class" will articulate their beliefs, their values, and even their art. Consciously and unconsciously they will then force these ideas, or what Marx calls their **ideology**, upon the working class. In such a system, the rich become richer, while the poor become poorer and more and more oppressed. To rid society of this situation, Marx believes that the government must own all industries and control the economic production of a country to protect the people from the oppression of the bourgeoisie.

Taken together, *The Communist Manifesto* and *Das Kapital* provide us with a theory of history, economics, politics, sociology, and even metaphysics. In these writings, little or no mention of literature, literary theory, or practical analysis of how to arrive at an interpretation of a text emerges. The link between the Marxism of its founding fathers and literary theory resides in Marx's concept of history and the sociological leanings of Marxism itself. Since Marx believed that the history of a people is directly based on the production of goods and the social relationships that develop from this situation, he necessarily assumed that the totality of a people's experience—social interactions, employment, and other day-to-day activities—were directly responsible for the shaping and the development of an individual's personal consciousness. That our place in society and our social interactions determine our consciousness or who we really are is a theme Marx highlights throughout his writings.

Since the literary approach to a text that was common during Marx's time made similar sociological assumptions, as did his own theories of society and the individual, Marx had no difficulty accepting his literary peers' methodology for interpreting a text. Known today as the "traditional historical approach," this critical position declares that a critic must place a work in its historical setting, paying attention to the author's life, the time period in which the work was written, and the cultural milieu of both the text and the author, all of these concerns being related to sociological issues. To these criteria, however, Marx and Engels add another element to be considered: the economic means of production. This fourth factor addresses such concerns as who decides what texts should be published or the date of publication or the distribution of any text. Such questions necessitate an understanding of the social forces at work at the time a text is written or is being interpreted. In addition, this added criterion forces the critic to investigate the scheme of social relationships not only within the text itself but also outside the text and within the world of the author. By adding this sociological dimension, Marxism expands the traditional, historical approach to literary analysis by dealing with sociological issues that concern not only the characters in a work of fiction but also the authors and the readers. This added dimension, Marx believed, links literature and society and shows how literature reflects society and how it reveals truths concerning our social interactions.

Not surprisingly, American and European critics took particular interest in the sociological implications of literature and Marxist principles during the first few decades of the twentieth century, especially at the end of the 1920s and throughout the 1930s, the time of the Great Depression. Called the Red Decade, the 1930s saw many American and continental intellectuals turn to Marxism, with its sociological concerns, as a way to help their countries out of economic depression. In America, for example, Marxism provided scholars with a ready-made doctrine and a pragmatic plan for reshaping their country. Using Marxism's emphases on economic production, social relationships, and the individual, American critics such as Vernon Louis Parrington began reinterpreting their country's cultural past, articulating its present conditions, and prophesying about its future. The time for change was now, they declared, and Marxism provided them a definition of reality and a methodology whereby humankind could redefine itself, society, and the future.

After the 1930s and with the passing of the Great Depression, Marxist criticism faded into the literary background, championed, so it seemed, only by "leftist" critics who many declared were out of touch with the rest of literary scholarship. Not until another period of social upheaval, the 1960s and early 1970s, did American and European critics once again recognize Marxism as a viable option for solving the social unrest and political turmoil caused by the Vietnam War, the Algerian conflict, the Cuban missile crisis, and a variety of social problems in America and Europe stemming from the racial and sexual revolutions of this period.

During this time Marxist criticism was once again thrust to the forefront of the academic world by a variety of intellectuals who held key positions in American universities, such as Berkeley, Columbia, and San Diego. An assortment of scholarly journals that loudly proclaimed Marxist principles, such as *Telos*, also appeared. In Europe in the early 1970s, a group of academics known as the Frankfurt School banded together to rejuvenate Marxist doctrine and revive the writings of Marx and Engels.

From the mid-1970s to the present, Marxism has continued to challenge what it deems the bourgeoisie concerns of its literary counterparts through the voices of such critics as Terry Eagleton and Frank Lentricchia. Critical movements and theories like structuralism, deconstruction, feminism, and New Historicism have all examined Marxism's basic tenets and share some of its social, political, and revolutionary concerns. Like Marxism, these contemporary schools of criticism want to change the way we think about literature and life. And from these various schools of thought present-day Marxism has borrowed many ideas. It has now evolved into an array of differing theories, with the result that there no longer exists a single school of Marxist thought, but a variety of Marxist critical positions. Common to all these theoretical positions, however, is the assumption that Marx, no matter how he is interpreted by any of his followers, believed that change for the better in a society is possible if we will only stop and examine our culture through the eyes of its methods of economic production.

Assumptions

Marxism is not primarily a literary theory that can be used to interpret a text. Unlike other schools of criticism, it is first a set of social, economic, and political ideas that its followers believe will enable them to interpret and, more importantly, change their world. Although a variety of Marxist positions exist, most Marxists adhere to a similar understanding of the world.

Ultimate reality, declares Marxism, is material, not spiritual. What we know beyond any doubt is that human beings exist and live in social groups. All of our actions and responses to such activities as eating, working, and even playing are related in some way to our culture and society. In order to understand ourselves and our world, we must first acknowledge the interrelatedness of all our actions within society. If, for example, we want to know who we are and how we should live, we must stop trying to find answers by looking solely to religion or philosophy; instead we must begin by examining all aspects of our daily activities within our own culture. Upon examining our daily routines, including our beliefs and values, we will discover that it is our cultural and social circumstances that determine who we are. What we believe, what we value, and in many ways what we think are a direct result of our culture and our society, not our religion or our supposed philosophy of life.

When we examine our society, declares Marxism, we will discover that its structure is built on a series of ongoing conflicts between social classes. The chief reason for these conflicts lies in the varying ways members of society work and utilize their economic resources. According to Marx, the various methods of economic production and the social relationships they engender form the economic structure of society, called the **base**. In America, for example, the capitalists exploit the working classes, determining for them their salaries and their working conditions, among a host of other elements of their lives. From this base, maintains Marx, arises the **superstructure**—a multitude of social and legal institutions, political and educational systems, religious beliefs, values, and a body of art and literature that one social class (the capitalists in America, for instance) uses to keep members of the working class in check.

The exact relationship between the base and the superstructure, however, is not easily defined. Some early Marxists believed that the base directly affected the superstructure and, in essence, determined its existence (a position known as **vulgar Marxism** or the **reflection theory** whereby the superstructure reflects or mirrors the base). Other Marxists assert that even Marx and Engels changed their opinions concerning this relationship and attest that the elements contained in the superstructure have a reality of their own, with each element affecting the other elements of the superstructure while simultaneously affecting the base. Whatever the position held by Marxists today, most would agree that the relationship between the base and the superstructure is a complex one and will continue to remain a contentious point in Marxist theories.

The relationship between the base and the superstructure becomes clearer when we consider capitalistic America. Marxism declares that in America the capitalists hold the economic purse strings and therefore control the base, making the capitalists the center of power in society. In addition to controlling the base, the capitalists also decree what beliefs are acceptable, what values are to be held, and what laws are to be formed. In other words, the capitalists, not the working classes, control their society's superstructure and its **ideology**, the direct expression of any society's superstructure. A much debated term in Marxist criticism, ideology often refers to a culture's collective or social consciousness (as opposed to the material reality on which experience is based), or its personal awareness of a body of laws or codes governing its politics, law, religion, philosophy, and art to which that culture's bourgeoisie and therefore its superstructure subscribes. According to Marx and Engels, a culture's ideology is more frequently than not synonymous with "false consciousness," for such an ideology has been defined and established by the bourgeoisie and therefore represents a set of false assumptions or illusions used by the elite to dominate the working classes and to maintain social stability. An ideology, then, may be a conscious stating of a society's philosophy, its laws, or its acceptable customs or it may be a somewhat vaguer and implicit understanding of its beliefs.

Consciously and unconsciously, this social elite inevitably forces its ideas upon the working classes. Almost without their knowing it, the working classes have become trapped in an economic system that decrees how much money they will earn, when they will take vacations, how they will spend their leisure time, what entertainment whey will enjoy, and even what they believe concerning the nature of humanity itself. Indeed, their system of values and meanings by which they live, work, and play, their **hegemony**, is dictated by the bourgeoisie.

It is to the working classes that Marxism addresses its rallying cry. All working men and women can free themselves from the chains of social, economic, and political oppression if they will only recognize that they are presently not free agents but individuals controlled by an intricate social web dominated by a self-declared, self-empowered, and self-perpetuating social elite.

Since this social elite, or the bourgeoisie, shapes a society's superstructure and its ideology, this social class necessarily controls its literature, for literature is one of many elements contained in the superstructure itself. From this perspective, literature, like any other element of the superstructure, becomes involved in the social process by means of which the bourgeoisie indoctrinate the working class with their elite ideology as reflected in the literature. What becomes natural and acceptable behavior in that society is now depicted in its literature and, in essence, controlled by the bourgeoisie, who control the economic means of production.

Because literature is part of a society's superstructure, its relationship to other elements of the superstructure and to the base becomes the central focus in varying Marxist literary theories. If, for example, a Marxist holds to the reflection theory concerning the relationship of the base to the superstructure, then this theorist posits that the economic base directly determines the literature. For such a critic, literature will mirror the economic base. On the other hand, if a Marxist theorist believes that elements of the superstructure have realities of their own and affect each other and also affect the base, a text may be responsible for altering not only other elements within the superstructure but also the base. And even the critics who adhere to this position hold differing opinions concerning the definition of a text and its relationship to other elements of the superstructure and to the base.

Although all Marxists assert that a text must be interpreted in the light of its culture, how they define the text and its social relationships provides us with an array of Marxist literary theories and differing methods of analysis. There exists, then, no single Marxist theory of literature, but many, each hoping to change society.

Methodology

Since there exists no absolute voice of authority expounding "pure" Marxist principles, there can exist no single Marxist approach to literary analysis. Like other methods of interpretation, Marxism includes an array of differing voices, with each voice articulating particular interests. These differing voices all agree, however, that Marxism, with its concerns for the working class and the individual, provides the most workable and satisfying framework for understanding our world. Recognizing the interrelatedness of all human activities, Marxism, they believe, enables us to understand ourselves and how we as individuals relate to and are affected by our society. And these voices all assert that we must help direct and change our society, our culture, our nation, and our world by leading humanity towards an understanding and an acceptance of socialism.

As an approach to literary analysis, Marxism's methodology is a dynamic process declaring that a proper critique (*proper* being defined as one that agrees with socialistic or Marxist beliefs) of a text cannot exist isolated from the cultural situation in which the text evolved. Necessarily, Marxists argue, the study of literature and the study of society are intricately bound together. Such a relationship demands that a Marxist approach to a text must deal with more than the conventional literary themes—matters of style, plot, characterization, and the usual emphasis on figures of speech and other literary devices utilized by other approaches to literary analysis; Marxism must move beyond these literary elements and must uncover the author's world and his or her worldview. By placing the text in its historical context and by analyzing the author's view of life, Marxist critics arrive at one of their chief concerns: ideology. It is the ideology expressed by the author as evidenced through his or her fictional world, and how this ideology interacts with the reader's personal ideology, that interests these critics.

Such an ideological and obviously political investigation, assert Marxist critics, will expose class conflict, with the dominant class and its accompanying ideology being imposed either consciously or unconsciously upon the proletariat. The task of the critic, then, is to uncover and denounce such anti-proletariat ideology and show how such a destructive ideology entraps the working classes and oppresses them in every area of their lives. Most important, through such an analysis the Marxist critic wishes to reveal to the working classes how they may end their oppression by the bourgeoisie through a commitment to socialism.

A Marxist critic may begin such an analysis by showing how an author's text reflects his or her ideology through an examination of the fictional world's characters, settings, society, or any other aspect of the text. From this starting point, the critic may then launch an investigation into that particular author's social class and its effects upon the author's society. Or the critic may choose to begin textual analysis by examining the history and the culture of the times as reflected in the text, and then investigate how the author either correctly or incorrectly pictures this historical period.

To gain a working understanding of a Marxist approach to literary analysis, Ira Shor, a Marxist critic and writer, suggests that we ask certain questions of any text, questions that will enable us to see the Marxist concerns that are evidenced or ignored in the text and therefore by the author. The following questions, Shor believes, will provide the framework for a close analysis of a text and will demonstrate Marxism's concern for the direct relationship between literature and society: Is there an outright rejection of socialism in the work? Does the text raise fundamental criticism about the emptiness of life in bourgeois society? In portraying society, what approximation of totality does the author achieve? What is emphasized, what is ignored? How well is the fate of the individual linked organically to the nature of societal forces? What are the work's conflicting forces? At what points are actions or solutions to problems forced or unreal? Are characters from all social levels equally well-sketched? What are the values of each class in the work? Are the main problems or solutions in the text individual or collective? and Which values allow effective action? (See *College English*, November 1972, volume 34 for a complete listing of Shor's questions and other perspectives on Marxism.)

Whether the critic asks these questions or follows a variety of other methods of textual analysis, a Marxist approach seeks to expose the dominant class, show how its ideology controls and oppresses all actions of the working class, and finally highlights those elements of society most affected by such oppression. Such an analysis, hopes the Marxist critic, will lead to action, to social change, to revolution, and to the rise of socialism.

In the essay that follows, note how the student applies Marxist principles in her interpretation of Browning's "My Last Duchess." What is her main interest—class struggle, economics, social behavior? Does she use any of Shor's questions in her analysis? If so, which ones? Does she successfully show the dynamic relationship between society and literature? And where in her analysis might she strengthen her interpretation?

Further Reading

Eagleton, Terry. *Criticism and Ideology: A Study in Marxist Literary Theory.* London: New Left Books, 1976.

———. *Literary Theory: An Introduction.* Minneapolis: University of Minnesota Press, 1983.

———. *Marxism and Literary Theory.* Berkeley: University of California Press, 1976.

Hicks, Granville. *The Great Tradition*. New York: Macmillan, 1933; revised 1935.
Jameson, Fredric. *Marxism and Form: Twentieth-Century Dialectical Theories of Literature*. Princeton: Princeton University Press, 1971.
McMurtry, John. *The Structure of Marx's World-View*. Princeton: Princeton University Press, 1978.

Student Essay

A Marxist Interpretation of "My Last Duchess"

Marxist doctrine posits the existence in every society of a base and a superstructure. In each society, the economic base (capitalism or communism, for example) affects and is affected by the superstructure (art, politics, the psychological views of individuals and classes, etc.). Much Marxist literary criticism is therefore directed toward the class influences of the society in which a particular author lives and writes; such criticism, however, can be applied to an author's secondary world; i.e., in this case Browning's created social order established in "My last Duchess."

Browning's dramatic poem "My Last Duchess" contains four characters of differing social class: the envoy of the Count of Tyrol, a working-class man; Frà Pandolf the artist, a monk; the deceased duchess, a female aristocrat; and the Duke of Ferrara who voices this dramatic poem. Placing himself at the top of the economic chain, the duke perceives himself, others, and the world around him in relation to his own social position. Without question, his membership in the bourgeoisie and his perception of himself within this socioeconomic class affects his attitudes toward and treatment of the people and the arts in his world.

Apart from the duke, the characters in "My Last Duchess" exist in subservient socioeconomic positions. Representing the lower classes of society, the envoy of the Count of Tyrol listens to the extensive speech of the duke. Unlike the duke, the envoy works for his living (in this case arranging a marriage between the duke and the count's daughter), and therefore the envoy *must* listen to the duke (all emphases added). We, the readers, see this envoy only through the eyes of the duke, a person we thoroughly mistrust by the end of the poem; but through the unintended revelations of the duke's speech we learn the reactions of the envoy. Immediately after the duke reveals his murder of the duchess, the duke says, "Will't please you rise?" perhaps indicating that the envoy has risen in horrified disgust. Although of a lower class, the envoy seems to possess a higher moral standard than the duke; wanting to get away from the murderer, he forgets his social "place" and starts to leave the room ahead of this aristocratic duke. To reassert his position, however, the duke says, "Nay, we'll go / Together down, sir." Because his ideology defines and controls acceptable social behavior, he commands the right to leave the room ahead of the envoy. Although the envoy may be morally superior to the duke, the envoy's oppressed social situation requires that he defer to the wishes of the aristocracy and do as the duke commands.

Socially greater than the envoy but subordinate to the duke, Fra Pandolf comes from the class of the clergy. Conversing with the duchess in a class-conscious manner, Fra Pandolf addresses her as "my lady," and he says (according to the duke), "Paint / Must never hope to reproduce the faint / Half-flush that dies along her throat." In complimenting a woman of higher economic status than he, the monk fulfills his social obligations to his moneyed superiors.

In societal rank, the duchess is second only to her husband. By the standards of her time, she exists as both a social and a sexual inferior to the duke. Her true nature, however, can be discerned through the warped speech of the duke: she seems to be young, naive, and accepting ("She had / A heart . . . too soon made glad / Too easily impressed"). She is a woman trained according to her social position to flatter others with thanks and to blush at the praise of men ("such stuff / Was courtesy, she thought, and cause enough / For calling up that spot of joy"). Like the monk and the envoy, the duchess performs as her economic rank dictates.

With his past and present monetary wealth (or, as he puts it, his "nine-hundred-years-old name"), the duke commands the ultimate socioeconomic position in Browning's poem. His self-worth derives from this position. Since birth, he has possessed power by virtue of his wealth and the resulting family prestige. Because he is used to such power, he chooses "Never to stoop." He, like his sculpture of Neptune taming the sea-horse, must control his world. His economic status and his ideology apparently demand that he reign over the world around him: the envoy, the monk, his wife and even art itself. When he discovers, however, that he cannot control his youthful wife as he does everyone else, he destroys her. Unquestionably, his bourgeoisie opinion of himself and his accompanying economic wealth directly affect his desire to manipulate and control his world.

The duke's language betrays this obsession with power. Throughout his conversation he uses numerous first-person pronouns ("*my* last duchess") and references to himself ("*I* call," "none puts by / The curtain *I* have drawn for you, but *I*"). Emphasizing his power over others, he states that people ask him about his painting only "if they durst." And when he speaks of his relationship to the duchess, he expresses his role in terms such as "will" and "commands" and "lessoned."

Beyond word choice, the duke's language expresses socioeconomic dominance in more subtle ways. In the midst of what he well knows to be an overwhelming and lengthy speech, the duke professes to lack eloquence; he uses pretended self-deprecation to emphasize the power he is exercising even at that moment over the envoy; i.e., the duke says he has no skill in speech, when, in reality, the power of his crazed speech allows the envoy no opportunity to respond. The duke thus manipulates the envoy by subjecting him to this long, artificial, maniacal speech, at the end of which he reasserts his social position over the envoy, as discussed earlier.

Acting upon his hunger for power, the duke manipulates not only the envoy but also the monk, the duchess, and any art in his possession. Perhaps the duke chose Fra Pandolf to paint the portrait because of the monk's artistic skill; more likely, however, he chose the monk because of this clergy's specific social position as a sexually powerless male. Fra Pandolf presents no threat to the duke, unlike all the other men who bring a "spot of joy" to the cheek of the duchess. Because of his own social predilection to power, the duke relates to the monk on a social class level rather than an aesthetic or personal one.

As part of a society's superstructure, art exists on an aesthetic level and as such can be assigned value, however that may be defined. But for the duke, art (good or bad) is simply another thing to control; he does not perceive or care about the aesthetic quality of art. His perception of good art seems erroneous: he believes the portrait of the duchess to be "a wonder," but that is difficult to accept when he tells us that Fra Pandolf completed it in a mere day. Compounding his misunderstanding of art, the duke makes himself the only person who may reveal the portrait to observers, thereby controlling the viewing of his art. When he refers the envoy to another piece of art, the duke says, "Notice Neptune, though, / Taming a sea-horse, thought a rarity, / Which Claus of Innsbruck cast in bronze *for me*!" In emphasizing himself as the motivation behind an artist's creation, the duke reveals that he possesses art not for art's sake, but so that he might control it.

The center of the duke's class power struggle ultimately revolves around the duchess. Like the duke's art, the duchess, the duke believes, existed to be controlled by him. Because she, as his wife, reflected his control to the general public, he needed mastery over her love, her emotions, and even her words. He demanded that his physical love elicit more gratitude from her than flowers given by "some officious fool." Behaving as a lady of her class should have behaved, the duchess played the coquette with the courtiers around her, seemingly placing the duke's "gift of a nine-hundred-years-old name / *With anybody's gift*." Unfortunately for her, something in her "depth and passion," her youthful joy, and her blushing thankfulness to all who praised her angered the duke: he saw her behavior as existing apart from his authority. To subjugate his wife, the duke imposed his will on her, and when he thought she refused to bend to it, "all smiles stopped together." Having been murdered, the duchess ceased to exist except on canvas. Now the duke has achieved total control over his framed wife; others can see her only when he chooses to pull the curtain away from her portrait.

Revealed through the language of his conversation, the duke's lust for economic and class power pervades his relationships both with artistic matters and with the people around him. With his bourgeoisie attitudes and beliefs, he believes he deserves to be respected, obeyed, and loved while at the same time he oppresses, belittles, and even murders those around him.

KATHLEEN STOCKIN

10

∽∽∽∽∽∽∽∽∽∽∽∽∽∽∽∽∽∽∽∽∽∽∽∽∽∽∽∽∽∽∽∽∽∽∽∽

New Historicism

Introduction

The ringing bell having signaled the start of class, Professor Wellington began his lecture. "Today, class, we will quickly review what we learned about Elizabethan beliefs from our last lecture so that we can apply this knowledge to our understanding of Act I of Shakespeare's *King Lear*. As you remember, the Elizabethans believed in the interconnectedness of all life. Having created everything, God imposed on creation a cosmic order. At all costs, this cosmic order was not to be upset. Any element of the created universe that portended change in this order, such as a violent storm, eclipses of the sun or moon, or even disobedient children within the family structure, suggested chaos that could possibly lead to anarchy and the destruction of the entire earth. Nothing, believed the Elizabethans, should break any link in this Great Chain of Being, the name given to this created cosmic order. With God and the angels in their place, with the King governing his obedient people in their places, and the animals being subdued and utilized by humankind in theirs, all would be right in the world and operate as ordained by God."

"Having gained an understanding of the Elizabethan worldview, let's turn to act 1, scene ii, lines 101–12 of Shakespeare's *King Lear*. You will recall that in this scene Edmund, the illegitimate son of the Duke of Gloucester, has persuaded the Duke that Edgar, the Duke's legitimate son and heir to the dukedom, wants his father dead so that he may inherit the Duke's title, lands, and wealth. Believing his natural son has betrayed both him and Edmund, Edgar's half brother, the Duke says, 'These late eclipses in the sun and moon portend no good to us. Though the wisdom of nature can reason it thus and thus, yet nature finds itself scourged by the sequent effects. Love cools, friendship falls off, brothers divide. . . . ' "

"What we see in these lines, class, is the Elizabethan worldview in operation. The Duke obviously believes in the interrelatedness of the created cosmic order and the concept of the Great Chain of Being. The significance of the eclipses of the sun and moon therefore rests in their representing change and chaos. Because the Duke believes that the macrocosm (the universe) directly affects the microcosm (the world of humanity on earth), he blames these natural occurrences (the eclipses) for interfering in familial relationships and destroying love between brothers, between father and daughters (King Lear having already banished his most beloved daughter Cordelia), and between King and servant (Kent, King Lear's loyal courtier also having being expelled from the kingdom)."

Professor Wellington's method of literary analysis represents what is known today as the "old historicism." In this methodology, history serves as a background to literature. Of primary importance is the text, the art object itself. The historical background of the text is only secondarily important, for it is the aesthetic object (the text) that mirrors the history of its times. The historical context, then, serves to shed light upon the object of primary concern, the text.

Underlying Professor Wellington's methodology (the old historicism) is a view of history that declares that history, as written, is an accurate view of what really occurred. Such a view assumes that historians are able to write objectively about any given historical time period and are able to state definitively the truth about that era. Through various means of historical analysis, such historians are also capable of discovering the mindset, the worldview, or the beliefs of any group of people. For example, when Professor Wellington describes the beliefs of the Elizabethans at the beginning of his lecture, he is articulating the Elizabethan worldview—the unified set of presuppositions or assumptions that all Elizabethans supposedly held concerning their world. By applying these assertions to the Elizabethan text *King Lear,* Professor Wellington believes he can formulate a more accurate interpretation of the play then if he did not know the play's historical context.

That historians can articulate a unified and internally consistent worldview of any given people, country, or time period and can reconstruct an accurate and objective picture of any historical event are key assumptions that **New Historicism,** the most recent approach to literary analysis, challenges. Appearing as an alternative approach to textual interpretation in the late 1970s and early 1980s, New Historicism declares that all history is subjective, written by people whose personal biases affect their interpretation of the past. History, asserts New Historicism, can never provide us with the "truth" or give us a totally accurate picture of past events or the worldview of a group of people. Disavowing the old historicism's autonomous view of history, New Historicism declares that history is one of many **discourses** or ways of seeing and thinking about the world. By highlighting and viewing history as one of many equally important discourses, such as sociology and politics, and by closely examining how all discourses (including that of textual analysis itself) affect a text's interpretation, New Historicism proclaims that it provides its adherents with a practice of literary analysis that highlights the interrelatedness of all human activities, admits its own prejudices, and gives a more complete understanding of a text than does the old historicism and other interpretative approaches.

Historical Development

Since the 1960s, critical theories such as deconstruction, Marxism, feminism, and Lacanian psychoanalysis have successfully challenged the assumptions of the New Criticism that dominated literary theory and practice for the first half of the twentieth century. Rejecting New Criticism's claim that the meaning of a text can be found, for the most part, in the text alone, poststructural critics have been developing a variety of theoretical positions concerning the nature of the reading process, the part the reader plays in that process, and the definition of a text or the actual work of art. The most recent critical voice to be heard in this discussion is New Historicism.

Influenced by sociological and cultural studies, New Historicism challenges the supposed objectivity of history, redefines the meaning of a text, and asserts that all critics must acknowledge and openly declare their own biases when interpreting a work. That consensus can be found among New Historicists concerning theories of art, various terminology, and practical methods of interpretation, however, would be an invalid assumption. Embracing different theories and a variety of methodologies, New Historicism is best thought of as a practice of literary interpretation that is still in process, one that is continuously exploring new interests, gaining new followers, and formulating its philosophy and practices.

Although New Historical assumptions and practices have been employed by critics for several decades, the beginnings of New Historicism date to 1979–80 with the publication of several essays such as "Improvisation and Power" and texts (*Renaissance Self-Fashioning*, for example) by the Renaissance scholar Stephen Greenblatt, and a variety of works by Louis Montrose and others. Wishing to remain open to differing politics, theories, and ideologies, these critics share a similar set of concerns, not a codified theory or school of criticism. Of chief interest is their shared view that the mid-nineteenth to early-twentieth-century historical methods of literary analysis are erroneous; history, they believe, should not serve merely as background information for textual analysis, nor can it ever objectively reproduce "how it really was." In disclaiming this old historicism and formulating its own theories of history and interpretative analysis, New Historicism was aptly named by Stephen Greenblatt in the introduction to a collection of Renaissance essays in a 1982 volume of the journal *Genre*.

Throughout the 1980s and up to the present, critics such as Catherine Gallagher, Jonathan Dollimore, Jerome McGann, Frank Lentricchia, and many others have voiced their concerns that the study of literature and its relationship to history has been too narrow. Viewing a text as culture in action, these critics blur the distinction between an artistic production and any other kind of social production or event. Greenblatt and other New Historicists wish us to see, for example, that the publication of Swift's "A Modest Proposal" is a political act, while noting that the ceremonies surrounding the inauguration of a United States president is an aesthetic event with many of the trappings of symbolism and structure found in any poem. Many similar examples highlighting their critical practices can be found in their chief public voice, the journal *Representations*.

Called a "bastard child of history," considered by some to be hostile to American values, and heralded as subversive and destructive to theory and literary studies, New Historicism does not present a unified front to its opponents, and is in the process of articulating a clear declaration of its purposes and its philosophy. Yet its followers continue to call for a reawakening of our historical consciousness and an understanding that while we are researching and learning about different societies that provide the historical context for various texts, we are simultaneously learning about ourselves, our own habits, and our own beliefs.

Assumptions

Like other poststructuralist practices, New Historicism begins by challenging the long-held belief that a text is an autonomous work of art that contains in itself all the elements necessary to arrive at a supposedly correct interpretation. Disavowing the old historical assumption that a text simply reflects its historical context (the mimetic view of art and history) and that such historical information provides an interesting and sometimes useful backdrop for literary analysis, New Historicism redirects our attention to a series of philosophical and practical concerns that it believes will highlight the complex interconnectedness of all human activities. It redefines, for example the definition of a text and of history while simultaneously redefining the relationship between a text and history. Unlike the old historicism, New Historicism asserts that there exists an intricate connection between an aesthetic object (a text or any work of art) and society, while denying that a text can be evaluated in isolation from its cultural context. We must know, it declares, the societal concerns of the author, of the historical times evidenced in the work, and of other cultural elements exhibited in the text before we can devise a valid interpretation. And this new approach to textual analysis questions the very way we arrive at meaning for any human activity such as a text, a social event, a long-held tradition, or a political act.

New Historicism finds the basis for its concerns and a coherent body of assumptions in the writings of the twentieth-century French archaeologist, historian, and philosopher Michel Foucault. Foucault begins his rather complex and sometimes paradoxical theoretical structure by redefining the concept of history. Unlike many past historians, Foucault declares that history is not **linear,** for it does not have a definite beginning, middle, and end, nor is it necessarily **teleological,** purposefully going forward toward some known end. Nor can it be explained as a series of causes and effects that are controlled by some mysterious destiny or all-powerful deity. For Foucault, history is the complex interrelationship of a variety of discourses (the various ways—artistic, social, political, and so forth—in which people think and talk about their world). How these various discourses interact in any given historical period is not random but is dependent upon a unifying principle or pattern Foucault calls the **episteme:** through language and thought, each period in history develops its own perceptions concerning the nature of reality (or what it defines as truth) and sets up its own standards of acceptable and unacceptable behavior, in addition to its criteria for judging what it deems good or bad, and what group of people articulate, protect, and defend the yardstick whereby all established truths, values, and actions will be deemed acceptable.

To unearth the episteme of any given historical period, Foucault borrows techniques from archaeology. Just as an archaeologist must slowly and meticulously dig through various layers of earth to uncover the symbolic treasures of the past, historians must expose each of the layers of discourse that come together to shape a people's episteme. And just as an archaeologist must date each finding and then piece together the artifacts that define and help explain that culture, so must the historian piece together the various discourses and their interconnections among themselves and with nondiscursive practices (any cultural institution such as a form of government, for example) that will assist in articulating the episteme under investigation.

Seen from this point of view, history is a form of power. Since each historical era develops its own episteme, it is, in actuality, the episteme that controls how that era and its people will view reality. History, then, becomes the study and unearthing of a vast, complex web of interconnecting forces that ultimately determines what takes place in each culture or society. Why or how epistemes change from one historical period to another is basically unclear. That they change seemingly without warning is certain. Such a change occurred, for example, at the beginning of the nineteenth century (the change from the Age of Reason to romanticism) and initiated a new episteme. In this new historical era a variety of different relationships developed among discourses that had not evolved or did exist and were deemed unacceptable in the previous historical period. Foucault asserts that such radical and abrupt changes that cause breaks from one episteme to another are neither good nor bad, neither valid nor invalid. Like the discourses that help produce them, different epistemes exist in their own right; they are neither moral nor immoral, but amoral.

According to Foucault, historians must realize that they are influenced and prejudiced by the episteme(s) in which they live. Since their thoughts, customs, habits, and other actions are colored by their own epistemes, historians, Foucault argues, must realize that they can never be totally objective about their own or any other historical period. To be a historian, then, means one must be able to confront and articulate one's own set of biases before examining the various discourses (the material evidence of past events) that comprise the episteme of any given period. Such an archaeological uncovering of the various discourses, Foucault believes, will not unearth a monological view of an episteme that presupposes a single, overarching political vision or design, but will uncover a set of inconsistent, irregular, and often contradictory discourses that will help to explain the development of that episteme, including what elements were accepted, changed, or rejected to form the "truth" and set the acceptable standards for that era.

In addition to borrowing many of its ideas from Foucault, New Historicism also utilizes theories and methodologies from cultural anthropologists such as Clifford Geertz and Victor Turner. Along with Geertz, New Historicists believe that there exists "no human nature independent of culture," culture being defined by Geertz as "a set of control mechanisms— plans, recipes, rules, instructions" for the governing of behavior. Adapting Geertz's anthropological methodology for describing culture as "thick description," New Historicists declare that each separate discourse of a culture must be uncovered and analyzed in hopes of showing how all discourses interact with each other and with institutions, peoples, and other elements of culture. It is this interaction between various discourses that shapes a culture and thus interconnects all human activities, including the writing, reading, and interpretation of a text that the New Historicist wishes to emphasize.

Since texts are simply one of many elements that help shape a culture, New Historicists believe that all texts are really social documents that not only reflect but also, and more importantly, respond to their historical situation. And since any historical situation is an intricate web of oftentimes competing discourses, New Historicists necessarily put history at the center and declare that any interpretation of a text will be incomplete if we do not consider the text's relationship to the various discourses that helped fashion it and to which the text is a response. From this point of view, a text becomes a battleground of competing ideas among the author, society, customs, institutions, and social practices that are all eventually negotiated by the author and the reader and influenced by each contributor's episteme. Only by allowing history a prominent place in the interpretative process and by examining the various convoluted webbings of discourses found both within a text and in its historical setting, can we hope, declares the New Historicist, to negotiate a text's meaning.

Overall, New Historicists posit the interconnectedness of all our actions. In our search to attach meaning to our actions, they believe that we can never be fully objective, for we are all biased by cultural forces. Only by examining the complex web of these interlocking forces or discourses that empower and shape culture, and by realizing that no one discourse reveals the pathway to absolute truth concerning ourselves or our world, can we begin to interpret either our world or a text.

For the New Historicist, the goal of interpretative analysis is really the formation and an understanding of a "poetics of culture," a process that sees life and its sundry activities as being more like art than we think, more a metaphorical interpretation of reality than an analytic one. Through the practice of New Historical analysis, New Historicists believe that we will discover not only the social world of the text but also the present-day social forces working upon us as we negotiate meaning with printed material. Like history itself, however, our interaction with any text is a dynamic, ongoing process that will always be somewhat incomplete.

Methodology

Like other approaches to literary analysis, New Historicism includes an array of techniques and strategies in its interpretative inquiries, with no one method being designated as the correct form of investigation. No matter what the technique, however, New Historicists begin by assuming that language shapes and is shaped by the culture that uses it. By language, New Historicists mean much more than spoken words. For them, language includes discourse, writing, literature, social actions, and any social relationship whereby a person or a group imposes their ideas or actions upon another.

Included in this definition of language is history. Like literature, writing, or other relationships that involve a transfer or a relationship of power, history now becomes a narrative discourse. As in literature or any other narrative discourse, history must now be viewed as a "language" that can never be fully articulated or completely explained. From this perspective, history and literature are nearly synonymous terms, both being narrative discourses that interact with their historical situations, their authors, their readers, and their present-day cultures. Neither can claim a complete or an objective understanding of its content or historical situation, for, in actuality, both are ongoing conversations with their creators, readers, and cultures.

Since New Historicists view history, literature, and other social activities as forms of discourse, they strongly reject the old historicism that sees history as necessary background material for the study of literature. For New Historicists, a work of art (a text) is like any other social discourse that interacts with its culture to produce meaning. No longer is one discourse superior to another, but all are necessary components that shape and are shaped by society. And no longer do clear lines of distinction exist among literature, history, literary criticism, anthropology, art, the sciences, and other disciplines. Blurring the boundaries between the disciplines, New Historicists investigate all discourses that affect any social production. Since they believe that meaning evolves from the interaction of the variously interwoven social discourses, no hierarchy of discourses can exist, for all are necessary and must be investigated in the process of textual analysis. Included in this interpretative process must also be a questioning of the methodological assumptions for discerning meaning for each discourse and for every practitioner, for no one discourse or method or critic can reveal the "truth" about any social production in isolation from other discourses.

Since New Historicists view an aesthetic work as a social production, a text's meaning resides for them in the cultural system composed of the interlocking discourses of its author, the text, and its reader. To unlock textual meaning, the New Historicist investigates three areas of concern: (1) the life of the author; (2) the social rules and dictates found within a text; and (3) the reflection of a work's historical situation as evidenced in the text. Since an actual person authors a text, his or her actions and beliefs reflect both individual concerns and those of the society, and are therefore essential elements of the text itself. In addition, the standards of behavior as reflected in a society's rules of decorum must also be investigated, since these behavioral codes simultaneously helped shape and were shaped by the text. And the text must also be viewed as an artistic work that reflects upon these behavioral social codes. To begin to understand a text's significance and to realize the complex social structure of which it is a part, New Historicists declare that all three areas of concern must be investigated. If one area is ignored, the risk of returning to the old historicism, with its lack of understanding concerning a text as a social production, is great. And during this process of textual analysis critics must not forget to question their own assumptions and methods, for they too are products of and shaping influences upon their culture.

To avoid the old historicism's "error" of thinking that each historical period evidences a single, political worldview, New Historicism avoids sweeping generalizations and seeks out the seemingly insignificant details and manifestations of culture that are more frequently than not ignored by most historians or literary critics. Because New Historicists view history and literature as social discourses and therefore as battlegrounds for conflicting beliefs, actions, and customs, a text becomes "culture in action." By highlighting seemingly insignificant happenings, such as a note written by Thomas Jefferson to one of his slaves or a sentence etched on a glass window by Hawthorne, these critics hope to uncover the competing social codes and forces that mold a given society. Emphasizing a particular moment or incident rather than an overarching vision of society, a New Historicist will often point out nonconventional connections, such as that between Sophia Hawthorne's having a headache after reading *The Scarlet Letter* and the ending of Nathaniel Hawthorne's next romance *The House of the Seven Gables,* or between the production of cottage cheese and Flannery O'Connor's *Wise Blood.* The New Historicists believe that an investigation into these and similar happenings will demonstrate the complex relationships that exist among all discourses and how the various narrative discourses such as history, literature, and other social productions interact, define, and are in turn shaped by their culture.

In the following essay, entitled "Hawthorne's Ambiguity: A New Historical Point of View," ask yourself whether the critic investigates the three major areas of concern for New Historicists. Is one area emphasized more than another? Does the writer highlight a historical moment or a culture's single vision of reality? Does the critic admit his own prejudices and methodology? Is history used as background or is it brought to the center of the literary analysis? And what would be different about this essay if it were written from the point of view of the old historicism?

Further Reading

Collier, Peter, and Helga Geyer-Ryan, eds. *Literary Theory Today.* Ithaca, NY: Cornell University Press, 1990.

Greenblatt, Stephen. Introduction. "The Forms of Power and the Power of Forms in the Renaissance." *Genre* 15 (Summer 1982): 3–6.

———. *Renaissance Self-Fashioning: From More to Shakespeare.* Chicago: University of Chicago Press, 1980.

Murfin, Ross C., ed. *Heart of Darkness: A Case Study in Contemporary Criticism.* New York: St. Martin's, 1989.

Robertson, D. W. Jr. "Historical Criticism," in *English Institute Essays: 1950,* ed. Alan S. Downer. New York: Columbia University Press, 1951. 3–31.

Thomas, Brook. "The Historical Necessity for—and Difficulties with—New Historical Analysis in Introductory Literature Courses." *College English* 49 (September 1987): 509–22.

Vesser, H. Aram, ed. *The New Historicism.* New York: Routledge, 1989.

Student Essay

Hawthorne's Ambiguity: A New Historical Point of View

Nathaniel Hawthorne's use of ambiguity in "Young Goodman Brown" is commonly interpreted to represent Hawthorne's own indecision regarding the nature of humankind. Still other critics render his ambiguity as a device to portray the unsure road of doubt and devotion to God. But if we apply the principles of New Historicism, we will discover that Hawthorne's ambiguity functions on two levels in the text. On one hand, Hawthorne will allow the reader to share the Puritanical perspective of humankind, but throughout the tale, the reader will simultaneously recognize the blind limitations of that worldview. By considering both the text and its historical context as forms of narrative discourse, we can conclude that Hawthorne's ambiguity may no longer be ambiguous.

New England Magazine first published "Young Goodman Brown" in April, 1835, but Hawthorne probably wrote the work in 1828 or 1829, it being considered one of the *Provincial Tales.* At this time Hawthorne was by no means accepted as an author of great repute; in fact, the magazine published Hawthorne's "Young Goodman Brown" anonymously as it did all of his work prior to 1837. We cannot, then, regard "Young Goodman Brown" as representative of the mature Hawthorne's later acclaimed romances and tales, nor can we consider this tale in the context of Hawthorne's later literary influences. Works like "Nature," "The Fall of the House of Usher," *Walden, Moby-Dick,* and *Leaves of Grass* had not yet entered the literary milieu upon "Young Goodman Brown's" publication. This story, then, must not be considered the key that unlocks the supposedly Hawthornesque world view, but this tale must stand as a separate and complex entity for our examination.

An important link exists between Hawthorne's ancestors and the story's fictional time frame. The fictional setting occurs during the witch trials of Salem, Massachusetts. In reference to his great-grandfather, John Hathorne, a judge in these infamous trials, Hawthorne writes in the "Custom House": "Their blood may fairly be said to have left a stain upon him." Apparently, Hawthorne knew of a family tradition that one of the witches had cursed Judge Hathorne and all of the judge's posterity. Knowing of the family tradition, Hawthorne held a superstitious respect for the curse and half seriously attributed to its influence what he perceived to be a subsequent decline in the family's notoriety. Furthermore, the administrative tradition of the Hathorne lineage had ended with Joseph, Judge Hathorne's oldest son, who became a farmer. Following Joseph's generation there would not appear a high-level administrator. Some speculate that Hawthorne added the *w* to his last name in order to evade resemblance to the cursed family appellation.

In "The Custom House" Hawthorne writes specifically about his great-great-grandfather, William Hathorne:

> The figure of that first ancestor, invested by family tradition with a dim and dusky grandeur, was present to my boyish imagination as far back as I can remember. It still haunts me, and induces a sort of home feeling with the past. . . . I seem to have a stronger claim to residence here (in Salem) on account of this grave, bearded, sable-cloaked and steeple-crowned progenitor—who came so early, with his Bible and his sword, and trod the unworn street with such a stately port, and made so large a figure, as a man of war and peace—a stronger claim than for myself. . . . He was a soldier, a legislator, judge; he was a ruler in the church; he had all the Puritanic traits both good and bad. He was likewise a bitter persecutor, as witness the Quakers, who have remembered him in their histories, and relate an incident of his hard severity towards a woman of their sect, which will last longer, it is to be feared, than any record of his better deeds, although these were many.

First, let us note the parallels between the text of "Young Goodman Brown" and Hawthorne's consideration of William in "The Custom House." Recalling an incident when William dragged a Quaker woman down a street in Salem, Hawthorne refers to William as a "bitter persecutor." Brown, too, has an ancestor who "lashed the Quaker women so smartly through the streets of Salem." In addition, Hawthorne realizes that William, his own ancestor, is susceptible to error in spite of his many leadership roles: church leader, legislator, and judge. Similarly, Hawthorne challenges Brown to recognize that the Governor, the church leaders, and Brown's ancestors are fallible despite their status as models of the Puritan worldview.

In the same passage, Hawthorne sees that William, a model of the Puritan worldview, hurts others (namely the Quakers) rather than loving them. Because Puritanism encourages its followers to love humankind, Hawthorne seemingly questions here the consistency of the Puritan's philosophical framework. He neither condemns, however, the Quaker beliefs, nor does he maintain the Puritan view as the model of correctness, for Puritanism has "both good and bad" traits. Accordingly, Hawthorne does not grant William moral superiority to the Quakers by merit of his world view, but judges William's character by merit of his actions. Because Hawthorne questions William's concepts and values in "The Custom House," we can expect him to do the same in "Young Goodman Brown," a work bearing distinct similarities to "The Custom House."

The exact historical time frame of "Young Goodman Brown" also aids us in our interpretation. Hawthorne fixes the fictional time frame by providing an allusion to Sir William Phips, the Royal Governor of Massachusetts from 1692–1694. Into that time frame Hawthorne introduces a character usually identified as Satan. The age of this character, whom I will call the pedagogue, is "about fifty." By more than coincidence the pedagogue's date of birth, *c.* 1642–1644, rests in the heat of the English Revolution. Hawthorne notes that the pedagogue wears "grave and decent attire" and has a "general acquaintance" in Puritan New England among the prominent figures of the community. We are also told that the pedagogue and Brown "might have been taken for father and son." The pedagogue, I believe, represents Brown's Puritan forefather who, we will find, learns a grave lesson about his Puritan faith. Because of the pedagogue's Puritan garb and many acquaintances, we can dub him a Puritan. And since he was born at the time of the English Revolution, we will say that he embodies the defeated Puritan of that revolution.

The English Revolution (1642–1649) consisted of the civil wars fought in England and Scotland between Royalist supporters of King Charles I and the Parliamentarians who protested the king's taxation not approved by the English citizenry and the king's religious policies, to name a few of many causes. Among those who joined the Parliamentarian alliance were members of the Puritan sect, sections of the land-owning gentry, and members of the merchant class. In 1642, the English Revolution continued chaotically at a time when compromise was not less than imperative, but compromise did not appear on the agenda of the groups involved. Both English and Scottish Presbyterians felt no security in anything less than a complete Presbyterian victory. Charles I regarded any proposal as a betrayal of his God-given monarchy, and the Independent Army of the Puritans refused compromise as avidly as any.

Our concern will be with the Puritan interest in this revolution. The Puritans believed that after the time of the apostles there had been thirteen or fourteen centuries of ignorance of God's will. During that period humankind had experienced its peak of depravity for reasons known only to God. Puritans felt sure that they would be God's answer to this long period of perceived unenlightenment; they hoped to find new revelation in themselves, serving as a lighthouse to a society in a long age of darkness. Having been summoned to create a holy community, the Puritans found hope in the secular revolution of England to effect such a change. But the hope of the Puritan would not be recognized in England, for they found that they would have to take new hopes to North America, at least the Puritans who did not lose faith after disappointment in Europe.

The pedagogue's Puritanic philosophy had allowed him to hope for new revelation and a new Zion, but after defeat in the revolution, he realizes that these were false hopes. As a result, he loses his faith and questions his own beliefs, exactly what he will challenge Brown to do. In assuming that the Puritans were the sole witnesses of God's will among an unenlightened world, he believed that the non-Puritan members of England were uninformed of God's will and consequently among the damned. His beliefs, then, offered him moral superiority; he had hoped to be the salvation of the English society. But when his hopes were not recognized, he could no longer claim that God's will included Puritan victory in the revolution. He realized that the new Zion was only a dream for the English Puritan; he was not God's answer to the problems in English society. He then questioned the belief in the elect, for his election was connected with his ability to provide a society purified of humankind's depravity. If he could not create a society any purer than that of the damned, then he could not very well see a difference in the moralities of the damned and the elect.

Being a historian, Hawthorne knew of the revolutionary Puritans' failed attempt to achieve a purified society (embodied in the pedagogue), and he has already commented on the failures of both William and John's purity. Hawthorne will now attempt to reveal these inconsistencies to Goodman Brown, who represents the Puritan's New World attempt at a new Zion utopia in New England.

Hawthorne provides, in abundance, reason for Brown to require such a lesson about his faith. As Brown considers returning to Faith, his wife, he contemplates, "And what calm sleep would be his that very night, which was to have been spent so wickedly, but so purely and sweetly now, in the arms of Faith!" Here, playing on the word *faith,* Hawthorne refers to the name of Brown's wife as well as to Brown's Puritan faith. Hawthorne seemingly equates the Puritan faith with calm sleep, as Brown prefers to sleep in the arms of that faith. If Brown's faith represents sleep, then his faith apparently becomes ignorance. Even the name Young Goodman Brown implies a simplistic, uneducated, and inexperienced character. And Brown further reveals his apparent naivete in saying to his wife, "Say thy prayers . . . and go to bed at dusk, and no harm will come to thee." Once again, Hawthorne compares the Puritan faith to sleep, for Brown's prescription is one of avoidance: to go to bed before night and escape the uncertain darkness.

Brown's slumberous faith remains intact until the pedagogue challenges Brown's reasoning. Brown, then, endures a fearful paranoia and finally becomes "maddened with despair." In his despondency, confusion and terror overtake him: "the road grew wilder and drearier and more faintly traced," and "the whole forest was peopled with frightful sounds—

the creaking of the trees, the howling of wild beasts, and the yells of Indi-ans." Brown's fear becomes malicious when he roars, "Think not to frighten me with your deviltry. Come witch, come wizard, come Indian powwow, come devil himself, and here comes Goodman Brown. You may as well fear him as he fears you." From this passage, we gain insight into Brown's concept of evil. He is frightened into believing that his surround-ings are evil. First, he is confronted by "frightful sounds" of the forest and becomes afraid. Then he considers the frightening unknown to be "devil-ish" and evil. His final reaction to his fear is hostility as he threatens the imagined Indians and witches. We should also note that Brown threatens the devil in the same sentence as the imaginary Indians. It is likely, then, that the devil too is an imaginary enemy. If Brown fears what he is igno-rant of and calls evil that which he fears, then that which he is ignorant of is evil to him. By saying that the Puritan concept of evil comes from igno-rance, Hawthorne refutes the Puritan idea of evil, including Indians, wiz-ards, and the Devil.

We know, now, not only that Hawthorne refuses to endorse the abso-lute correctness of the Puritan world view, but that he also equates the Puritan concept of evil with fearful ignorance. We can thus safely assume that Hawthorne will not fear the things that Brown fears—the forest, the Indians, and the myth of witchery—for the romantic Hawthorne worships the natural beauty of the forest, for him the Indian becomes a noble savage, and he declares the Salem witch trials to be a tragic result of ignorance. If Hawthorne, then, refutes the Puritan idea of evil, then the pedagogue, who is Satan to Brown, is not likely to be Satan at all to Hawthorne, allow-ing us to see the two levels of understanding upon which the text oper-ates—that of Brown's and of Hawthorne's.

Hawthorne's distinctive use of ambiguity, then, acts as a mediator be-tween these two levels of understanding. Hawthorne not accidentally af-fords double meaning throughout the text to accommodate simulta-neously Brown, who believes that he confronts actual evil, and the reader, who realizes that Brown struggles with his own ignorance and fear and not with supposedly universal evil. We see the story through Brown's Pu-ritan eyes; for him, there is the devil: "What if the devil himself should be at my very elbow!" We are offered Brown's understanding of the pedagogue's character, but Hawthorne does not demand that the reader agree with Brown's ignorance. Though Hawthorne makes it obvious that Brown believes "he of the serpent" to be Satan, we are free to see that Satan is a concept of Brown's limited understanding. When Brown accuses the pedagogue of being wicked, the pedagogue responds by saying, "Wicked-ness or not, I have a very general acquaintance here in New England," not admitting to be evil, yet allowing Brown and the Puritan mind to keep this option as well.

We can now deduce that the pedagogue cannot be the literal devil when he realizes, in his discourse with Brown, "that his arguments seemed rather to spring up in the bosom of his auditor [Brown] than to be suggested by himself." We know that if the character in question were the devil, then all evil would supposedly arise from him rather than being contained within the bosom of Brown. Unfortunately, the Puritans attributed all that is feared or unfavorable to the devil instead of looking within themselves or their society for answers to their questions and their behavior. Hawthorne's answer to the devil is that "The fiend in his own shape is less hideous than when he rages in the breast of man." In other words, it is easier for the Puritans to attribute all that seems negative to a scapegoat entity called the devil than to admit to own all human qualities, both good and bad, with no one to blame.

After Hawthorne debunks the Puritan concepts of evil and the devil, he refutes the Puritan concept of the damned and the elect. While in the forest Brown hears and recognizes the voices of the "pious and ungodly," the "sinners" and "saints" intermingled and conversing among one another. Brown recognizes that these people, "many of whom he had met at the communion table, and had seen others rioting at the tavern," were not separated by a status of damned or elect. And Hawthorne draws a common ground for the now-intermingled group. The communion table and the tavern provide a similar image of conversation and wine. By repeatedly mentioning "the communion of your race," Hawthorne solidifies the unity of both groups. Furthermore, we know that this communion of the human race cannot be united under the Puritan idea that all humankind is fallen because Hawthorne has already refuted the Puritan concept of evil and fallenness.

Hawthorne's use of ambiguity can now be explained as the intermediary between the seventeenth-century Puritan understanding of evil and the reader's elevated understanding of the limitations of Puritan assumptions. Hawthorne offers the reader insight into the Puritans' failed attempt at creating the purified new Zion. Although the Puritan claims to be a morally superior messenger of God's will, Hawthorne and I contend that this Puritan view is fallible, noting the failures of the Puritan beliefs as held by Hawthorne's Puritan ancestors, the Puritans of the English Revolution, and the fictional Puritans of "Young Goodman Brown." By viewing history, religion, and literature as various discourses, we see that Hawthorne does not endorse the Puritan idea that we are fallen, but on the contrary, comments on the fallible quality of Puritan doctrine.

KEVIN A. EATON

LITERARY
SELECTIONS

Young Goodman Brown

NATHANIEL HAWTHORNE

Young Goodman Brown came forth at sunset into the street at Salem village; but put his head back, after crossing the threshold, to exchange a parting kiss with his young wife. And Faith, as the wife was aptly named, thrust her own pretty head into the street, letting the wind play with the pink ribbons on her cap while she called to Goodman Brown.

"Dearest heart," whispered she, softly and rather sadly, when her lips were close to his ear, "prithee put off your journey until sunrise and sleep in your own bed to-night. A lone woman is troubled with such dreams and such thoughts that she's afeared of herself sometimes. Pray tarry with me this night, dear husband, of all nights in the year."

"My love and my Faith," replied young Goodman Brown, "of all nights in the year, this one night must I tarry away from thee. My journey, as thou callest it, forth and back again, must needs be done 'twixt now and sunrise. What, my sweet, pretty wife, dost thou doubt me already, and we but three months married?"

"Then God bless you!" said Faith, with the pink ribbons; "and may you find all well when you come back."

"Amen!" cried Goodman Brown. "Say thy prayers, dear Faith, and go to bed at dusk, and no harm will come to thee."

So they parted; and the young man pursued his way until, being about to turn the corner by the meeting-house, he looked back and saw the head of Faith still peeping after him with a melancholy air, in spite of her pink ribbons.

"Poor little Faith!" thought he, for his heart smote him. "What a wretch am I to leave her on such an errand! She talks of dreams, too. Methought as she spoke there was trouble in her face, as if a dream had warned her what work is to be done to-night. But no, no; 'twould kill her to think it. Well, she's a blessed angel on earth; and after this one night I'll cling to her skirts and follow her to heaven."

With this excellent resolve for the future, Goodman Brown felt himself justified in making more haste on his present evil purpose. He had taken a dreary road, darkened by all the gloomiest trees of the forest, which barely stood aside to let the narrow path creep through, and closed immediately behind. It was all as lonely as could be; and there is this peculiarity in such a solitude, that the traveller knows not who may be concealed by the innumerable trunks and the thick boughs overhead; so that with lonely footsteps he may yet be passing through an unseen multitude.

"There may be a devilish Indian behind every tree," said Goodman Brown to himself; and he glanced fearfully behind him as he added, "What if the devil himself should be at my very elbow!"

His head being turned back, he passed a crook of the road, and, looking forward again, beheld the figure of a man, in grave and decent attire, seated at the foot of an old tree. He arose at Goodman Brown's approach and walked onward side by side with him.

"You are late, Goodman Brown," said he. "The clock of the Old South was striking as I came through Boston, and that is full fifteen minutes agone."

"Faith kept me back a while," replied the young man, with a tremor in his voice, caused by the sudden appearance of his companion, though not wholly unexpected.

It was now deep dusk in the forest, and deepest in that part of it where these two were journeying. As nearly as could be discerned, the second travel-ler was about fifty years old, apparently in the same rank of life as Goodman Brown, and bearing a considerable resemblance to him, though perhaps more in expression than features. Still they might have been taken for father and son. And yet, though the elder person was as simply clad as the younger, and as simple in manner too, he had an indescribable air of one who knew the world, and who would not have felt abashed at the governor's dinner table or in King William's court, were it possible that his affairs should call him thither. But the only thing about him that could be fixed upon as remarkable was his staff, which bore the likeness of a great black snake, so curiously wrought that it might almost be seen to twist and wriggle itself like a living serpent. This, of course, must have been an ocular deception, assisted by the uncertain light.

"Come, Goodman Brown," cried his fellow-traveller, "this is a dull pace for the beginning of a journey. Take my staff, if you are so soon weary."

"Friend," said the other, exchanging his slow pace for a full stop, "having kept covenant by meeting thee here, it is my purpose now to return whence I came. I have scruples touching the matter thou wot'st of."

"Sayest thou so?" replied he of the serpent, smiling apart. "Let us walk on, nevertheless, reasoning as we go; and if I convince thee not thou shalt turn back. We are but a little way in the forest yet."

"Too far! too far!" exclaimed the goodman, unconsciously resuming his walk. "My father never went into the woods on such an errand, nor his father before him. We have been a race of honest men and good Christians since the days of the martyrs; and shall I be the first of the name of Brown that ever took this path and kept"—

"Such company, thou wouldst say," observed the elder person, interpre-ting his pause. "Well said, Goodman Brown! I have been as well acquainted with your family as with ever a one among the Puritans; and that's no trifle to say. I helped your grandfather, the constable, when he lashed the Quaker woman so smartly through the streets of Salem; and it was I that brought your father a pitch-pine knot, kindled at my own hearth, to set fire to an Indian village, in King Philip's war. They were my good friends, both; and many a pleasant walk have we had along this path, and returned merrily after midnight. I would fain be friends with you for their sake."

"If it be as thou sayest," replied Goodman Brown, "I marvel they never spoke of these matters; or verily, I marvel not, seeing that the least rumor of the sort would have driven them from New England. We are a people of prayer, and good works to boot, and abide no such wickedness."

"Wickedness or not," said the traveller with the twisted staff, "I have a very general acquaintance here in New England. The deacons of many a church have drunk the communion wine with me; the selectmen of divers towns make me their chairman; and a majority of the Great and General Court are firm supporters of my interest. The governor and I, too—But these are state secrets."

"Can this be so?" cried Goodman Brown, with a stare of amazement at his undisturbed companion. "Howbeit, I have nothing to do with the governor and council; they have their own ways, and are no rule for a simple husbandman like me. But, were I to go with thee, how should I meet the eye of that good old man, our minister, at Salem village? Oh, his voice would make me tremble both Sabbath day and lecture day."

Thus far the elder traveller had listened with due gravity; but now burst into a fit of irrepressible mirth, shaking himself so violently that his snake-like staff actually seemed to wriggle in sympathy.

"Ha! ha! ha!" shouted he again and again; then composing himself, "Well, go on, Goodman Brown, go on; but, prithee, don't kill me with laughing."

"Well, then, to end the matter at once," said Goodman Brown, considerably nettled, "there is my wife, Faith. It would break her dear little heart; and I'd rather break my own."

"Nay, if that be the case," answered the other, "e'en go thy ways, Goodman Brown. I would not for twenty old women like the one hobbling before us that Faith should come to any harm."

As he spoke he pointed his staff at a female figure on the path, in whom Goodman Brown recognized a very pious and exemplary dame, who had taught him his catechism in youth, and was still his moral and spiritual adviser, jointly with the minister and Deacon Gookin.

"A marvel, truly, that Goody Cloyse should be so far in the wilderness at nightfall," said he. "But with your leave, friend, I shall take a cut through the woods until we have left this Christian woman behind. Being a stranger to you, she might ask whom I was consorting with and whither I was going."

"Be it so," said his fellow-traveller. "Betake you to the woods, and let me keep the path."

Accordingly the young man turned aside, but took care to watch his companion, who advanced softly along the road until he had come within a staff's length of the old dame. She, meanwhile, was making the best of her way, with singular speed for so aged a woman, and mumbling some indistinct words—a prayer, doubtless—as she went. The traveller put forth his staff and touched her withered neck with what seemed the serpent's tail.

"The devil!" screamed the pious old lady.

"Then Goody Cloyse knows her old friend?" observed the traveller, confronting her and leaning on his writhing stick.

"Ah, forsooth, and is it your worship indeed?" cried the good dame. "Yes, truly is it, and in the very image of my old gossip, Goodman Brown, the grandfather of the silly fellow that now is. But—would your worship believe it?—my broomstick hath strangely disappeared, stolen, as I suspect, by that unhanged witch, Goody Cory, and that, too, when I was all anointed with the juice of smallage, and cinquefoil, and wolf's bane"—

"Mingled with fine wheat and the fat of a new-born babe," said the shape of old Goodman Brown.

"Ah, your worship knows the recipe," cried the old lady, cackling aloud. "So, as I was saying, being all ready for the meeting, and no horse to ride on, I made up my mind to foot it, for they tell me there is a nice young man to be taken into communion tonight. But now your good worship will lend me your arm, and we shall be there in a twinkling."

"That can hardly be," answered her friend. "I may not spare you my arm, Goody Cloyse; but here is my staff, if you will."

So saying, he threw it down at her feet, where, perhaps, it assumed life, being one of the rods which its owner had formerly lent to the Egyptian magi. Of this fact, however, Goodman Brown could not take cognizance. He had cast up his eyes in astonishment, and, looking down again, beheld neither Goody Cloyse nor the serpentine staff, but his fellow-traveller alone, who waited for him as calmly as if nothing had happened.

"That old woman taught me my catechism," said the young man; and there was a world of meaning in this simple comment.

They continued to walk onward, while the elder traveller exhorted his companion to make good speed and persevere in the path, discoursing so aptly that his arguments seemed rather to spring up in the bosom of his auditor than to be suggested by himself. As they went, he plucked a branch of maple to serve for a walking stick, and began to strip it of the twigs and little boughs, which were wet with evening dew. The moment his fingers touched them they became strangely withered and dried up as with a week's sunshine. Thus the pair proceeded, at a good free pace, until suddenly, in a gloomy hollow of the road, Goodman Brown sat himself down on the stump of a tree and refused to go any farther.

"Friend," said he, stubbornly, "my mind is made up. Not another step will I budge on this errand. What if a wretched old woman do choose to go to the devil when I thought she was going to heaven: is that any reason why I should quit my dear Faith and go after her?"

"You will think better of this by and by," said his acquaintance, composedly. "Sit here and rest yourself a while; and when you feel like moving again, there is my staff to help you along."

Without words, he threw his companion the maple stick, and was as speedily out of sight as if he had vanished into the deepening gloom. The young man sat a few moments by the roadside, applauding himself greatly, and thinking with how clear a conscience he should meet the minister in his morning walk, nor shrink from the eye of good old Deacon Gookin. And what calm sleep would be his that very night, which was to have been spent so wickedly, but so purely and sweetly now, in the arms of Faith! Amidst these pleasant and praiseworthy meditations, Goodman Brown heard the tramp of horses along the road, and deemed it advisable to conceal himself within the verge of the forest, conscious of the guilty purpose that had brought him thither, though now so happily turned from it.

On came the hoof tramps and the voices of the riders, two grave old voices, conversing soberly as they drew near. These mingled sounds appeared to pass along the road, within a few yards of the young man's hiding-place; but, owing doubtless to the depth of the gloom at that particular spot, neither the travellers nor their steeds were visible. Though their figures brushed the small boughs by the wayside, it could not be seen that they intercepted, even for a moment, the faint gleam from the strip of bright sky athwart which they must have passed. Goodman Brown alternately crouched and stood on tiptoe, pulling aside the branches and thrusting forth his head as far as he durst without discerning so much as a shadow. It vexed him the more, because he could have sworn, were such a thing possible, that he recognized the voices of the minister and Deacon Gookin, jogging along quietly, as they were wont to do, when bound to some ordination or ecclesiastical council. While yet within hearing one of the riders stopped to pluck a switch.

"Of the two, reverend sir," said the voice like the deacon's, "I had rather miss an ordination dinner than to-night's meeting. They tell me that some of our community are to be here from Falmouth and beyond, and others from Connecticut and Rhode Island besides several of Indian powwows, who, after their fashion, know almost as much deviltry as the best of us. Moreover, there is a goodly young woman to be taken into communion."

"Mighty well, Deacon Gookin!" replied the solemn old tones of the minister. "Spur up, or we shall be late. Nothing can be done you know until I get on the ground."

The hoofs clattered again; and the voices, talking so strangely in the empty air, passed on through the forest, where no church had ever been gathered or solitary Christian prayed. Whither, then, could these holy men be journeying so deep into the heathen wilderness? Young Goodman Brown caught hold of a tree for support, being ready to sink down on the ground, faint and overburdened with the heavy sickness of his heart. He looked up to the sky, doubting whether there really was a heaven above him. Yet there was the blue arch, and the stars brightening in it.

"With heaven above and Faith below, I will yet stand firm against the devil!" cried Goodman Brown.

While he still gazed upward into the deep arch of the firmament and had lifted his hands to pray, a cloud, though no wind was stirring, hurried across the zenith and hid the brightening stars. The blue sky was still visible, except directly overhead, where this black mass of cloud was sweeping swiftly northward. Aloft in the air, as if from the depths of the cloud, came a confused and doubtful sound of voices. Once the listener fancied that he could distinguish the accents of townspeople of his own, men and women, both pious and ungodly, many of whom he had met at the communion table, and had seen others rioting at the tavern. The next moment, so indistinct were the sounds, he doubted whether he had heard aught but the murmur of the old forest, whispering without a wind. Then came a stronger swell of those familiar tones, heard daily in the sunshine at Salem village, but never until now from a cloud of night. There was one voice of a young woman uttering lamentations, yet with an uncertain sorrow, and entreating for some favor, which perhaps, it would grieve her to obtain; and all the unseen multitude, both saints and sinners, seemed to encourage her onward.

"Faith!" shouted Goodman Brown, in a voice of agony and desperation; and the echoes of the forest mocked him, crying, "Faith! Faith!" as if bewildered wretches were seeking her all through the wilderness.

The cry of grief, rage, and terror was yet piercing the night, when the unhappy husband held his breath for a response. There was a scream, drowned immediately in a loud murmur of voices, fading into far-off laughter, as the dark cloud swept away, leaving the clear and silent sky above Goodman Brown. But something fluttered lightly down through the air and caught on the branch of a tree. The young man seized it, and beheld a pink ribbon.

"My Faith is gone!" cried he, after one stupefied moment. "There is no good on earth; and sin is but a name. Come, devil; for to thee is this world given."

And, maddened with despair, so that he laughed loud and long, did Goodman Brown grasp his staff and set forth again, at such a rate that he seemed to fly along the forest path rather than to walk or run. The road grew wilder and drearier and more faintly traced, and vanished at length, leaving him in the heart of the dark wilderness, still rushing onward with the instinct that guides mortal man to evil. The whole forest was peopled with frightful sounds—the creaking of the trees, the howling of wild beasts, and the yells of Indians; while sometimes the wind tolled like a distant church bell, and sometimes gave a broad roar around the traveller, as if all Nature were laughing him to scorn. But he was himself the chief horror of the scene, and shrank not from its other horrors.

"Ha! ha! ha!" roared Goodman Brown when the wind laughed at him. "Let us hear which will laugh loudest. Think not to frighten me with your deviltry. Come witch, come wizard, come Indian powwow, come devil himself, and here comes Goodman Brown. You may as well fear him as he fears you."

In truth, all through the haunted forest there could be nothing more frightful than the figure of Goodman Brown. On he flew among the black pines, brandishing his staff with frenzied gestures, now giving vent to an inspiration of horrid blasphemy, and now shouting forth such laughter as set all the echoes of the forest laughing like demons around him. The fiend in his own shape is less hideous than when he rages in the breast of man. Thus sped the demoniac on his course, until, quivering among the trees, he saw a red light before him, as when the felled trunks and branches of a clearing have been set on fire, and throw up their lurid blaze against the sky, at the hour of midnight. He paused, in a lull of the tempest that had driven him onward, and heard the swell of what seemed a hymn, rolling solemnly from a distance with the weight of many voices. He knew the tune; it was a familiar one in the choir of the village meeting-house. The verse died heavily away, and was lengthened by a chorus, not of human voices, but of all the sounds of the benighted wilderness pealing in awful harmony together. Goodman Brown cried out, and his cry was lost to his own ear by its unison with the cry of the desert.

In the interval of silence he stole forward until the light glared full upon his eyes. At one extremity of an open space, hemmed in by the dark wall of the forest, arose a rock, bearing some rude, natural resemblance either to an altar or a pulpit, and surrounded by four blazing pines, their tops aflame, their stems untouched, like candles at an evening meeting. The mass of foliage that had overgrown the summit of the rock was all on fire, blazing into the night and fitfully illuminating the whole field. Each pendent twig and leafy festoon was in a blaze. As the red light arose and fell, a numerous congregation alternately shone forth, then disappeared in shadow, and again grew, as it were, out of the darkness, peopling the heart of the solitary woods at once.

"A grave and dark-clad company," quoth Goodman Brown.

In truth they were such. Among them, quivering to and fro between gloom and splendor, appeared faces that would be seen next day at the council board of the province, and others which, Sabbath after Sabbath, looked devoutly heavenward, and benignantly over the crowded pews, from the holiest pulpits in the land. Some affirm that the lady of the governor was there. At least there were high dames well known to her, and wives of honored husbands, and widows, a great multitude, and ancient maidens, all of excellent repute, and fair young girls, who trembled lest their mothers should espy them. Either the sudden gleams of light flashing over the obscure field bedazzled Goodman Brown, or he recognized a score of the church members of Salem village famous for their special sanctity. Good old Deacon Gookin had arrived, and waited at the skirts of that venerable saint, his revered pastor. But, irreverently consorting with these grave, reputable, and pious people, these elders of the church, these chaste dames and dewy virgins, there were men of dissolute lives and women of spotted fame, wretches given over to all mean and filthy vice, and suspected even of horrid crimes. It was strange to see that the good shrank not from the wicked, nor were the sinners abashed by the saints. Scattered also among their pale-faced enemies were the Indian priests, or powwows, who had often scared their native forest with more hideous incantations than any known to English witchcraft.

"But where is Faith?" thought Goodman Brown; and, as hope came into his heart, he trembled.

Another verse of the hymn arose, a slow and mournful strain, such as the pious love, but joined to words which expressed all that our nature can conceive of sin, and darkly hinted at far more. Unfathomable to mere mortals is the lore of fiends. Verse after verse was sung; and still the chorus of the desert swelled between like the deepest tone of a mighty organ; and with the final peal of that dreadful anthem there came a sound, as if the roaring wind, the rushing streams, the howling beasts, and every other voice of the unconcerted wilderness were mingling and according with the voice of guilty man in homage to the prince of all. The four blazing pines threw up a loftier flame, and obscurely discovered shapes and visages of horror on the smoke wreaths above the impious assembly. At the same moment the fire on the rock shot redly forth and formed a glowing arch above its base, where now appeared a figure. With reverence be it spoken, the figure bore no slight similitude, both in garb and manner, to some grave divine of the New England churches.

"Bring forth the converts!" cried a voice that echoed through the field and rolled into the forest.

At the word, Goodman Brown stepped forth from the shadow of the trees and approached the congregation, with whom he felt a loathful brotherhood by the sympathy of all that was wicked in his heart. He could have well-nigh sworn that the shape of his own dead father beckoned him to advance, looking downward from a smoke wreath, while a woman, with dim features of despair, threw out her hand to warn him back. Was it his mother? But he had no power to retreat one step, nor to resist, even in thought, when the minister and good old Deacon Gookin seized his arms and led him to the blazing rock. Thither came also the slender form of a veiled female, led between Goody Cloyse, that pious teacher of the catechism, and Martha Carrier, who had received the devil's promise to be queen of hell. A rampant hag was she. And there stood the proselytes beneath the canopy of fire.

"Welcome, my children," said the dark figure, "to the communion of your race. Ye have found thus young your nature and your destiny. My children, look behind you!"

They turned; and flashing forth, as it were, in a sheet of flame, the fiend worshippers were seen; the smile of welcome gleamed darkly on every visage.

"There," resumed the sable form, "are all whom ye have reverenced from youth. Ye deemed them holier than yourself, and shrank from your own sins, contrasting it with their lives of righteousness and prayerful aspirations heavenward. Yet here are they all in my worshipping assembly. This night it shall be granted you to know their secret deeds: how hoary-bearded elders of the church have whispered wanton words to the young maids of their households; how many a woman, eager for widows' weeds, has given her husband a drink at bedtime and let him sleep his last sleep in her bosom; how beardless youths have made haste to inherit their fathers' wealth, and how fair damsels—blush not, sweet ones—have dug little graves in the garden, and bidden me, the sole guest to an infant's funeral. By the sympathy of your human hearts for sin ye shall scent out all the places—whether in church, bed-chamber, street, field, or forest—where crime has been committed, and shall exult to behold the whole earth one stain of guilt, one mighty blood spot. Far more than this. It shall be yours to penetrate, in every bosom, the deep mystery of sin, the fountain of all wicked arts, and which inexhaustibly supplies more evil impulses than human power—than my power at its utmost—can make manifest in deeds. And now, my children, look upon each other."

They did so; and, by the blaze of the hell-kindled torches, the wretched man beheld his Faith, and the wife her husband, trembling before that unhallowed altar.

"Lo, there ye stand, my children," said the figure, in a deep and solemn tone, almost sad with its despairing awfulness, as if his once angelic nature could yet mourn for our miserable race. "Depending upon one another's hearts, ye had still hoped that virtue were not all a dream. Now are ye undeceived, Evil is the nature of mankind. Evil must be your only happiness. Welcome again, my children, to the communion of your race."

"Welcome," repeated the fiend worshippers, in one cry of despair and triumph.

And there they stood, the only pair, as it seemed, who were yet hesitating on the verge of wickedness in this dark world. A basin was hollowed, naturally, in the rock. Did it contain water, reddened by the lurid light? or was it blood? or, perchance, a liquid flame? Herein did the shape of evil dip his hand and prepare to lay the mark of baptism upon their foreheads, that they might be partakers of the mystery of sin, more conscious of the secret guilt of others, both in deed and thought, than they could now be of their own. The husband cast one look at his pale wife, and Faith at him. What polluted wretches would the next glance show them to each other, shuddering alike at what they disclosed and what they saw!

"Faith! Faith!" cried the husband, "look up to heaven, and resist the wicked one."

Whether Faith obeyed he knew not. Hardly had he spoken when he found himself amid calm night and solitude, listening to a roar of the wind which died heavily away through the forest. He staggered against the rock, and felt it chill and damp; while a hanging twig, that had been all on fire, besprinkled his cheek with the coldest dew.

The next morning young Goodman Brown came slowly into the street of Salem village, staring around him like a bewildered man. The good old minister was taking a walk along the graveyard to get an appetite for breakfast and meditate his sermon, and bestowed a blessing, as he passed, on Goodman Brown. He shrank from the venerable saint as if to avoid an anathema. Old Deacon Gookin was at domestic worship, and the holy words of his prayer were heard through the open window. "What God does the wizard pray to?" quoth Goodman Brown. Goody Cloyse, that excellent old Christian, stood in the early sunshine at her own lattice, catechizing a little girl who had brought her a pint of morning's milk. Goodman Brown snatched away the child as from the grasp of the fiend himself. Turning the corner by the meeting-house, he spied the head of Faith, with the pink ribbons, gazing anxiously forth, and bursting into such joy at sight of him that she skipped along the street and almost kissed her husband before the whole village. But Goodman Brown looked sternly and sadly into her face, and passed on without a greeting.

Had Goodman Brown fallen asleep in the forest and only dreamed a wild dream of a witch-meeting?

Be it so if you will; but, alas! it was a dream of evil omen for young Goodman Brown. A stern, a sad, a darkly meditative, a distrustful, if not a desperate man did he become from the night of that fearful dream. On the Sabbath day, when the congregation were singing a holy psalm, he could not listen because an anthem of sin rushed loudly upon his ears and drowned all the blessed strain. When the minister spoke from the pulpit with power and fervid eloquence, and, with his hand on the open Bible, of the sacred truths of our religion, and of saint-like lives and triumphant death and of future bliss or misery unutterable, then did Goodman Brown turn pale, dreading lest the roof should thunder down upon the gray blasphemer and his hearers. Often, waking suddenly at midnight, he shrank from the bosom of Faith; and at morning or eventide, when the family knelt down at prayer, he scowled and muttered to himself, and gazed sternly at his wife, and turned away. And when he had lived long, and was borne to his grave a hoary corpse, followed by Faith, an aged woman, and children and grandchildren, a goodly procession, besides neighbors not a few, they carved no hopeful verse upon his tombstone, for his dying hour was gloom.

My Last Duchess

ROBERT BROWNING

That's my last Duchess painted on the wall,
Looking as if she were alive. I call
That piece a wonder, now: Frà Pandolf's hands
Worked busily a day, and there she stands.
Will't please you sit and look at her? I said
"Frà Pandolf" by design, for never read
Strangers like you that pictured countenance,
The depth and passion of its earnest glance,
But to myself they turned (since none puts by
The curtain I have drawn for you, but I)
And seemed as they would ask me, if they durst,
How such a glance came there; so, not the first
Are you to turn and ask thus. Sir, 'twas not
Her husband's presence only, called that spot
Of joy into the Duchess' cheek: perhaps
Frà Pandolf chanced to say, "Her mantle laps
Over my lady's wrist too much," or "Paint
Must never hope to reproduce the faint
Half-flush that dies along her throat": such stuff
Was courtesy, she thought, and cause enough
For calling up that spot of joy. She had
A heart—how shall I say?—too soon made glad,
Too easily impressed; she liked whate'er
She looked on, and her looks went everywhere.
Sir, 'twas all one! My favor at her breast,
The dropping of the daylight in the West,
The bough of cherries some officious fool
Broke in the orchard for her, the white mule
She rode with round the terrace—all and each
Would draw from her alike the approving speech,
Or blush, at least. She thanked men,—good! but thanked
Somehow—I know not how—as if she ranked
My gift of a nine-hundred-years-old name
With anybody's gift. Who'd stoop to blame

This sort of trifling? Even had you skill
In speech—(which I have not)—to make your will
Quite clear to such an one, and say, "Just this
Or that in you disgusts me; here you miss,
Or there exceed the mark"—and if she let
Herself be lessoned so, nor plainly set
Her wits to yours, forsooth, and made excuse,
—E'en then would be some stooping; and I choose
Never to stoop. Oh sir, she smiled, no doubt,
Whene'er I passed her; but who passed without
Much the same smile? This grew; I gave commands:
Then all smiles stopped together. There she stands
As if alive. Will't please you rise? We'll meet
The company below, then. I repeat,
The Count your master's known munificence
Is ample warrant that no just pretense
Of mine for dowry will be disallowed;
Though his fair daughter's self, as I avowed
At starting, is my object. Nay, we'll go
Together down, sir. Notice Neptune, though,
Taming a sea-horse, thought a rarity,
Which Claus of Innsbruck cast in bronze for me!

Trifles

SUSAN GLASPELL

CAST OF CHARACTERS
George Henderson, *county attorney*
Henry Peters, *sheriff*
Lewis Hale, *a neighboring farmer*
Mrs. Peters
Mrs. Hale

SCENE. *The kitchen in the now abandoned farmhouse of* JOHN WRIGHT, *a gloomy kitchen, and left without having been put in order—unwashed pans under the sink, a loaf of bread outside the bread-box, a dish-towel on the table—other signs of incompleted work. At the rear the outer door opens and the* SHERIFF *comes in followed by the* COUNTY ATTORNEY *and* HALE. *The* SHERIFF *and* HALE *are men in middle life, the* COUNTY ATTORNEY *is a young man; all are much bundled up and go at once to the stove. They are followed by the two women—the* SHERIFF'S *wife first; she is a slight wiry woman, a thin nervous face.* MRS. HALE *is larger and would ordinarily be called more comfortable looking, but she is disturbed now and looks fearfully about as she enters. The women have come in slowly, and stand close together near the door.*

COUNTY ATTORNEY. [*Rubbing his hands.*] This feels good. Come up to the fire, ladies.

MRS. PETERS. [*After taking a step forward.*] I'm not—cold.

SHERIFF. [*Unbuttoning his overcoat and stepping away from the stove as if to mark the beginning of official business.*] Now, Mr. Hale, before we move things about, you explain to Mr. Henderson just what you saw when you came here yesterday morning.

COUNTY ATTORNEY. By the way, has anything been moved? Are things just as you left them yesterday?

SHERIFF. [*Looking about.*] It's just the same. When it dropped below zero last night I thought I'd better send Frank out this morning to make a fire for us—no use getting pneumonia with a big case on, but I told him not to touch anything except the stove—and you know Frank.

COUNTY ATTORNEY. Somebody should have been left here yesterday.

SHERIFF. Oh—yesterday. When I had to send Frank to Morris Center for that

man who went crazy—I want you to know I had my hands full yesterday.
I knew you could get back from Omaha by today and as long as I went
over everything here myself—

COUNTY ATTORNEY. Well, Mr. Hale, tell just what happened when you came
here yesterday morning.

HALE. Harry and I had started to town with a load of potatoes. We came along
the road from my place and as I got here I said, "I'm going to see if I can't
get John Wright to go in with me on a party telephone." I spoke to Wright
about it once before and he put me off, saying folks talked too much anyway, and all he asked was peace and quiet—I guess you know about how
much he talked himself; but I thought maybe if I went to the house and
talked about it before his wife, though I said to Harry that I didn't know
as what his wife wanted made much difference to John—

COUNTY ATTORNEY. Let's talk about that later, Mr. Hale. I do want to talk about
that, but tell now just what happened when you got to the house.

HALE. I didn't hear or see anything; I knocked at the door, and still it was all
quiet inside. I knew they must be up, it was past eight o'clock. So I
knocked again, and I thought I heard somebody say, "Come in." I wasn't
sure, I'm not sure yet, but I opened the door—this door [*Indicating the door
by which the two women are still standing.*] and there in that rocker—[*Pointing to it.*] sat Mrs. Wright.

[*They all look at the rocker.*]

COUNTY ATTORNEY. What—was she doing?

HALE. She was rockin' back and forth. She had her apron in her hand and was
kind of—pleating it.

COUNTY ATTORNEY. And how did she—look?

HALE. Well, she looked queer.

COUNTY ATTORNEY. How do you mean—queer?

HALE. Well, as if she didn't know what she was going to do next. And kind of
done up.

COUNTY ATTORNEY. How did she seem to feel about your coming?

HALE. Why, I don't think she minded—one way or other. She didn't pay
much attention. I said, "How do, Mrs. Wright, it's cold, ain't it?" And she
said, "Is it?"—and went on kind of pleating at her apron. Well, I was sur-
prised; she didn't ask me to come up to the stove, or to set down, but just
sat there, not even looking at me, so I said, "I want to see John." And then
she—laughed. I guess you would call it a laugh. I thought of Harry and
the team outside, so I said a little sharp: "Can't I see John?" "No," she says,
kind o'dull like. "Ain't he home?" says I. "Yes," says she, "he's home."
"Then why can't I see him?" I asked her, out of patience. "Cause he's
dead," says she. "*Dead?*" says I. She just nodded her head, not getting a bit
excited, but rockin' back and forth. "Why—where is he?" says I, not
knowing what to say. She just pointed upstairs—like that. [*himself pointing
to the room above.*] I got up, with the idea of going up there. I walked from
there to here—then I says, "Why, what did he die of?" "He died of a rope
round his neck," says she, and just went on pleatin' at her apron. Well, I

went out and called Harry. I thought I might—need help. We went upstairs and there he was lyin'—

COUNTY ATTORNEY. I think I'd rather have you go into that upstairs, where you
can point it all out. Just go on now with the rest of the story.

HALE. Well, my first thought was to get that rope off. It looked . . . [*Stops, his
face twitches.*] . . . but Harry, he went up to him, and he said, "No, he's dead
all right, and we'd better not touch anything." So we went back down-
stairs. She was still sitting that same way. "Has anybody been notified?" I
asked. "No," says she, unconcerned. "Who did this, Mrs. Wright?" said
Harry. He said it businesslike—and she stopped pleatin' of her apron. "I
don't know," she says. "You don't *know?*" says Harry. "No," says she.
"Weren't you sleepin' in the bed with him?" says Harry. "Yes," says she,
"but I was on the inside." "Somebody slipped a rope around his neck and
strangled him and you didn't wake up?" says Harry. "I didn't wake up,"
she said after him. We must 'a looked as if we didn't see how that could
be, for after a minute she said, "I sleep sound." Harry was going to ask her
more questions but I said maybe we ought to let her tell her story first to
the coroner, or the sheriff, so Harry went fast as he could to Rivers' place,
where there's a telephone.

COUNTY ATTORNEY. And what did Mrs. Wright do when she knew that you
had gone for the coroner?

HALE. She moved from that chair to this one over here [*Pointing to a small chair
in the corner.*] and just sat there with her hands held together and looking
down. I got a feeling that I ought to make some conversation, so I said I
had come in to see if John wanted to put in a telephone, and at that she
started to laugh, and then she stopped and looked at me—scared. [*The
COUNTY ATTORNEY, who has had his notebook out, makes a note.*] I dunno,
maybe it wasn't scared. I wouldn't like to say it was. Soon Harry got back,
and then Dr. Lloyd came, and you, Mr. Peters, and so I guess that's all I
know that you don't.

COUNTY ATTORNEY. [*Looking around.*] I guess we'll go upstairs first—and then
out to the barn and around there. [*To the SHERIFF.*] You're convinced that
there was nothing important here—nothing that would point to any motive.

SHERIFF. Nothing here but kitchen things.

[*The COUNTY ATTORNEY, after again looking around the kitchen, opens the door of a
cupboard closet. He gets up on a chair and looks on a shelf. Pulls his hand away,
sticky.*]

COUNTY ATTORNEY. Here's a nice mess.

[*The women draw nearer.*]

MRS. PETERS. [*To the other woman.*] Oh, her fruit; it did freeze. [*To the LAWYER.*]
She worried about that when it turned so cold. She said the fire'd go out
and her jars would break.

SHERIFF. Well, can you beat the women! Held for murder and worryin' about
her preserves.

COUNTY ATTORNEY. I guess before we're through she may have something more serious than preserves to worry about.

HALE. Well, women are used to worrying over trifles.

[*The two women move a little closer together.*]

COUNTY ATTORNEY. [*With the gallantry of a young politician.*] And yet, for all their worries, what would we do without the ladies? [*The women do not unbend. He goes to the sink, takes a dipperful of water from the pail and pouring it into a basin, washes his hands. Starts to wipe them on the roller-towel, turns it for a cleaner place.*] Dirty towels! [*Kicks his foot against the pans under the sink.*] Not much of a housekeeper, would you say, ladies?

MRS. HALE. [*Stiffly.*] There's a great deal of work to be done on a farm.

COUNTY ATTORNEY. To be sure. And yet [*with a little bow to her.*] I know there are some Dickson county farmhouses which do not have such roller towels.

[*He gives it a pull to expose its full length again.*]

MRS. HALE. Those towels get dirty awful quick. Men's hands aren't always as clean as they might be.

COUNTY ATTORNEY. Ah, loyal to your sex, I see. But you and Mrs. Wright were neighbors. I suppose you were friends, too.

MRS. HALE. [*Shaking her head.*] I've not seen much of her of late years. I've not been in this house—it's more than a year.

COUNTY ATTORNEY. And why was that? You didn't like her?

MRS. HALE. I liked her all well enough. Farmers' wives have their hands full, Mr. Henderson. And then—

COUNTY ATTORNEY. Yes—?

MRS. HALE. [*Looking about.*] It never seemed a very cheerful place.

COUNTY ATTORNEY. No—it's not cheerful. I shouldn't say she had the homemaking instinct.

MRS. HALE. Well, I don't know as Wright had, either.

COUNTY ATTORNEY. You mean that they didn't get on very well?

MRS. HALE. No, I don't mean anything. But I don't think a place'd be any cheerfuller for John Wright's being in it.

COUNTY ATTORNEY. I'd like to talk more of that a little later. I want to get the lay of things upstairs now.

[*He goes to the left, where three steps lead to a stair door.*]

SHERIFF. I suppose anything Mrs. Peters does'll be all right. She was to take in some clothes for her, you know, and a few little things. We left in such a hurry yesterday.

COUNTY ATTORNEY. Yes, but I would like to see what you take, Mrs. Peters, and keep an eye out for anything that might be of use to us.

MRS. PETERS. Yes, Mr. Henderson.

[*The women listen to the men's steps on the stairs, then look about the kitchen.*]

MRS. HALE. I'd hate to have men coming into my kitchen, snooping around and criticising.

[*She arranges the pans under sink which the LAWYER had shoved out of place.*]

MRS. PETERS. Of course it's no more than their duty.

MRS. HALE. Duty's all right, but I guess that deputy sheriff that came out to make the fire might have got a little of this on. [*Gives the roller towel a pull.*] Wish I'd thought of that sooner. Seems mean to talk about her for not having things slicked up when she had to come away in such a hurry.

MRS. PETERS. [*Who has gone to a small table in the left rear corner of the room, and lifted one end of a towel that covers a pan.*] She had bread set.

[*Stands still.*]

MRS. HALE. [*Eyes fixed on a loaf of bread beside the breadbox, which is on a low shelf at the other side of the room. Moves slowly toward it.*] She was going to put this in there. [*Picks up loaf, then abruptly drops it. In a manner of returning to familiar things.*] It's a shame about her fruit. I wonder if it's all gone. [*Gets up on the chair and looks.*] I think there's some here that's all right, Mrs. Peters. Yes— here; [*Holding it toward the window.*] this is cherries, too. [*Looking again.*] I declare I believe that's the only one. [*Gets down, bottle in her hand. Goes to the sink and wipes it off on the outside.*] She'll feel awful bad after all her hard work in the hot weather. I remember the afternoon I put up my cherries last summer.

[*She puts the bottle on the big kitchen table, center of the room. With a sigh, is about to sit down in the rocking-chair. Before she is seated realizes what chair it is; with a slow look at it, steps back. The chair which she has touched rocks back and forth.*]

MRS. PETERS. Well, I must get those things from the front room closet. [*She goes to the door at the right, but after looking into the other room, steps back.*] You coming with me, Mrs. Hale? You could help me carry them.

[*They go in the other room; reappear, MRS. PETERS carrying a dress and skirt, MRS. HALE following with a pair of shoes.*]

MRS. PETERS. My, it's cold in there.

[*She puts the clothes on the big table and hurries to the stove.*]

MRS. HALE. [*Examining the skirt.*] Wright was close. I think maybe that's why she kept so much to herself. She didn't even belong to the Ladies Aid. I suppose she felt she couldn't do her part, and then you don't enjoy things when you feel shabby. She used to wear pretty clothes and be lively, when she was Minnie Foster, one of the town girls singing in the choir. But that—oh, that was thirty years ago. This all you was to take in?

MRS. PETERS. She said she wanted an apron. Funny thing to want, for there isn't much to get you dirty in jail, goodness knows. But I suppose just to make her feel more natural. She said they was in the top drawer in this cupboard. Yes, here. And then her little shawl that always hung behind the door. [*Opens stair door and looks.*] Yes, here it is.

[*Quickly shuts door leading upstairs.*]

Mrs. Hale. [*Abruptly moving toward her.*] Mrs. Peters?
Mrs. Peters. Yes, Mrs. Hale?
Mrs. Hale. Do you think she did it?
Mrs. Peters. [*In a frightened voice.*] Oh, I don't know.
Mrs. Hale. Well, I don't think she did. Asking for an apron and her little shawl. Worrying about her fruit.
Mrs. Peters. [*Starts to speak, glances up, where footsteps are heard in the room above. In a low voice.*] Mr. Peters says it looks bad for her. Mr. Henderson is awful sarcastic in a speech and he'll make fun of her sayin' she didn't wake up.
Mrs. Hale. Well, I guess John Wright didn't wake when they was slipping that rope under his neck.
Mrs. Peters. No, it's strange. It must have been done awful crafty and still. They say it was such a—funny way to kill a man, rigging it all up like that.
Mrs. Hale. That's just what Mr. Hale said. There was a gun in the house. He says that's what he can't understand.
Mrs. Peters. Mr. Henderson said coming out that what was needed for the case was a motive; something to show anger, or—sudden feeling.
Mrs. Hale. [*Who is standing by the table.*] Well, I don't see any signs of anger around here. [*She puts her hand on the dish towel which lies on the table, stands looking down at table, one half of which is clean, the other half messy.*] It's wiped to here. [*Makes a move as if to finish work, then turns and looks at loaf of bread outside the breadbox. Drops towel. In that voice of coming back to familiar things.*] Wonder how they are finding things upstairs. I hope she had it a little more red-up up there. You know, it seems kind of *sneaking*. Locking her up in town and then coming out here and trying to get her own house to turn against her!
Mrs. Peters. But Mrs. Hale, the law is the law.
Mrs. Hale. I s'pose 'tis. [*Unbuttoning her coat.*] Better loosen up your things, Mrs. Peters. You won't feel them when you go out.

[*Mrs. Peters takes off her fur tippet, goes to hang it on hook at back of room, stands looking at the under part of the small corner table.*]

Mrs. Peters. She was piecing a quilt.

[*She brings the large sewing basket and they look at the bright pieces.*]

Mrs. Hale. It's log cabin pattern. Pretty, isn't it? I wonder if she was goin' to quilt it or just knot it?

[*Footsteps have been heard coming down the stairs. The Sheriff enters followed by Hale and the County Attorney.*]

SHERIFF. They wonder if she was going to quilt it or just knot it!

[*The men laugh; the women look abashed.*]

COUNTY ATTORNEY. [*Rubbing his hands over the stove.*] Frank's fire didn't do much up there, did it? Well, let's go out to the barn and get that cleared up.

[*The men go outside.*]

MRS. HALE. [*Resentfully.*] I don't know as there's anything so strange, our takin' up our time with little things while we're waiting for them to get the evidence. [*She sits down at the big table smoothing out a block with decision.*] I don't see as it's anything to laugh about.
MRS. PETERS. [*Apologetically.*] Of course they'e got awful important things on their minds.

[*Pulls up a chair and joins MRS. HALE at the table.*]

MRS. HALE. [*Examining another block.*] Mrs. Peters, look at this one. Here, this is the one she was working on, and look at the sewing! All the rest of it has been so nice and even. And look at this! It's all over the place! Why, it looks as if she didn't know what she was about!

[*After she has said this they look at each other, then start to glance back at the door. After an instant MRS. HALE has pulled at a knot and ripped the sewing.*]

MRS. PETERS. Oh, what are you doing, Mrs. Hale?
MRS. HALE. [*Mildly.*] Just pulling out a stitch or two that's not sewed very good. [*Threading a needle.*] Bad sewing always made me fidgety.
MRS. PETERS. [*Nervously.*] I don't think we ought to touch things.
MRS. HALE. I'll just finish up this end. [*Suddenly stopping and leaning forward.*] Mrs. Peters?
MRS. PETERS. Yes, Mrs. Hale?
MRS. HALE. What do you suppose she was so nervous about?
MRS. PETERS. Oh—I don't know. I don't know as she was nervous. I sometimes sew awful queer when I'm just tired. [*MRS. HALE starts to say something, looks at MRS. PETERS, then goes on sewing.*] Well I must get these things wrapped up. They may be through sooner than we think. [*Putting apron and other things together.*] I wonder where I can find a piece of paper, and string.
MRS. HALE. *In that cupboard, maybe.*
MRS. PETERS. [*Looking in cupboard.*] Why, here's a bird-cage. [*Holds it up.*] Did she have a bird, Mrs. Hale?
MRS. HALE. Why, I don't know whether she did or not—I've not been here for so long. There was a man around last year selling canaries cheap, but I don't know as she took one; maybe she did. She used to sing real pretty herself.
MRS. PETERS. [*Glancing around.*] Seems funny to think of a bird here. But she must have had one, or why would she have a cage? I wonder what happened to it.

MRS. HALE. I s'pose maybe the cat got it.

MRS. PETERS. No, she didn't have a cat. She's got that feeling some people have about cats—being afraid of them. My cat got in her room and she was real upset and asked me to take it out.

MRS. HALE. My sister Bessie was like that. Queer, ain't it?

MRS. PETERS. [*Examining the cage.*] Why, look at this door. It's broke. One hinge is pulled apart.

MRS. HALE. [*Looking too.*] Looks as if someone must have been rough with it.

MRS. PETERS. Why, yes.

[*She brings the cage forward and puts it on the table.*]

MRS. HALE. I wish if they're going to find any evidence they'd be about it. I don't like this place.

MRS. PETERS. But I'm awful glad you came with me, Mrs. Hale. It would be lonesome for me sitting here alone.

MRS. HALE. It would, wouldn't it? [*Dropping her sewing.*] But I tell you what I do wish, Mrs. Peters. I wish I had come over sometimes when *she* was here. I—[*Looking around the room.*]—wish I had.

MRS. PETERS. But of course you were awful busy, Mrs. Hale—your house and your children.

MRS. HALE. I could've come. I stayed away because it weren't cheerful—and that's why I ought to have come. I—I've never liked this place. Maybe because it's down in a hollow and you don't see the road. I dunno what it is, but it's a lonesome place and always was. I wish I had come over to see Minnie Foster sometimes. I can see now—

[*Shakes her head.*]

MRS. PETERS. Well, you mustn't reproach yourself, Mrs. Hale. Somehow we just don't see how it is with other folks until—something comes up.

MRS. HALE. Not having children makes less work—but it makes a quiet house, and Wright out to work all day, and no company when he did come in. Did you know John Wright, Mrs. Peters?

MRS. PETERS. Not to know him; I've seen him in town. They say he was a good man.

MRS. HALE. Yes—good; he didn't drink, and kept his word as well as most, I guess, and paid his debts. But he was a hard man, Mrs. Peters. Just to pass the time of day with him—[*Shivers.*] Like a raw wind that gets to the bone. [*Pauses, her eye falling on the cage.*] I should think she would 'a wanted a bird. But what do you suppose went with it?

MRS. PETERS. I don't know, unless it got sick and died.

[*She reaches over and swings the broken door, swings it again, both women watch it.*]

MRS. HALE. You weren't raised round here, were you? [*MRS. PETERS shakes her head.*] You didn't know—her?

MRS. PETERS. Not till they brought her yesterday.

MRS. HALE. She—come to think of it, she was kind of like a bird herself—real sweet and pretty, but kind of timid and—fluttery. How—she—did—change. [*Silence; then as if struck by a happy thought and relieved to get back to everyday things.*] Tell you what, Mrs. Peters, why don't you take the quilt in with you? It might take up her mind.

MRS. PETERS. Why, I think that's a real nice idea, Mrs. Hale. There couldn't possibly be any objection to it, could there? Now, just what would I take? I wonder if her patches are in here—and her things.

[*They look in the sewing basket.*]

MRS. HALE. Here's some red. I expect this has got sewing things in it. [*Brings out a fancy box.*] What a pretty box. Looks like something somebody would give you. Maybe her scissors are in here. [*Opens box. Suddenly puts her hand to her nose.*] Why—[MRS. PETERS *bends nearer, then turns her face away.*] There's something wrapped up in this piece of silk.

MRS. PETERS. Why, this isn't her scissors.

MRS. HALE. [*Lifting the silk.*] Oh, Mrs. Peters—its—

[MRS. PETERS *bends closer.*]

MRS. PETERS. It's the bird.

MRS. HALE. [*Jumping up.*] But, Mrs. Peters—look at it! Its neck! Look at its neck! It's all—other side *to.*

MRS. PETERS. Somebody—wrung—its—neck.

[*Their eyes meet. A look of growing comprehension, of horror. Steps are heard outside. MRS. HALE slips box under quilt pieces, and sinks into her chair. Enter SHERIFF and COUNTY ATTORNEY. MRS. PETERS rises.*]

COUNTY ATTORNEY. [*As one turning from serious things to little pleasantries.*] Well, ladies, have you decided whether she was going to quilt it or knot it?

MRS. PETERS. We think she was going to—knot it.

COUNTY ATTORNEY. Well, that's interesting, I'm sure. [*Seeing the bird-cage.*] Has the bird flown?

MRS. HALE. [*Putting more quilt pieces over the box.*] We think the—cat got it.

COUNTY ATTORNEY. [*Preoccupied.*] Is there a cat?

[MRS. HALE *glances in a quick covert way at* MRS. PETERS.]

MRS. PETERS. Well, not *now.* They're superstitious, you know. They leave.

COUNTY ATTORNEY. [*To* SHERIFF PETERS, *continuing an interrupted conversation.*] No sign at all of anyone having come from the outside. Their own rope. Now let's go up again and go over it piece by piece. [*They start upstairs.*] It would have to have been someone who knew just the—

[MRS. PETERS *sits down. The two women sit there not looking at one another, but as if peering into something and at the same time holding back. When they talk now it is in the manner of feeling their way over strange ground, as if afraid of what they are saying, but as if they cannot help saying it.*]

Mrs. Hale. She liked the bird. She was going to bury it in that pretty box.

Mrs. Peters. [*In a whisper.*] When I was a girl—my kitten—there was a boy took a hatchet, and before my eyes—and before I could get there—[*Covers her face an instant.*] If they hadn't held me back I would have—[*Catches herself, looks upstairs where steps are heard, falters weakly*]—hurt him.

Mrs. Hale. [*With a slow look around her.*] I wonder how it would seem never to have had any children around. [*Pause.*] No, Wright wouldn't like the bird—a thing that sang. She used to sing. He killed that, too.

Mrs. Peters. [*Moving uneasily.*] We don't know who killed the bird.

Mrs. Hale. I knew John Wright.

Mrs. Peters. It was an awful thing was done in this house that night, Mrs. Hale. Killing a man while he slept, slipping a rope around his neck that choked the life out of him.

Mrs. Hale. His neck. Choked the life out of him.

[*Her hand goes out and rests on the bird-cage.*]

Mrs. Peters. [*With rising voice.*] We don't know who killed him. We don't know.

Mrs. Hale. [*Her own feeling not interrupted.*] If there'd been years and years of nothing, then a bird to sing to you, it would be awful—still, after the bird was still.

Mrs. Peters. [*Something within her speaking.*] I know what stillness is. When we homesteaded in Dakota, and my first baby died—after he was two years old, and me with no other then—

Mrs. Hale. [*Moving.*] How soon do you suppose they'll be through, looking for the evidence?

Mrs. Peters. I know what stillness is. [*Pulling herself back.*] The law has got to punish crime, Mrs. Hale.

Mrs. Hale. [*Not as if answering that.*] I wish you'd seen Minnie Foster when she wore a white dress with blue ribbons and stood up there in the choir and sang. [*A look around the room.*] Oh, I *wish* I'd come over here once in a while! That was a crime! That was a crime! Who's going to punish that?

Mrs. Peters. [*Looking upstairs.*] We mustn't—take on.

Mrs. Hale. I might have known she needed help! I know how things can be— for women. I tell you, it's queer, Mrs. Peters. We live close together and we live far apart. We all go through the same things—it's all just a different kind of the same thing. [*Brushes her eyes, noticing the bottle of fruit, reaches out for it.*] If I was you I wouldn't tell her her fruit was gone. Tell her it *ain't.* Tell her it's all right. Take this in to prove it to her. She—she may never know whether it was broke or not.

Mrs. Peters. [*Takes the bottle, looks about for something to wrap it in; takes petticoat from the clothes brought from the other room, very nervously begins winding this around the bottle. In a false voice.*] My, it's a good thing the men couldn't hear us. Wouldn't they just laugh! Getting all stirred up over a little thing like a—dead canary. As if that could have anything to do with—with—wouldn't they *laugh!*

[*The men are heard coming down stairs.*]

MRS. HALE. [*Under her breath.*] Maybe they would—maybe they wouldn't.
COUNTY ATTORNEY. No, Peters, it's all perfectly clear except a reason for doing it. But you know juries when it comes to women. If there was some definite thing. Something to show—something to make a story about—a thing that would connect up with this strange way of doing it—

[*The women's eyes meet for an instant. Enter HALE from outer door.*]

HALE. Well, I've got the team around. Pretty cold out there.
COUNTY ATTORNEY. I'm going to stay here a while by myself. [*To the SHERIFF.*] You can send Frank out for me, can't you? I want to go over everything. I'm not satisfied that we can't do better.
SHERIFF. Do you want to see what Mrs. Peters is going to take in?

[*The COUNTY ATTORNEY goes to the table, picks up the apron, laughs.*]

COUNTY ATTORNEY. Oh, I guess they're not very dangerous things the ladies have picked out. [*Moves a few things about, disturbing the quilt pieces which cover the box. Steps back.*] No, Mrs. Peters doesn't need supervising. For that matter, a sheriff's wife is married to the law. Ever think of it that way, Mrs. Peters?
MRS. PETERS. Not—just that way.
SHERIFF. [*Chuckling.*] Married to the law. [*Moves toward the other room.*] I just want you to come in here a minute, George. We ought to take a look at these windows.
COUNTY ATTORNEY. [*Scoffingly.*] Oh, windows!
SHERIFF. We'll be right out, Mr. Hale.

[*HALE goes outside. The SHERIFF follows the COUNTY ATTORNEY into the other room. Then MRS. HALE rises, hands tight together, looking intensely at MRS. PETERS, whose eyes make a slow turn, finally meeting MRS. HALE'S. A moment MRS. HALE holds her, then her own eyes point the way to where the box is concealed. Suddenly MRS. PETERS throws back quilt pieces and tries to put the box in the bag she is wearing. It is too big. She opens box, starts to take bird out, cannot touch it, goes to pieces, stands there helpless. Sound of a knob turning in the other room. MRS. HALE snatches the box and puts it in the pocket of her big coat. Enter COUNTY ATTORNEY and SHERIFF.*]

COUNTY ATTORNEY. [*Facetiously.*] Well, Henry, at least we found out that she was not going to quilt it. She was going to—what is it you call it, ladies?
MRS. HALE. [*Her hand against her pocket.*] We call it—knot it, Mr. Henderson.

CURTAIN

Glossary

Absolutist Critic   One who believes that there is one and only one theory or set of principles a reader may utilize when interpreting a text.

Aesthetic Reading   A term used by Louise M. Rosenblatt in *The Reader, the Text, the Poem: The Transactional Theory of the Literary Work* to describe the act of reading or the process whereby a reader interacts with a text. During this "event," the "object of aesthetic contemplation is what perceivers or readers make of their responses to the artistic stimulus, no matter whether this be a physical object, such as a statue, or a set of verbal symbols. Readers contemplate their own shaping of their responses to the text." The term thus refers to each reader's personal response to a text and how individual readers find and create meaning when interacting with printed material. Such a process assumes an active role on the part of the reader to create meaning or individual interpretations with and from a text.

Aesthetics   That branch of philosophy that deals with the concept of the beautiful and strives to determine the criteria for beauty in any work of art. It asks such questions as Where is the source of beauty? In the object? In the perceiver? What is beauty? and How is beauty recognized?

Affective Fallacy   A term used by New Critics to explain that a reader's emotional response to a text is neither important nor equivalent to its interpretation. Believing those who evaluate a work of art on the basis of its emotional effect upon its perceiver to be incorrect, New Critics assert that the Affective Fallacy confuses what a poem is (its meaning) and what it does. The term was first introduced by W. K. Wimsatt, Jr. and M. C. Beardsley.

Ambiguity   A stylistic error in everyday speech in which a word or expression has multiple meanings. Since the publication of William Empson's

Seven Types of Ambiguity (1930) and the specialized use of this term adopted by New Criticism, ambiguity is now synonymous with *plurisignation,* both terms implying the complexity and richness of poetic language that allows for a word or expression to simultaneously have two or more distinct meanings. New Critics believe that ambiguity becomes one of the chief tools great poets use effectively to demonstrate the various valid meanings contained in a word or expression. See **Connotation** and **Denotation.**

Anal Stage The second stage of child development as articulated by Sigmund Freud. In this stage, the anus becomes the object of pleasure when the child learns the delights of defecation.

Applied Criticism Applies the theories and tenets of theoretical criticism to a particular work of art. Also known as practical criticism. In applied criticism, the critic defines the standards of taste and explains, evaluates, or justifies a particular text.

Archetypal Criticism An approach to literary analysis that applies the theories of Carl Jung and/or Northrop Frye to literary analysis. An archetypal critic studies images or patterns of repeated human experiences (archetypes) found within a specific text and common to other works of art. See **Archetype.**

Archetype Refers to a recurrent plot pattern, image, descriptive detail, or character that evokes from the reader strong but illogical responses. This term was brought into literary criticism via the psychological writings of Carl Jung. Jung believed that the mind was composed of three parts: the personal conscious, the personal unconscious, and the collective unconscious. Lying deep within the mind in the collective unconscious is the collective knowledge of humanity, the memories of humanity's past. Formed through the repeated experiences of humankind, this knowledge can be tapped through images of birth, death, rebirth, the seasons, etc. within a text and can cause profound emotions to surface within a reader.

Archi-écriture (Arche-writing) A term used by the deconstructionist Jacques Derrida in *Of Grammatology* to assert that language is a kind of writing. Writing and language, he declares, share common characteristics. Although Western culture privileges or prefers speech to writing, Derrida proclaims that writing should be preferred or privileged to speech, for speech is a kind of writing. Derrida argues that without language or arche-writing, there can be no consciousness, for consciousness presupposes language. It is therefore through arche-writing that we impose human consciousness upon the world.

Aspirated A linguistic term designating a sound such as the *p* in *pat* in which a brief delay occurs before pronouncing the vowel sound with an accompanying release of air.

Base A term used by Karl Marx to designate the economic structure of society. According to Marx, the various methods of economic production and the social relationships they engender form the base. In America, for example, Marxism asserts that the capitalists exploit the working classes, determining for them their salaries and their working conditions.

Bourgeoisie According to Karl Marx and Friedrich Engels in *The Communist Manifesto,* this term refers to the social elite, or members of the upper class who control and therefore define the economic base of society through economic policies and the production of goods. It is the bourgeoisie who also define a society's superstructure.

Castration Complex   According to Sigmund Freud, if a child's sexual development is to proceed normally, each must pass through the castration complex. Boys, for example, know they have a penis like their fathers while their mother and sisters do not. What stops the male child from having incestuous desires for his mother is fear of castration by his father. The child therefore represses his sexual desire, identifies with his father, hopes to possess a woman as his father now possesses his mother, and unconsciously makes a successful transition to manhood. The female child, however, realizes that she is already castrated like her mother. Knowing that her father possesses what she desires (a penis), she turns her attention away from her mother and toward her father. After unsuccessfully attempting to seduce her father, she turns back toward her mother, identifies with her, and successfully makes her transition to womanhood.

Catalyst   An agent or element that causes but is not affected by a reaction.

Catharsis   A term used by Aristotle in the *Poetics* concerning the nature and function of tragedy. Although its meaning is highly controversial and by no means clear, *catharsis* had both a medical and a religious meaning in Aristotle's day. Medically, it referred to a body's discharge of excess elements during sickness and its subsequent return to health. In a religious sense, catharsis is the soul's method of purification, freeing itself from the body and becoming unfettered. Concerning its use in tragedy, Aristotle writes, "through pity and fear effecting the proper purgation (catharsis) of these emotions." By witnessing a tragedy, then, the audience's emotions would somehow be purified. How this process actually occurs, however, is open to debate.

Collective Unconscious   A term brought into literary criticism via the psychology of Carl Jung. The collective unconscious is that part of the mind that contains the cumulative knowledge, experiences, and images of the human race. This knowledge evidences itself as "primordial images" in humankind's religions, myths, dreams, and literature and can be tapped by writers through the use of archetypes. See **Archetype.**

Condensation   A term used by Sigmund Freud in psychoanalysis and dream interpretation to designate the process whereby one compacts a feeling or emotion toward a variety of people and objectifies it into a simple sentence, phrase, or symbol.

Connotation   The implied meaning of a word as opposed to its dictionary definition. See **Denotation.**

Conscious   A term brought into psychoanalysis by Carl Jung that refers to one of the three parts of the human psyche, a person's waking state. See **Personal Unconscious** and **Collective Unconscious.**

Deconstruction   Introduced in America in 1966 by Jacques Derrida's speech at Johns Hopkins University, this poststructural approach to literary analysis is best considered a "strategic device" for interpreting a text rather than a critical theory, a school of criticism, or a philosophy. Such theories, schools of criticism, and philosophies, Derrida asserts, must identify with a body of knowledge that they decree to be true or at least to contain truth. That truth or a core of metaphysical ideals can be definitely believed, articulated, and supported is exactly what Derrida and deconstruction wish to "deconstruct."

Considered to be the most intellectually formidable approach to literary analysis, deconstruction bases its ideas on the linguistics of Ferdinand de Saussure and his assertion that language is a system based on differences; for example, we know the difference between the sounds /b/ and /p/ because we have heard both and can note the difference. Derrida enlarges this concept of difference by declaring that knowing concepts is also a matter of difference.

Denying any "center" of truth such as God, humanity, or self, deconstruction maintains that we can never be sure about our values, beliefs, and assumptions. If this is the case, then we can never be certain about a text's meaning, and we can therefore never declare a text to have but one meaning. The undecidability of a text's meaning is a cardinal rule of deconstruction.

Denotation   The dictionary definition of a word as distinct from its *connotation*, or its suggestive and/or emotional meaning(s).

Diachronic   A linguistic term used to designate a process of language study that involves tracing language change through long expanses of time and discovering, for example, how a particular phenomenon in one language has changed throughout several centuries and if a similar change could be noted in other languages.

Différance   Introduced by the French deconstructionist Jacques Derrida. *Différance* is derived from the French word *différer*, meaning (1) to defer, postpone, or delay, and (2) to differ, to be different from. Derrida deliberately coined this word to be ambiguous, taking on both meanings simultaneously. One of the keys to understanding deconstruction, *différance* is Derrida's "What if" question. What if there is no ultimate truth? What if there is no essence, being, or inherently unifying element in the universe? What then? Derrida's answer is that all meaning or interpretations of a text are undecidable, for a text can have innumerable meanings and interpretations.

Discourse   A way of seeing and thinking about the world. Bound by ideology, culture, education, politics, and a variety of other influences, a discourse refers not only to speech patterns but also to a particular mind-set bound by philosophical assumptions that predisposes a person to interpret the world in a particular fashion.

Displacement   A term used by Sigmund Freud in psychoanalysis to designate the process whereby we suppress wishes and desires that are too hard for our psyches to handle by concealing them in symbols that take the place of the original desire. Our unconscious mind may switch, for example, a person's hatred of another onto a rotting apple in a dream.

Écriture Féminine   A term used in feminist criticism to refer specifically to "women's writing." Modern feminist critics speculate that a style of writing peculiar to women exists, and that this écriture féminine is fundamentally different from the way males write and obtain meaning through the writing process.

Efferent Reading   A term used by Louise M. Rosenblatt in *The Reader, the*

Text, the Poem to refer to that type of reading "in which the primary concern of the reader is with what he/she will carry away from the reading." We read efferently, for example, when we read solely for information such as when we read the directions on how to heat a can of soup. During this process we are interested only in newly gained information. This is different from aesthetic reading in which the reader "lives through" and experiences the reading process. See **Aesthetic Reading.**

Ego   A term used by Sigmund Freud to designate the rational, logical, waking part of the psyche as differentiated from the id and the superego.

Eme   A linguistic term used by Ferdinand de Saussure to designate the basic units or building blocks of language. All languages, for example, are composed of basic sounds called phonemes. When these phonemes combine to form meaningful or grammatical units called morphemes, another eme is established.

Episteme   A term borrowed from the French writer, philosopher, and critic Michel Foucault and used by New Historicists to define the unifying principle or pattern that develops in each historical epoch. Through language and thought, each period in history develops its own perceptions concerning the nature of reality (or what it defines as truth) and sets up its own standards of behavior.

Esoteric Work   A text meant for private as opposed to public circulation.

Exoteric Work   A text meant for general publication.

Expressive School   Emphasizes the individuality of the artist and the reader's privilege to share in this individuality. Disavowing rhetorical or objective theories of art, expressive critics emphasize the subjective experience of sharing emotions. Wordsworth and other nineteenth-century romantics are prime examples of this school of thought.

Extrinsic Analysis   The process of examining elements outside the text (such as historical events and biographies) to uncover the text's meaning.

Feminism   An approach to textual analysis having its roots in the Progressive Era in the early decades of the twentieth century. Some of its earliest and major philosophical tenets are articulated by the British feminist Virginia Woolf (*A Room of One's Own*, published in 1919) and the French feminist Simone de Beauvoir (*The Second Sex*, published in 1949). Feminists assert that Western societies are patriarchal, being controlled by men. Either consciously or unconsciously, men have oppressed women, allowing them little or no voice in the political, social, or economic issues of their society. By not giving voice and therefore value to women's opinions, responses, and writings, men have suppressed the female, defined what it means to be feminine, and thereby de-voiced, devalued, and trivialized what it means to be a woman. Men have made women the "nonsignificant Other."

A goal of feminism is to change this degrading view of women so that each woman will realize that she is a valuable person possessing the same privileges and rights as every man. Women must therefore define themselves and assert their own voices in politics, education, the arts, and other elements of society. By debunking stereotypical images of women found throughout the literary canon, by rediscovering and publishing texts written by females but suppressed by men, by rereading the canonized works of male authors from a woman's point of view, and by engaging in the discussion of literary theory, women can begin to challenge the concept of male superiority and work toward creating equality between the sexes.

Since feminism is more an approach or mind-set rather than a school of criticism, feminist theory and thought have been embraced by scholars belonging to a variety of critical schools, such as Marxism, deconstruction, psychoanalysis, and New Historicism. Some of the leading twentieth-century feminists are Virginia Woolf, Simone de Beauvoir, Elaine Showalter, Hélène Cixous, Sandra Gilbert, and Gayatri Chakravorty Spivak.

Formalism   A term used to designate those critics who rely upon a work's form or structure to determine its meaning. The term is often applied to the New Critics who insist that the interpretation of a work of art must evolve from the work's structure, not extrinsic elements such as the author's life or historical context.

Grammar   The system of rules that govern the production and interpretation of language. *Prescriptive* grammar refers to matters of "correctness" such as not using the word *ain't* or saying, "It is *I*," and not "It is *me.*" *Descriptive* grammar refers to the process of describing how actual speakers use their language for communication.

Gynocriticism   A term coined by the feminist scholar/critic Elaine Showalter that has become synonymous with the study of women as writers. It provides critics with four models concerning the nature of women's writing that help answer some of the chief concerns of feminist criticism. Each of Showalter's models are sequential, subsuming and developing the preceding model(s): (1) biological, (2) linguistic, (3) psychoanalytic, (4) cultural.

Hamartia   A term used by Aristotle in the *Poetics* that refers to the tragic hero's mistake or error that leads to a downfall. Literally, the word means "missing the mark." According to Aristotle, the hero of a tragedy will commit some action or exhibit some frailty (*hamartia*) that will lead to a reversal of fortune.

Hegemony   A term used in Marxist criticism that refers to the system of beliefs, values, and meanings to which most people in a given society subscribe. Usually the bourgeoisie control or dictate the hegemony of a culture. According to the Italian Marxist Antonio Gramsci, a given society's hegemony may be successful, but never complete. Rather than one all-encompassing ruling class, there usually exist several, interconnecting yet somewhat divergent classes, each influencing the superstructure at different times and in different ways. Marxist revolutions, then, can begin within alternative hegemonies rather than direct political action.

Heresy of Paraphrase   A term used by New Critics and others to suggest that a work of art is not equal to its paraphrase. A poem, for example, is not the same as its paraphrased version, for the paraphrased version will miss the poem's uniqueness with its many connotations and various complexities of thought.

Hermeneutics   First defined by religious scholars as the art and science of biblical interpretation, this term now refers to any theory and practice of interpretation.

Holistic Approach   An approach to literary study that investigates, analyzes, and interprets all elements of the artistic situation (text, author, historical context, etc.) instead of concentrating on one or more specific aspects.

Id   A term used by Sigmund Freud to designate the irrational, instinctual, unknown, and unconscious part of the psyche as differentiated from the ego and superego.

Ideology   A much debated term in Marxist criticism, ideology often refers to a culture's collective or social consciousness (as opposed to the material reality on which experience is based), or its personal awareness of a body of laws or codes governing its politics, law, religion, philosophy, and art to which that culture's bourgeoisie and therefore its superstructure subscribes. According to Marx and Engels, a culture's ideology is more frequently than not synonymous with "false consciousness," for it has been defined and established by the bourgeoisie and therefore represents a set of false assumptions or illusions used by the elite to dominate the working classes and to maintain stability. An ideology, then, may be a conscious stating and shaping of a society's philosophy, its laws, or its acceptable customs or it may be a somewhat vaguer and implicit understanding of its controlling beliefs.

Impressionistic Critics   Those critics who believe that how we feel and what we personally see in a work of art are what really matters. Capturing what we see from a particular point of view and at a specific moment in time is what is important, not an objective, lengthy investigation of a work of art or an aesthetic object. The term *impressionism* was first used by nineteenth-century French painters such as Monet and Renoir and referred to the impressions an object makes upon the artist rather than the actual representation of an objective picture of that object.

In Medias Res   From the Latin, meaning "in the middle of things." This term refers to a story or narrative such as *The Iliad* that begins in the middle rather than at its chronological starting point in time.

Intentional Fallacy   A term used by New Critics to refer to what they believe is the erroneous assumption that the interpretation of a literary work can be equated to the author's stated or implied intentions and/or private meanings. Claiming such external information to be irrelevant in ascertaining a text's meaning, the New Critics base their interpretation on the text itself. The term was first used by W. K. Wimsatt and Monroe C. Beardsley in "The Intentional Fallacy" (1946).

Irony   The use of words whereby a writer or speaker suggests the opposite of what is actually stated. According to New Critics such as Cleanth Brooks, John Crowe Ransom, and I. A. Richards, irony is *the* key to the "dramatic structure" of poetry and unlocks the door to show how meaning is contained in and evolves from a poem's structure. According to New Criticism, a poem's meaning is structurally determined and created by the tension between the denotative meaning of a poem's words and their connotations, which are, in turn, determined by the context of that particular poem. Irony, then, is "an equilibrium of [these] opposing attitudes and evaluations," which ultimately determine the poem's meaning.

Language   Defined by the linguist Thomas Pyles as "a systematized combination of sounds that have meaning for all people in a given cultural community." Broadly speaking, *language* may be considered any system of signs or codes that convey meaning, such as road signs, the language of fashion (wearing different clothes in different social settings), or even the language of eating.

Langue   The linguistic term used by Ferdinand de Saussure to refer to the rules that comprise a language or the structure of the language that is mastered and shared by all its speakers. By the age of five or six, children have mastered their language's langue, although they have not mastered the exceptions. For example, a six-year-old may say, "I drinked a glass of milk, and I climbed a tree." Having mastered his or her langue, the child has learned that most English verbs form their past tense by adding -*d* or -*ed*. What the child has not mastered is the many exceptions to this rule, in this case the past tense of the irregular verb *to drink.*

Latent Content   A term used by Sigmund Freud in psychoanalytic dream interpretation. According to Freud, the ego or the rational part of the psyche hides the true wish or *latent content* of our dreams, thereby allowing the dreamer to remember a somewhat changed and often radically different dream than the one that actually occurred.

Libido   A term used by Sigmund Freud in psychoanalysis that has become synonymous with sexual drive. Freud used this term to refer to emotional energy that springs from primitive biological urges and is usually directed toward some goal.

Linear   A term used to refer to something that has a definite beginning, a middle, and an end. A philosophy of life or one's worldview, for example, may be considered linear.

Linguistic Sign   A term used in linguistics in reference to words. As used by Ferdinand de Saussure, a *sign* is composed of two parts: the signifier (a written or spoken mark) and the signified (the concept it represents).

Literacy Experience   An event that occurs when reader and print interact.

Literary Criticism   According to Matthew Arnold, *literary criticism* is "a disinterested endeavor to learn and propagate the best that is known and thought in the world." It is therefore a disciplined activity that attempts to study, analyze, interpret, and evaluate a work of art.

Literary Theory   A term that refers to a set of principles or assumptions upon which our interpretation of a text is based. Our personal literary theory is our conscious or unconscious development of a mind-set (including values, sense of aesthetics, morals, etc.) concerning our expectations when reading any type of literature. To articulate this framework and piece together the various elements of our practical criticism into a coherent, unified body of knowledge is our *literary theory.*

Logocentrism   A term used by the French deconstructionist Jacques Derrida that refers to Western culture's proclivity for desiring absolute truths, or what Derrida calls "centers." *Logocentrism* is therefore the belief that there is an ultimate reality or center of truth that can serve as the basis for all our thoughts and actions.

Manifest Content   A term used by Sigmund Freud in psychoanalytic dream interpretation. According to Freud, the ego or the rational part of the psyche hides the true wish or latent content of our dreams and allows the dreamer to remember a somewhat changed and often radically different dream than the one that actually occurred. This changed dream is the *manifest content* that the dreamer remembers and tells his or her dream analyst.

Marxism   An approach to literary analysis founded on principles articulated by Friedrich Engels and Karl Marx. Unlike other schools of criticism, Marxism is not primarily a literary theory that can be used to interpret a text, for it is first a set of social, economic, and political ideas that its followers believe will enable them to interpret and change their world. Ultimate reality, they declare, is material, not spiritual. What we know beyond any doubt is that human beings exist and live in social groups. In order to understand ourselves and our world, we must first acknowledge the interrelatedness of all our actions within society. Once understood properly, we will note that it is our cultural and our social circumstances that determine who we are. What we believe, what we value, and how we think are a direct result of our society. And our society, says Marxism, is built upon a series of ongoing conflicts between the "haves" and the "have nots."

In *The Communist Manifesto,* Engels and Marx declare that the "haves" (the capitalists or the bourgeoisie) have successfully enslaved the "have nots" (the working class or the proletariat) through economic policies and control of the production of goods. In addition, the bourgeoisie have established society's beliefs, its values, and even its art. Now the proletariat must revolt and strip the bourgeoisie of their economic and political power and place the ownership of all property in the hands of the government, which will fairly distribute the people's wealth.

Since the bourgeoisie controls a society's art and therefore its literature, Marxist critics believe they must move beyond the usual analysis of literary devices, themes, and style and concentrate on determining an author's worldview, the historical context of the work, and the sociological concerns of the text to see if such an analysis of the author's ideology advances either the bourgeoisie's or the proletariat's concerns.

Some of the leading Marxist critics of the twentieth century are Georg Lukacs, Raymond Williams, Walter Benjamin, Fredric Jameson, and Terry Eagleton.

Metaphor   A figure of speech that directly compares two unlike objects (without using "like" or "as") where the qualities of one object are ascribed to the other. For example, in the sentence, "My love is a rose," the qualities of the rose are directly ascribed to "my love."

Metaphysics of Presence   A term coined by the French deconstructionist Jacques Derrida to encompass those ideas such as logocentrism, phonocentrism, the operation of binary oppositions, and other notions that Western thought and culture hold concerning the nature of language and metaphysics. Derrida's objective is to demonstrate the shaky foundations upon which such beliefs have been established and thereby "deconstruct" or take apart what Western culture values, and to show how such a deconstructive process will lead to new and exciting interpretations of a text.

Metatheory   An overarching or all-inclusive literary theory that can encompass all possible interpretations of a text suggested by its readers.

Mimetic Theory   A term used in literary criticism to refer to art as being an imitation of various elements of the universe. In linguistics, the *mimetic theory of language* asserts that words are symbols for things in the world; i.e., each word has its own referent—the object, concept, or idea that is represented or symbolized by that word. Accordingly, a word equals a thing. See **Referent.**

Modernism   A literary movement in both England and America considered by some to have begun with the influence of the French Symbolist poetry of Baudelaire and Valéry at the beginning of the twentieth century. Some assert this period begins in 1914, with the start of the First World War, and ends right after the Second World War, while still others mark its ending around 1965. Whatever its dating, Modernism is marked, as T. S. Eliot notes, by an "impersonal" view of humanity and a literature that is distinctly anti-romantic and anti-expressionistic. In its ardent search for meaning through form, Modernism typically employs "hard, dry" language which asserts that feeling or emotions are elicited by the text itself through the textual arrangement of its images. By rejecting a sheerly personal reading of a work, Modernism declares that a text's meaning can be found by examining its structure, a technique that is especially true for poetry. The Modernist Period thus provides literary criticism with a formal explanation for how a poem or any other work of literature achieves or produces meaning through its form.

Monomyth   A term used in the archetypal criticism of Northrop Frye. According to Frye, all literature comprises one complete and whole story called the *monomyth.* This monomyth can best be diagrammed as a circle containing four separate phases, with each phase corresponding to a season of the year and to peculiar cycles of human experiences. The phases are romance (the summer story of total happiness and wish fulfillment), anti-romance (the winter story of bondage, imprisonment, frustration, and fear), comedy (the spring story that tells of our rise from frustration to freedom and happiness), and tragedy (the fall story, narrating our fall from happiness to disaster). According to Frye, all stories fall somewhere within these categories.

Mythemes   A term coined by the structuralist critic Claude Lévi-Strauss that refers to the many recurrent themes running through humankind's countless myths. These basic structures, he maintains, are similar to the individual sounds of language, the primary building blocks of language itself. Like these sounds, *mythemes* find meaning in and through their relationships within the mythic structure, not in their own individuality. The meaning of any individual myth, then, depends upon the interaction and order of the mythemes found within the story.

Narratology   A form of structuralism espoused by Vladimir Propp, Tzvetan Todorov, Roland Barthes, and Gerard Genette, that illustrates how a story's meaning develops from its overall structure (its *langue,* rather than each individual story's isolated theme). To ascertain a text's meaning, narratologists emphasize such textual elements as the function of the narrator, various grammatical elements such as verb tenses, and the relationships and configurations of figures of speech within the story.

Naturalism   A term that refers to the late nineteenth- and early twentieth-century view of life that emphasizes the importance of scientific thought and determinism in literary study. A naturalistic critic views humans as animals who respond in deterministic ways to their environment and internal drives.

New Criticism   A loosely structured "school" of criticism that dominated American literary criticism from the early 1930s to the 1960s. Named after John Crowe Ransom's 1941 book *The New Criticism*, New Criticism asserts that a work of art or a text is a concrete object that can, like any other concrete object, be analyzed to discover its meaning independent of its author's intention or the emotional state and/or values of either its author or reader. For the New Critic, a poem's meaning must reside within its own structure (in New Criticism, the word *poem* refers to any text, not only a poem). By giving a poem a "close reading," the New Critics believe they can ascertain the text's correct meaning.

Often referred to as "the text and text alone" approach to literary analysis, New Criticism has found many practitioners, such as John Crowe Ransom, René Wellek, W. K. Wimsatt, R. P. Blackmur, I. A. Richards, Cleanth Brooks, and Robert Penn Warren. With the publication of Brooks and Warren's 1938 college text *Understanding Poetry*, New Criticism became the dominant approach to textual analysis until the 1960s.

New Historicism   Appearing in the late 1970s and early 1980s, New Historicism is the most recent approach of textual analysis to appear on the literary scene. Led by such scholars as Stephen Greenblatt and Louis Montrose, New Historicism challenges the "old historicism" founded in nineteenth-century thought that declares (1) that history serves as a background to literature, (2) that history, as written, is an accurate view of what really occurred, and (3) that historians can articulate a unified and internally consistent worldview of any people, country, or era.

New Historicism declares that all history is subjective and that historians can therefore never provide us with the "truth" or give us a totally accurate picture of past events or the worldview of a people. Like language, history is one of many discourses or ways of viewing the world. By highlighting and viewing history as one of several important discourses that directly affect the interpretation of a text, New Historicism asserts that it provides its followers with a practice of literary analysis that highlights the interrelatedness of all human activities, admits its own prejudices, and gives a more complete understanding of a text than do the old historicism and other interpretative approaches.

New Humanists   A school of twentieth-century American literary critics who value the moral qualities of art. Declaring that human experience is basically ethical, these critics demand that literary analysis be based on the moral values exhibited in a text.

Objective Correlative   A term coined by T. S. Eliot that refers to a set of objects, a situation, a chain of events or reactions that can serve to awaken in the reader the emotional response which the author desires without being a direct statement of that emotion.

Objective Theory of Art   A term introduced by M. H. Abrams that declares that the literary work itself is an object. Every work of art must therefore be a public text that can be understood by applying the standards of public discourse, not the private experience, intentions, and vocabulary of its author or a particular audience.

Oedipus Complex   According to Sigmund Freud's theory of child development, all children between the ages of three and six develop sexual or libidinal feelings towards the parent of the opposite sex and hostile feelings towards the parent of the same sex. In young boys, this is known as the *Oedipus Complex*, named after the legendary Thebian Oedipus, who murdered his father and married his mother. In young girls, this period is called the *Electra complex,* named after the legendary Electra, who avenged her father's death by killing her mother and her mother's lover.

Ontological   The term used by New Critics in recognition of their belief that a work of art is a concrete entity (one that really exists) and can therefore be analyzed and "dissected" like any other object to ascertain its meaning.

Oral Phase   The first stage of child development as postulated by Sigmund Freud. In this stage, a child sucks at its mother's breast to be fed, but simultaneously the child's sexuality or libido is activated. Our mouths become erotogenic zones that will later cause us to enjoy sucking our tongues and, still later, kissing.

Organic Unity   A term describing the concept that a text's structure is like a living plant with all its parts supporting each other and living in a complex interrelationship. First advanced by the nineteenth-century poet/critic Samuel Taylor Coleridge, the concept of the organic unity of a work of art or text declares that each part of the text reflects and helps support the text's central idea, or as the New Critics would call it, the work's chief paradox. No part of a text is superfluous, but like a living organism, each serves to enhance the whole. The whole is therefore greater than the sum of its parts.

Paradox   A term used by the New Critics (especially Cleanth Brooks) to help explain the nature and essence of poetry. According to Brooks, scientific language must be precise and exact. On the other hand, poetry's chief characteristic is its many rich connotations, not the scientific denotations of words. The meaning of a poem is therefore built on paradox, a juxtaposition of connotations and meaning that all support the poem's central idea.

Parole   A linguistic term used by Ferdinand de Saussure and others to refer to an individual's actual speech utterances, as opposed to *langue,* the rules that comprise a language. An individual can generate countless examples of *parole,* but all will be governed by the language's structure, its langue. For Saussure and other linguists, the proper study of linguistics is the system, the langue, not parole.

Patriarchal   A term used by feminist critics and others to describe a society or culture dominated by males. In these societies, the male defines what it means to be human, including what it means to be female.

Personal Unconscious   A term brought into literary criticism via the psychology of Carl Jung. According to Jung, the *personal unconscious* exists directly below the surface of the conscious, and contains elements of all those private affairs that occur daily in each of our lives. The personal unconscious is therefore peculiar to one individual and not shared with any other.

Personification   A figure of speech that attributes human qualities to animals, ideas, or inanimate objects.

Phallic Stage   The last stage of child development as theorized by Sigmund Freud. In this stage, the child's sexual desires or libido is directed toward the genitals.

Phenomenology   Founded by Edmund Husserl, *phenomenology* is a modern philosophical tendency that emphasizes the perceiver. Objects exist and achieve meaning if and only if we register them on our consciousness. Phenomenological critics are therefore concerned with the ways in which our consciousness perceives works of art.

Philologist   An earlier name given to linguists. A philologist is one who describes, compares, and analyzes the various languages of the world to discover their similarities and relationships.

Philology   An earlier name for the present-day science of linguistics, especially historical and comparative linguistics. Typically, philology approached the study of language diachronically, whereas linguistics uses both the diachronic and synchronic approaches. See **Diachronic** and **Synchronic.**

Phonemes   A linguistic term for the smallest distinct and significant sounds that comprise a language. Phonemes are the primary building blocks of language. American English, for example, contains approximately 45 phonemes, including /p/, /b/, /k/, and others.

Phonocentrism   A term coined by the French deconstructionist Jacques Derrida that asserts that Western culture privileges or prefers speech over writing.

Poem   A term used by Louise M. Rosenblatt that refers to the creation of a new interpretation each time a reader interacts with a text, be that interaction a first reading or any of countless rereadings of that same text. The interpretation thus becomes the poem, the new creation. New Critics also use this term to refer generically to any literary work.

Poststructuralism   A term applied to a variety of literary theories and practical criticisms developed after structuralism. Dating from the late 1960s, poststructuralism is often used synonymously with deconstruction, although the term is much broader and includes such critical schools of thought as feminism, psychoanalysis (especially the ideas of Jacques Lacan), Marxism or any of its revisionist forms, New Historicism, and others. Theoretically speaking, structuralism posits the objective reality of the text; that is, a structuralist believes one can examine a text using a standard and objective methodology and arrive at a conclusion. Poststructuralists, however, often assert undecidability concerning a text's meaning and declare that a text may not in and of itself have any objective reality. Poststructuralists also question the long-held assumptions concerning the processes involved in both reading and writing and the metaphysics of language.

Practical Critic   One who applies the theories and tenets of theoretical criticism to a particular work of art. It is the practical critic who often defines the standards of taste and explains, evaluates, or justifies a particular text.

Practical Criticism   See **Applied Criticism.**

Privileged   A term introduced into literary criticism by the French deconstructionist Jacques Derrida. According to Derrida, Western society bases its values and its metaphysical assumptions on opposites, such as good/bad, light/dark, true/false. In each of these pairs, Derrida asserts that Western culture values, or *privileges*, the first element while devaluing or un-privileging the second.

Proletariat   A term used by Karl Marx and Friedrich Engels to refer to the working class of society. According to Marxist theory, the bourgeoisie or upper class oppresses and enslaves the proletariat by controlling the economic policies and the production of goods. It is the bourgeoisie, not the proletariat, who define and articulate a society's ideology.

Prosody   The mechanical or structural elements that comprise poetry, such as rhythm, meter, rhyme, stanza, diction, alliteration, and so forth. Used synonymously with *versification.*

Psychoanalytic Criticism   The application of the methods of Sigmund Freud's psychoanalysis to interpreting works of literature. Because this approach to literary analysis attempts to explain the hows and whys of human actions without developing an aesthetic theory, a variety of critical approaches such as Marxism, feminism, and New Historicism utilize psychoanalytic methods in their interpretations without violating their own theoretical assumptions.

Central to psychoanalytic criticism is Freud's assumption that all artists are neurotic. Unlike other neurotics, the artist escapes many of the outward manifestations and end results of neurosis by finding in the act of creating art a pathway back to saneness and wholeness.

Freud believes that the literary text is really an artist's dream or fantasy. A text, then, can be analyzed like a dream. For Freud this means that we must assume that the dream is a disguised wish. Just as if he were counseling a patient and trying to uncover the meaning of the disguised wish as it evidences itself in a dream, Freud and we must apply the principles and methodology of psychoanalysis to a text to uncover its real meaning.

Although psychoanalytic criticism was founded by Freud, other critics such as Carl Jung, Northrop Frye, and Jacques Lacan have revised and expanded Freud's theories and developed their own methodologies for literary analysis.

Reader-Response Criticism   Rising to prominence in literary analysis in the early 1970s, reader-response criticism asserts that the reader is active, not passive, during the reading process. Both the reader and the text interact or share a transactional experience: the text acts as a stimulus for eliciting various past experiences, thoughts, and ideas of the reader, those found in both real life and in past reading experiences. Simultaneously, the text shapes the reader's experiences, selecting, limiting, and ordering those ideas that best conform to the text. The resulting interpretation is thus a new creation called a "poem." For reader-response critics, the reader + the text = meaning or the "poem."

Reader-response critics ask a variety of theoretical questions, such as What is a text? Who is the reader? Does the reader or the text or some combination of both determine the text's interpretation? What part does the author play in a work's interpretation? and perhaps most important, What is the reading process?

Composed of a diverse group of critics who emphasize different elements of the reading process, reader-response critics include Roland Barthes, Gerard Genette, Claude Lévi-Strauss, Wolfgang Iser, Louise Rosenblatt, Norman Holland, and David Bleich.

Referent   In linguistics, the entity (object, state of affairs, etc.) in the external world that is represented and/or symbolized by a word or term. For example, the referent for the word *desk* is the object desk.

Reflection Theory   One of the earliest theories developed by Marxist critics to explain the relationship between a society's base and its superstructure. A position held by Karl Marx early in his career, the reflection theory asserts that the base or economic structure of society directly affects and determines a society's values; its social, political, educational, and legal institutions; its art; and its beliefs (or, taken collectively, what Marx calls a society's superstructure). Simply put, the superstructure reflects or mirrors the base. Although a few Marxist critics still hold to this position, most now assert that the relationship between the base and the superstructure is much more complex than originally believed. The term **Vulgar Marxism** is used to describe the form of Marxism that still holds to the reflection theory.

Relativistic Critic   One who employs various and even contradictory theories in critiquing a work of art.

Rhetoric   Often defined as the art of speaking and writing effectively. Founded in Greece by Corax of Syracuse in the fifth century B.C., rhetoric set forth the principles and rules of composition for a speech. Today, the term is used by such critics as Kenneth Burke, Northrop Frye, Roland Barthes, and Jacques Derrida and refers to patterns of structure found within texts. It has become the basis for much modern criticism.

Romanticism   A literary movement that dates to the publication of William Wordsworth and Samuel Taylor Coleridge's *Lyrical Ballads* in 1798. As a reaction against the eighteenth-century Age of Reason, romanticism asserts that the world is like a living plant, ever growing, becoming, and aspiring. Denying reason as the sole path to truth, romanticists declare that intuition can lead them to an understanding of themselves and their world. Individual concerns, the emotions, and the imagination are to be valued. As an approach to a text, romanticism concerns itself with the artist's feelings and attitudes exhibited within the work of art.

Schools of Criticism   When a variety of readers and critics assert allegiance to a similar core of assumptions concerning an approach to textual analysis, they form a "school of criticism," a group of fellow believers who share common concerns about reading, writing, and interpretation. Examples of such schools are New Criticism, reader-response, structuralism, deconstruction, and New Historicism.

Semiology   Proposed by the structuralist Ferdinand de Saussure, this new science would study how we create meaning through signs or codes in all our social behavioral systems. Since language was the chief and most characteristic of these systems, Saussure declared that it was to be the main branch of this new science. Although semiology never became the important new science as Saussure envisioned it, **Semiotics,** a similar science, did develop and is still practiced today.

Semiotics   Founded by Charles Sanders Pierce and developing at the same time as Ferdinand de Saussure's proposed science of **Semiology,** semiotics borrows linguistic methods used by Saussure and applies them to all meaningful cultural phenomena. Semiotics declares that meaning in society can be systematically studied, both in terms of how this meaning occurs and in terms of the structures that allow it to operate. Because it uses methods employed by structuralism, semiotics and structuralism are often used interchangeably today, although the former denotes a particular field of study while the latter is more an approach to literary analysis.

Sign   A term used in linguistics and first used by the French structuralist Ferdinand de Saussure to denote the definition for a word. According to Saussure, a word is not a symbol that equals something else, but is a sign (something that has meaning) composed of both a signifier and a signified. For Saussure, a word does not represent a referent in the objective world, but a concept in our minds. See **Referent, Signifier,** and **Signified.**

Signification   A term used in literary criticism, theories of reading, and linguistics to denote the process by which we arrive at meaning through linguistic signs or other symbolic means.

Signified   A term used by the French structuralist Ferdinand de Saussure that denotes one part of a word. Saussure proposes that all words are really signs that are composed of two parts: the signifier and the signified. The signified is the concept to which the signifier, a written or spoken word or sound, refers. Like the two sides of a sheet of paper, the linguistic sign is the union of the signifier and the signified.

Signifier   A term used by the French structuralist Ferdinand de Saussure that denotes one part of a word. The signifier is the spoken or written constituent such as the sound /t/ and the orthographic (written) symbol *t*. See **Signified.**

Simile   A figure of speech that compares two unlike objects using *like* or *as*, such as "His nose is like a cherry." The objects being compared cannot be from the same class. For example, the statement "London is like Paris" contains no simile since the objects being compared are from the same class, both being cities.

Structuralism   An approach to literary analysis that flourished in the 1960s. By utilizing the techniques, methodologies, and vocabulary of linguistics as articulated by Ferdinand de Saussure, structuralism offers a scientific view of how we achieve meaning not only in literary works but in all forms of communication and social behavior.

Structuralists believe that codes, signs, and rules govern all social and cultural practices, including communication, the "language" of sports, friendships, education, and literature. They wish to discover those codes that they believe give meaning to all our social and cultural customs. The proper study of meaning and therefore reality is an examination of the system behind these practices, not the individual practices themselves.

For the structuralist, the proper study of literature becomes a study of the conditions surrounding the act of interpretation itself, not an in-depth investigation of an individual work. Structuralists believe that a study of the grammar, or the system of rules that govern literary interpretation, becomes the critic's primary task.

Practiced by such critics as Jonathan Culler, Tzvetan Todorov, Roland Barthes, and Gerard Genette, structuralism challenged New Criticism's methodology for finding meaning within a text.

Structuralist Narratology   A form of structuralism defined as the science of narrative and employed by such critics as Vladimir Propp, Tzvetan Todorov, Roland Barthes, and Gerard Genette. These narratologists illustrate how a story's meaning develops from its overall structure, including elements such as theme, persona, voice, style, grammatical structure, and tone.

Structural Linguistics   A term used synonymously with linguistics, the science of language.

Superego   A term used by Sigmund Freud to designate that part of the psyche that acts like an internal censor, causing us to make moral judgments in light of social pressures.

Superstructure   A term used by Karl Marx to designate that part of society that contains the social, legal, political, and educational systems along with the religious beliefs, values, and art of a society and that embodies a society's ideology. According to Marx, the economic structure of a society (called the base) is controlled by the bourgeoisie or upper class. By controlling the base, the bourgeoisie determines a society's superstructure and thus controls and oppresses the working class or proletariat.

Supplement   A term coined by the French deconstructionist Jacques Derrida to explain the relationship between two parts of any hierarchy upon which Western culture bases its metaphysics. For example, Derrida says Western society values light over darkness. The exact relationship between light and darkness, Derrida asserts, is not totally clear. Derrida uses the term supplement to refer to the unstable relationship between the two elements contained in this hierarchy. Rather than being two totally separate entities, light and dark supplement each other. Who, for example, can declare it to be light or dark when it is dusk? Each term thus helps define the other and is necessary for the other to exist.

Synchronic   A linguistic term introduced by the French structuralist Ferdinand de Saussure and used to designate a process of language analysis that studies one language at one particular time in its evolution, emphasizing how that language functions, not its historical development through a long expanse of time. See **Diachronic.**

Teleological   A philosophical term used to denote a worldview or philosophy of life that asserts a purposeful going forward toward some known end, especially one relating to nature.

Tension   A term used in literary criticism that is synonymous with conflict. It designates the opposition or conflicts operating with a text.

Theoretical Criticism   Formulates the theories, principles, and tenets of the nature and value of art. By citing general aesthetic and moral principles of art, theoretical criticism provides the necessary framework for **Practical Criticism.**

Tragedy   Although the term is used in many different ways, in literary criticism tragedy chiefly refers to Aristotle's definition found in the *Poetics.* Tragedy is "an imitation of a noble and complete action, having the proper magnitude; it employs language of linguistic adornment, applied separately in the various parts of the play; it is presented in dramatic, not narrative form, and achieves, through the representation of pitiable and fearful incidents, the catharsis of such pitiable and fearful incidents."

Transactional   A term introduced by Louise M. Rosenblatt to describe the process or "event" that takes place at a particular time and place when a reader interacts with a text. According to Rosenblatt, the text and the reader condition each other, for the text acts as a stimulus for eliciting various past experiences, thoughts, and ideas of the reader—those found in both real life and in past reading experiences. The end result of this experience or "transaction" is the creation of a "poem," or what has been traditionally called the interpretation.

Transcendental Signified   A term introduced into literary criticism by the French deconstructionist Jacques Derrida. In trying "to turn Western metaphysics on its head," Derrida asserts that from the time of Plato to the present, Western culture has been founded upon a classic, fundamental error: the searching for a transcendental signified, an external point of reference upon which one may build a concept or philosophy. Once found, this transcendental signified would provide ultimate meaning. It would guarantee to those who believe in it that they do exist and have meaning. It would also serve as the "center" of meaning, allowing those who believe in it to structure their ideas of reality around it. According to Derrida, Western metaphysics has invented a variety of such centers: God, reason, origin, being, truth, humanity, self, and so on.

Trope   A term synonymous with "figure of speech" or a word or phrase not meant to be taken literally. The term has now been employed by several schools of criticism in a variety of specialized meanings.

Unconscious   A term employed in Freudian psychoanalysis that refers to that part of the human psyche that receives and stores our hidden desires, ambitions, fears, passions, and irrational thoughts.

Unprivileged   A term introduced into literary criticism by the French deconstructionist Jacques Derrida. According to Derrida, Western society bases its values and its metaphysical assumptions on opposites, such as good/bad, light/dark, true/false. In each of these pairs, Derrida asserts that Western culture values or privileges the first element while devaluing or *unprivileging* the second.

Unvoiced   In linguistics, any sound made without vibrating the vocal folds, such as /t/, /p/, and /k/.

Voiced   In linguistics, any sound made during which the vocal folds are brought close together and made to vibrate, causing air to pass between them. Examples: /b/, /d/, and /g/.

Vulgar Marxism   A form of Marxism that holds to the reflection theory concerning the relationship of the base to the superstructure. Vulgar Marxism asserts that the superstructure directly reflects or mirrors the base. See **Reflection Theory.**

Worldview   According to James Sire in his book *The Universe Next Door,* a worldview is the set of assumptions or presuppositions that we all hold either consciously or unconsciously concerning the basic makeup of our world.

Bibliography

Introductory and General Surveys of Literary Criticism

Con Davis, Robert, and Laurie Finke. *Literary Criticism and Theory: The Greeks to the Present.* New York: Longman, 1989.

Con Davis, Robert, and Ronald Schleifer. *Contemporary Literary Criticism: Literary and Cultural Studies.* 2nd ed. New York: Longman, 1989.

Crane, R. S., ed. *Critics and Criticism: Ancient and Modern.* Chicago: U of Chicago P, 1952.

Daiches, David. *Critical Approaches to Literature.* 2nd ed. New York: Longman, 1981.

Danziger, Marlies, and W. Stacy Johnson. *An Introduction to Literary Criticism.* Boston: D. C. Heath, 1961.

Eagleton, Terry. *Literary Theory: An Introduction:* Minneapolis: U of Minnesota P, 1983.

Goldberg, Gerald Jay, and Nancy Marmer Goldberg, eds. *The Modern Critical Spectrum.* Englewood Cliffs, NJ: Prentice-Hall, 1962.

Jefferson, Ann, and David Robey, eds. *Modern Literary Theory: A Comparative Introduction.* Totowa, NJ: Barnes & Noble, 1982.

Lodge, David. *Modern Criticism and Theory: A Reader.* New York: Longman, 1988.

———. *20th Century Literary Criticism: A Reader.* New York: Longman, 1972.

Murfin, Ross, ed. *Heart of Darkness: A Case Study in Contemporary Criticism.* New York: St. Martin's, 1989.

———. *The Scarlet Letter: Case Studies in Contemporary Criticism.* Boston: St. Martin's, 1991.

Pritchard, John Paul. *Criticism in America.* Norman, OK: U of Oklahoma P, 1956.

Richter, David, ed. *The Critical Tradition: Classic Texts and Contemporary Trends.* New York: St. Martin's, 1989.

Schorer, Mark, Josephine Miles, and Gordon McKenzie, eds. *Criticism: The Foundations of Modern Literary Judgment.* Rev. ed. New York: Harcourt, 1958.

Scott, Wilbur S. *Five Approaches of Literary Criticism: An Arrangement of Contemporary Critical Essays.* New York: Macmillan, 1962.

Selden, Raman. *A Reader's Guide to Contemporary Literary Theory.* Lexington: UP of Kentucky, 1985.

———, ed. *The Theory of Criticism: From Plato to the Present.* New York: Longman, 1988.

Spingarn, J. E. *History of Literary Criticism in the Renaissance.* New York: Columbia UP, 1898.

Staton, Shirley, ed. *Literary Theories in Praxis.* Philadelphia: U of Pennsylvania P, 1987.

Sutton, Walter. *Modern American Criticism.* Englewood Cliffs, NJ: Prentice-Hall, 1963.

Watson, George. *The Literary Critics: A Study of English Descriptive Criticism.* 2nd ed. London: Woburn, 1973.

Wellek, René. *A History of Modern Criticism: 1750–1950.* New Haven: Yale UP, 1986.

Wimsatt, William K., and Cleanth Brooks. *Literary Criticism: A Short History.* New York: Knopf, 1964.

Advanced Theoretical Texts

Abrams, M. H. *The Mirror and the Lamp: Romantic Theory and the Critical Tradition.* New York: Oxford UP, 1953.

Atkins, J. W. H. *English Literary Criticism: 17th and 18th Centuries.* London: Methuen, 1951.

Atkins, G. Douglas, and Laura Morrow, eds. *Contemporary Literary Theory.* Amherst: U of Massachusetts P, 1989.

Bate, Walter Jackson. *From Classic to Romantic: Premises of Taste in Eighteenth Century England.* Cambridge: Harvard UP, 1946.

Beardsley, Monroe C. *The Possibility of Criticism.* Detroit: Wayne State UP, 1970.

Berman, Art. *From the New Criticism to Deconstruction: The Reception of Structuralism and Post-Structuralism.* Chicago: U of Illinois P, 1988.

Bové, Paul A. *Intellectuals in Power: A Genealogy of Critical Humanism.* New York: Columbia UP, 1986.

Brooker, Peter, ed. *Modernism/Postmodernism.* New York: Longman, 1992.

Brownell, W. C. *Criticism.* New York: Scribner's, 1914.

Bruss, Elizabeth W. *Beautiful Theories: The Spectacle of Discourse in Contemporary Criticism.* Baltimore: Johns Hopkins UP, 1982.

Dembo, L. S. *Criticism: Speculative and Analytical Essays.* Madison: U of Wisconsin P, 1968.

Dowling, William C. *The Critic's Hornbook: Reading for Interpretation.* New York: Crowell, 1977.

Ellis, John M. *The Theory of Literary Criticism: A Logical Analysis.* Berkeley: U of California P, 1974.

Goodheart, Eugene. *The Failure of Criticism.* Cambridge: Harvard UP, 1978.

———. *The Skeptic Disposition in Contemporary Criticism.* Princeton: Princeton UP, 1984.

Greene, William Chace. *The Choices of Criticism.* Cambridge, MA: MIT., 1965.

Hartman, Geoffrey H. *Criticism in the Wilderness.* New Haven: Yale UP, 1980.

Hawthorn, Jeremy, ed. *Criticism and Critical Theory.* London: Arnold, 1984.

Krieger, Murray. *Theory of Criticism: A Tradition and Its System.* Baltimore: Johns Hopkins UP, 1976.

Malone, David H. *The Frontiers of Literary Criticism.* Los Angeles: Hennessey, 1974.

Moore, Stephen D. *Literary Criticism and the Gospels: The Theoretical Challenge.* New Haven: Yale UP, 1989.

Moran, Charles, and Elizabeth F. Penfield, eds. *Conversations: Contemporary Critical Theory and the Teaching of Literature.* Urbana, IL: National Council of Teachers of English, 1990.

Natoli, Joseph. *Tracing Literary Theory.* Chicago: U of Illinois P, 1987.

Rawlinson, D. H. *The Practice of Criticism.* Cambridge: Cambridge UP, 1968.

Ray, William. *Literary Meaning: From Phenomenology to Deconstruction.* New York: Blackwell, 1984.

Smith, Paul. *Discerning the Subject.* Minneapolis: U of Minnesota P, 1988.

Spanos, William, Paul Bové, and Daniel O'Hara, eds. *The Question of Textuality: Strategies of Reading in Contemporary American Criticism.* Bloomington: Indiana UP, 1982.

Stovall, Floyd. *The Development of American Literary Criticism.* New Haven: College and UP, 1955.

Taylor, Mark C. *Erring: A Postmodern A/Theology.* Chicago: U of Chicago P, 1984.

Todorov, Tzvetan. *Literature and Its Theorists.* Trans. Catherine Porter. Ithaca, NY: Cornell UP, 1987.

Wellek, René, and Austin Warren. *Theory of Literature.* 3rd ed. San Diego: Harcourt, 1977.

References

CHAPTER 1

Beardsley, Monroe C., Robert W. Daniel, and Glenn H. Leggett. *Theme and Form: An Introduction to Literature.* Englewood Cliffs, NJ: Prentice-Hall, 1969.

Daiches, David. *Critical Approaches to Literature.* New York: Longman, 1981.

Danziger, Marlies, and W. Stacy Johnson. *An Introduction to Literary Criticism.* Boston: D. C. Heath, 1961.

Eagleton, Terry. *Literary Theory: An Introduction.* Minneapolis: U of Minnesota P, 1983.

Grebanier, Bernard. *The Enjoyment of Literature.* New York: Crown, 1975.

Holman, C. Hugh, and William Harmon. *A Handbook to Literature.* 6th ed. New York: Macmillan, 1992.

Lentricchia, Frank, and Thomas McLaughlin, eds. *Critical Terms for Literary Study.* Chicago: U of Chicago P, 1990.

Rosenblatt, Louise M. *The Reader, the Text, the Poem: The Transactional Theory of the Literary Work.* Carbondale, IL: Southern Illinois UP, 1978.

Sire, James W. *The Joy of Reading: A Guide to Becoming a Better Reader.* Portland, OR: Multnomah, 1978.

——. *The Universe Next Door.* 2nd ed. Downers Grove, IL: InterVarsity, 1988.

Staton, Shirley F., ed. *Literary Theories in Praxis.* Philadelphia: U of Pennsylvania P, 1987.

Stevens, Bonnie, and Larry Stewart. *A Guide to Literary Criticism and Research.* Fort Worth: Holt, 1992.

Twain, Mark. *The Adventures of Huckleberry Finn.* New York: Harcourt, 1961.

CHAPTER 2

Alighieri, Dante. *The Divine Comedy.* Trans. by Charles S. Singleton. Princeton: Princeton UP, 1975.

——. *Eleven Letters.* Trans. Charles Sterret Latham. Boston: Houghton, 1892.

Aristotle. *Poetics.* Trans. Leon Golden. Englewood Cliffs, NJ: Prentice-Hall, 1968.

——. *Poetics.* Trans. Ingram Bywater. *On the Art of Poetry.* Oxford: Clarendon, 1920.

Arnold, Matthew. *Essays in Criticism: First Series.* New York: Macmillan, 1895.

Auerbach, Erich. *Dante: Poet of the Secular World.* Trans. R. Manheim. Chicago: Chicago UP, 1961.

Bate, Walter J. *From Classic to Romantic.* Cambridge, MA: Harvard UP, 1946.

Bradley, A. C. *Oxford Lectures on Poetry.* London: Macmillan, 1909.

Brody, Jules. *Boileau and Longinus.* Geneva: Droz, 1953.

Butcher, S. H. *Aristotle's Theory of Poetry and Fine Art.* 3rd ed. London: Macmillan, 1902.

Casey, John. *The Language of Criticism.* London: Methuen, 1960.

Clubbe, John, and Ernest J. Lovell. *English Romanticism: The Grounds of Belief.* London: Macmillan, 1983.

Cooper, Lane. *The Poetics of Aristotle: Its Meaning and Influence.* New York: Cooper Square, 1963.

D'Alton, J. F. *Horace and His Age.* London: Longman Green, 1917.

Daugherty, Sarah B. *The Literary Criticism of Henry James.* Athens: Ohio UP, 1981.

Devereux, James A. "The Meaning of Delight in Sidney's Defense of Poesy." *Studies in the Literary Imagination* 15 (1982): 85–97.

Eliot, T. S. *John Dryden: The Poet, the Dramatist, the Critic: Three Essays.* New York: Haskell House, 1966.

Ells, John Shepard. *The Touchstones of Matthew Arnold.* New York: Bookman Associates, 1955.

Else, Gerald F. *Aristotle's Poetics: The Argument.* Cambridge, MA: Harvard UP, 1957.

——. *Plato and Aristotle on Poetry.* Chapel Hill: U of North Carolina P, 1986.

Fenner, Arthur, Jr. "The Unity of Pope's Essay on Criticism." *Philological Quarterly* 39 (1960): 435–56.

Fergusson, Francis. "On the Poetics." *Tulane Drama Review* 4 (1960): 23–32.

Garrod, Deathcote William. *Poetry and the Criticism of Life.* New York: Russell, 1963.

Goad, Caroline. *Horace in the English Literature of the Eighteenth Century.* New Haven: Yale UP, 1918.

Griffin, Dustin. *Alexander Pope: The Poet in the Poems.* Princeton: Princeton UP, 1978.

Grube, G. M. *Plato's Thought.* London: Methuen, 1935.

Hamilton, Paul. *Coleridge's Poetics.* Oxford: Blackwell, 1983.

Henn, T. R. *Longinus and English Criticism.* Cambridge: Cambridge UP, 1934.

Herrick, Marvin T. *The Fusion of Horatian and Aristotelian Literary Criticism.* Urbana: U of Illinois P, 1946.

Hill, John Spencer, ed. *The Romantic Imagination: A Casebook.* London: Macmillan, 1977.

Hirsch, E. D. *Wordsworth and Schelling.* New Haven: Yale UP, 1950.

Hollander, R. *Allegory in Dante's Commedia.* Princeton: Princeton UP, 1969.

Hughes, Herbert Leland. *Theory and Practice in Henry James.* Ann Arbor, MI: Edwards, 1926.

Hume, Robert D. *Dryden's Criticism.* Ithaca, NY: Cornell UP, 1970.

James, Henry. *The Art of the Novel: Critical Prefaces.* Introduction by R. P. Blackmur. New York: Scribner's, 1932.

Jones, Henry John. *The Egotistical Sublime: A History of Wordsworth's Imagination.* London: Chatto & Windus, 1970.

Lanser, Susan S. *The Narrative Act: Point of View in Prose Fiction.* Princeton: Princeton UP, 1981.

Lodge, Rupert C. *Plato's Theory of Art.* New York: Humanities Press, 1953.

Mason, H. A. "An Introduction to Literary Criticism by Way of Sidney's Apologie for Poetrie." *Cambridge Quarterly* 12, no. 2–3 (1984): 79–173.

Mishra, J. B. *John Dryden: His Theory and Practice of Drama.* New Delhi: Bahir, 1978.

Modrak, Deborah. *Aristotle: The Power of Perception.* Chicago: U of Chicago P, 1987.

Monk, S. *The Sublime: A Study of Critical Theories in XVIII-Century England.* Ann Arbor: U of Michigan P, 1960.

Olson, Elder. *Aristotle's Poetics and English Literature.* Chicago: U of Chicago P, 1965.

——. "The Argument of Longinus's *On the Sublime.*" In *On Value Judgments in the Arts and Other Essays.* Chicago: U of Chicago P, 1976.

Owen, W. J. B. *Wordsworth as Critic.* Toronto: Toronto UP, 1971.

Pechter, E. *Dryden's Classical Theory of Literature.* London: Cambridge UP, 1975.

Perkins, David. "Arnold and the Function of Literature." ELH 18 (1951); 287–309.

Plato. *The Republic.* Trans. B. Jowett. 3rd ed. Oxford: Clarendon, 1888.

Roberts, Morris. *Henry James's Criticism.* Cambridge, MA: Harvard UP, 1929.

Robinson, Forrest Glen. *The Shape of Things Known: Sidney's Apology in Its Philosophical Tradition.* Cambridge, MA: Harvard UP, 1972.

Rollinson, Philip. *Classical Theories of Allegory and Christian Culture.* Pittsburgh: Duquesne UP, 1981.

Russell, D. A., ed. *"Longinus" on the Sublime.* Oxford: Clarendon, 1964.

Sharma, L. S. *Coleridge: His Contribution to English Criticism.* New Delhi: Arnold-Heinemann, 1981.

Shorey, Paul. *What Plato Said.* Chicago: U of Chicago P, 1933.

Singleton, Charles S. *Dante Studies.* 2 vols. Cambridge, MA: Harvard UP, 1958.

Smith, Nowell C., ed. *Wordsworth's Literary Criticism.* Bristol, England: Bristol Classical P, 1980.

Stack, Frank. *Pope and Horace: Studies in Imitation.* New York: Cambridge UP, 1985.

Taine, Hippolyte A. *The History of English Literature.* 4 vols. Trans. H. Van Laun. Philadelphia: David McKay, 1908.

Taylor, A. E. *Plato.* Ann Arbor: U of Michigan P, 1960.

Thorpe, C. D. "Coleridge as Aesthetician and Critic." *Journal of the History of Ideas* I (1944): 387–414.

Trilling, Lionel. *Matthew Arnold.* New York: Norton, 1939.

Warren, Austin. *Alexander Pope as Critic and Humanist.* Princeton: Princeton UP, 1963.

——. *English Poetic Theory, 1825–1865.* Princeton: Princeton UP, 1950.

——. *Pope as Critic and Humanist.* Princeton: Princeton UP, 1929.

Watson, George. *John Dryden: Of Dramatic Poesy and Other Critical Essays.* 2 vols. London: J. Dent, 1962.

Wood, Allen G. *Literary Satire and Theory: A Study of Horace, Boileau, and Pope.* New York: Garland, 1985.

CHAPTER 3

Brooks, Cleanth. "In Search of the New Criticism." *American Scholar* 53 (Winter 1983/84): 41–53.

——. "My Credo: Formalist Critics." *Kenyon Review,* 13 (1951): 72–81.

——. *Modern Poetry and the Tradition.* Chapel Hill: U of North Carolina P, 1939.

——. *The Well-Wrought Urn: Studies in the Structure of Poetry.* New York: Harcourt, 1947.

Brooks, Cleanth, and Robert Penn Warren. *Understanding Poetry: An Anthology for College Students.* New York: Holt, 1938.

Eliot, T. S. "The Function of Criticism." *Selected Essays.* New York: Harcourt, 1950.

——. "Tradition and the Individual Talent." *The Sacred Wood.* London: Methuen, 1928.

Elton, William. *A Glossary of the New Criticism.* Chicago: Modern Poetry Association, 1949.

Empson, William. *Seven Types of Ambiguity.* New York: Noonday Press, 1958.

Handy, William J. *Kant and the Southern New Critics.* Austin: U of Texas P, 1963.

Lentricchia, Frank. *After the New Criticism.* Chicago: U of Chicago P, 1980.

Ransom, John Crowe. *Beating the Bushes: Selected Essays: 1941–1970.* New York: New Directions: 1972.

—— *The New Criticism.* New York: New Directions, 1941.

Richards, I. A. *Practical Criticism.* New York: Harcourt, 1929.

——. *Principles of Literary Criticism.* New York: Harcourt, 1924.

Schiller, Jerome P. *I. A. Richards' Theory of Literature.* New Haven: Yale UP, 1969.

Schorer, Mark. "Technique as Discovery." *Hudson Review* I (Spring 1948): 67–87.

Simpson, Lewis P., ed. *The Possibilities of Order: Cleanth Brooks and His Work.* Baton Rouge: Louisiana State UP, 1976.

Tate, Allen. "What I Owe to Cleanth Brooks," in *The Possibilities of Order: Cleanth Brooks and His Work,* ed. Lewis P. Simpson. Baton Rouge: Louisiana State UP, 1976.

——. *Reason in Madness.* New York: Putnam's, 1941.

Warren, Robert Penn. "Pure and Impure Poetry." *Kenyon Review* 5 (Spring 1943): 229–54.

Wimsatt, W. K. *The Verbal Icon.* Lexington: U of Kentucky P, 1954.

Winters, Yvor. *In Defense of Reason.* Denver: Swallow, 1947.

CHAPTER 4

Bleich, David. *Subjective Criticism.* Baltimore: Johns Hopkins UP, 1978.

——. *Readings and Feelings: An Introduction to Subjective Criticism.* New York: Harper, 1977.

Booth, Wayne C. *The Rhetoric of Fiction.* Chicago: U of Chicago P, 1978.

Eco, Umberto. *The Role of the Reader: Explorations in the Semiotics of Texts.* Blooming-ton: Indiana UP, 1979.

Fish, Stanley E. *Is There a Text in This Class? The Authority of Interpretive Communi-ties.* Cambridge, MA: Harvard UP, 1980.

———. "Literature in the Reader: Affective Stylistics." *New Literary History* 2 (1970); 123–61.

———. *Self-Consuming Artifacts: The Experience of Seventeenth-Century Literature.* Berkeley: U of California P, 1972.

Freund, Elizabeth. *The Return of the Reader: Reader-Response Criticism.* New York: Methuen, 1987.

Holland, Norman N. *The Dynamics of Literary Response.* New York: Oxford UP, 1968.

———. "Unity, Identity, Text, Self." *PMLA* 90 (1975): 813–22.

Holub, Robert C. *Reception Theory: A Critical Introduction.* New York: Methuen, 1984.

Iser, Wolfgang. *The Act of Reading: A Theory of Aesthetic Response.* Baltimore: Johns Hopkins UP, 1978.

———. *The Implied Reader: Patterns of Communication in Prose Fiction from Bunyan to Beckett.* Baltimore: Johns Hopkins UP, 1974.

Mailloux, Steven. *Interpretive Conventions: The Reader in the Study of American Fic-tion.* Ithaca, NY: Cornell UP, 1982.

———. "Learning to Read: Interpretation and Reader-Response Criticism." *Studies in the Literary Imagination* 12 (1979): 93–108.

———. "Reader-Response Criticism?" *Genre* 10 (1977): 413–31.

Ong, Walter, S. J. *Orality and Literacy.* New York: Methuen, 1982.

"Reading Interpretation, Response," special section of *Genre* 10 (1977): 363–453.

Rosenblatt, Louise M. "Towards a Transactional Theory of Reading." *Journal of Reading Behavior* 1 (1969): 31–47.

Suleiman, Susan R., and Inge Crosman, eds. *The Reader in the Text: Essays on Audi-ence and Interpretation.* Princeton: Princeton UP, 1980.

Tompkins, Jane O. *Reader-Response Criticism: From Formalism to Post-Structuralism.* Baltimore: Johns Hopkins UP, 1980.

CHAPTER 5

Bannet, Eve Tavor. *Structuralism and the Logic of Dissent.* Chicago: U of Illinois P, 1989.

Barthes, Roland. *Critical Essays.* Trans. R. Howard. Evanston, IL: Northwestern UP, 1972.

———. *Elements of Semiology.* Trans. A. Lavers and C. Smith. London: Cape, 1967.

———. *S/Z.* Trans. R. Miller, New York: Hill and Wang, 1971.

Crystal, David. *A Dictionary of Linguistics and Phonetics.* 2nd ed. Cambridge, MA: Basil Blackwell, 1985.

Culler, Jonathan. *Ferdinand de Saussure.* Baltimore: Penguin, 1976.

———. *Structuralist Poetics: Structuralism, Linguistics and the Study of Literature.* Lon-don: Routledge, 1975.

De George, Richard T., and Fernande M., eds. *The Structuralists from Marx to Lévi-Strauss.* Garden City, NY: Doubleday, 1972.

Detweiler, Robert. *Story, Sign, and Self: Phenomenology and Structuralism as Literary-Critical Methods.* Philadelphia: Fortress, 1978.

Ehrmann, Jacques, ed. *Structuralism.* Garden City, NY: Doubleday, 1970.

Genette, Gerard. *Narrative Discourse.* Oxford: Blackwell, 1980.

Hawkes, Terence. *Structuralism and Semiotics.* London: Methuen, 1977.

Jakobson, Roman. *Fundamentals of Language.* Paris: Mouton, 1975.

Jameson, Fredric. *The Prison-House of Language: A Critical Account of Structuralism and Russian Formalism.* Princeton: Princeton UP, 1972.

Krieger, Murray, and L. S. Dembo, eds. *Directions for Criticism: Structuralism and Its Alternatives.* Madison: U of Wisconsin P, 1977.

Lane, Michael, ed. *Introduction to Structuralism.* New York: Harper, 1972.

Lévi-Strauss, Claude. *Structural Anthropology.* Trans. C. Jacobson and B. G. Schoepf. London: Allen Lane, 1968.

Lodge, David. *Working with Structuralism: Essays and Reviews on Nineteenth- and Twentieth-Century Literature.* Boston: Routledge and Kegan Paul, 1981.

Macksey, Richard, and Eugenio Donato, eds. *The Structuralist Controversy.* Baltimore: Johns Hopkins UP, 1970.

Prince, Gerald. *Narratology: The Form and Functioning of Narrative.* New York: Mouton, 1982.

Propp, Vladimir. *The Morphology of the Folktale.* Austin: Texas UP, 1968.

Robey, David, ed. *Structuralism: An Introduction.* Oxford: Clarendon, 1973.

Saussure, Ferdinand de. *Course in General Linguistics.* Trans. W. Baskin. London: Collins, 1974.

Scholes, Robert. *Structuralism in Literature: An Introduction.* New Haven: Yale UP, 1974.

Sturrock, John. *Structuralism and Since.* New York: Oxford UP, 1979.

Tatham, Campbell. "Beyond Structuralism." *Genre* 10, no. 1 (1977): 131–55.

Todorov, Tzvetan. *The Fantastic: A Structural Approach to a Literary Genre.* Ithaca, NY: Cornell UP, 1973.

CHAPTER 6

Arac, Jonathan, Wlad Godzich, and Wallace Martin, eds. *The Yale Critics: Deconstruction in America. Theory and History of Literature,* vol. 6. Minneapolis: U of Minnesota Press, 1983.

Atkins, G. Douglas. *Reading Deconstruction: Deconstructive Reading.* Lexington: UP of Kentucky, 1983.

Barthes, Roland. *S/Z.* Trans. Richard Miller. New York: Hill, 1974.

Bloom, Harold, et al., eds. *Deconstruction and Criticism.* New York: Seabury P, 1979.

Bruns, Gerald L. "Structuralism, Deconstruction, and Hermeneutics." *Diacritics* 14 (1984): 12–23.

Cain, William E. "Deconstruction in America: The Recent Literary Criticism of J. Hillis Miller." *College English* 41 (1979): 367–82.

Cascardi, A. J. "Skepticism and Deconstruction." *Philosophy and Literature* 8 (1984): 1–14.

Con Davis, Robert, and Ronald Schleifer, eds. *Rhetoric and Form: Deconstruction at Yale.* Norman: U of Oklahoma P, 1985.

Crowley, Sharon. *A Teacher's Introduction to Deconstruction.* Urbana, IL: National Council of Teachers of English, 1989.

Culler, Jonathan. *On Deconstruction: Theory and Criticism after Structuralism.* Ithaca, NY: Cornell UP, 1982.

——. *The Pursuit of Signs: Semiotics, Literature, Deconstruction.* Ithaca, NY: Cornell UP, 1981.

——. *Structuralist Poetics: Structuralism, Linguistics and the Study of Literature.* Ithaca, NY: Cornell UP, 1975.

de Man, Paul. *Allegories of Reading.* New Haven: Yale UP, 1979.

——. *Blindness and Insight.* New York: Oxford UP, 1971.

Derrida, Jacques. *Of Grammatology.* Trans. Gayatri Spivak. Baltimore: Johns Hopkins UP, 1974. Trans. of *De la grammatologie.* 1967.

——. *Speech and Phenomena, and Other Essays on Husserl's Theory of Signs.* 1973. Trans. David B. Allison. Evanston, IL: Northwestern UP, 1978.

——. *Writing and Difference.* 1967.Trans. Alan Bass. Chicago: U of Chicago P, 1978.

Ellis, John M. *Against Deconstruction.* Princeton: Princeton UP, 1989.

Fisher, Michael. *Does Deconstruction Make Any Difference?* Bloomington: Indiana UP, 1987.

Flores, Ralph. *The Rhetoric of Doubtful Authority: Deconstructive Readings of Self-questioning Narratives, St. Augustine to Faulkner.* Ithaca, NY: Cornell UP, 1984.

Gasche, Rodolphe. "Deconstruction as Criticism." *Glyph* 6 (1979): 177–215.

Hartman, Geoffrey. *Saving the Text: Literature/Derrida/Philosophy.* Baltimore: Johns Hopkins UP, 1981.

Hartmann, Geoffrey H. et al. *Deconstruction and Criticism.* New York: Continuum, 1979.

Johnson, Barbara. *The Critical Difference: Essays in the Contemporary Rhetoric of Reading.* Baltimore: Johns Hopkins UP, 1980.

Leitch, Vincent B. *Deconstructive Criticism: An Advanced Introduction.* New York: Columbia UP, 1983.

——. "The Laterial Dance: The Deconstructive Criticism of J. Hillis Miller." *Critical Inquiry* 6 (1980): 593–607.

Miller, J. Hillis. Introduction. *Bleak House.* By Charles Dickens. Ed. Norman Page. Harmondsworth, England: Penguin, 1971. 11–13.

——. *Fiction and Repetition: Seven English Novels.* Cambridge, MA: Harvard UP, 1982.

——. "Tradition and Differance." *Diacritics* 2, No. 4 (1972): 6–13.

Norris, Christopher. *Deconstruction and the Interests of Theory.* Oklahoma Project for Discourse and Theory 4. Norman: U of Oklahoma P, 1989.

——. *Deconstruction: Theory and Practice.* New York: Methuen, 1982.

——. *The Deconstructive Turn: Essays in the Rhetoric of Philosophy.* New York: Methuen, 1983.

Rajnath, ed. *Deconstruction: A Critique.* New York: Macmillan, 1989.

Rorty, Richard. "Deconstruction and Circumvention." *Critical Inquiry* 11 (1984): 1–23.

Ryan, Michael. *Marxism and Deconstruction.* Baltimore: Johns Hopkins UP, 1982.

Scholes, Robert. "Deconstruction and Criticism." *Critical Inquiry* 14, (1988): 278–95.

Spivak, Gayatri. "Reading the World: Literary Studies in the 1980's." *College English* 43 (1981): 671–79.

Taylor, Mark C., ed. *Deconstruction in Context: Literature and Philosophy*. Chicago: U of Chicago P, 1986.

CHAPTER 7

Barrett, William. "Writers and Madness." *Literature and Psychoanalysis*. Edith Kurzweil and William Phillips, eds. New York: Columbia UP, 1983.

Basler, Roy P. *Sex, Symbolism, and Psychology in Literature*. New York: Octagon, 1975.

Bodkin, Maud. *Archetypal Patterns in Poetry*. New York: Vintage, 1958.

Campbell, Joseph. *The Hero with a Thousand Faces*. New York: Pantheon, 1949.

Caroll, David. "Freud and the Myth of Origins." *New Literary History* 6 (1975): 511–28.

Crews, Frederick C. *Out of My System*. New York: Oxford UP, 1975.

——, ed. *Psychoanalysis and Literary Process*. Cambridge, MA: Winthrop, 1970.

Davis, Robert Con, ed. *The Fictional Father: Lacanian Readings of the Text*. Amherst: U of Massachusetts P, 1981.

——, ed. Special issue on "Psychoanalysis and Pedagogy." *College English* 49 6/7 (1987).

Erikson, Erik. *Childhood and Society*. New York: Norton, 1963.

Freud, Sigmund. *The Interpretation of Dreams*. Trans. A. A. Brill. New York: Random, 1950.

——. *Introductory Lectures on Psycho-Analysis*. Trans. Joan Riviere. London: Allen, 1922.

——. *Totem and Taboo*. Trans. A. A. Brill. New York: Moffat, 1918.

Frye, Northrop. *Anatomy of Criticism*. Princeton: Princeton UP, 1957.

Gallop, Jane. *Reading Lacan*. Ithaca, NY: Cornell UP, 1985.

Gilman, Sander, ed. *Introducing Psychoanalytic Theory*. New York: Brunner-Mazel, 1982.

Gutheil, Emil. *The Handbook of Dream Analysis*. New York: Liveright, 1951.

Hartman, Geoffrey. *Psychoanalysis and the Question of the Text*. Baltimore: Johns Hopkins UP, 1979.

Hoffman, Frederick J. *Freudianism and the Literary Mind*. 2nd ed. Baton Rouge: Louisiana State UP, 1957.

Holland, Norman. *The Dynamics of Literary Response*. New York: Oxford UP, 1968.

——. *The I*. New Haven: Yale UP, 1985.

——. "Literary Interpretation and the Three Phases of Psychoanalysis." *Critical Inquiry* 3 (1976): 221–33.

——. "The 'Unconscious' of Literature." *Contemporary Criticism*. Ed. Norman Bradbury and David Palmer. Stratford-upon-Avon Series, vol. 12. New York: St. Martin's, 1970.

Kazin, Alfred. "Freud and His Consequences." *Contemporaries*. Boston: Little, Brown, 1962.

Klein, George. *Psychoanalytic Theory: An Exploration of Essentials*. New York: International Universities P, 1976.

Kurzweil, Edith, and William Phillips, eds. *Literature and Psychoanalysis.* New York: Columbia UP, 1983.

Lesser, Simon O. *Fiction and the Unconscious.* Boston: Beacon, 1957.

Meisel, Perry, ed. *Freud: A Collection of Critical Essays.* Englewood Cliffs, NJ: Prentice-Hall, 1981.

——, ed. *Freud: Twentieth Century Views.* Englewood Cliffs, NJ: Prentice-Hall, 1981.

Nagele, Rainer. *Reading after Freud.* New York: Columbia UP, 1987.

Natoli, Joseph, and Frederik L. Rusch, comps. *Psychocriticism: An Annotated Bibliography.* Westport, CT: Greenwood, 1984.

Porter, Laurence M. *The Interpretation of Dreams: Freud's Theories Revisited.* Twayne's Masterwork Studies Series. Boston: Hall, 1986.

Reppen, Joseph, and Maurice Charney. *The Psychoanalytic Study of Literature.* Hillsdale, NJ: Analytic, 1985.

Schafer, Ray. *The Analytic Attitude.* New York: Basic Books, 1982.

Skura, Meredith Anne. *The Literary Use of Psychoanalytic Process.* New Haven: Yale UP, 1981.

Strelka, Joseph P., ed. *Literary Criticism and Psychology.* University Park, PA: Pennsylvania State UP, 1976.

Tennenhouse, Leonard, ed. *The Practice of Psychoanalytic Criticism.* Detroit: Wayne State UP, 1976.

Trilling, Lionel. *Freud and the Crisis of Our Culture.* Boston: Beacon, 1955.

Wright, Elizabeth. *Psychoanalytic Criticism: Theory in Practice.* London: Methuen, 1984.

CHAPTER 8

Abel, Elizabeth, ed. *Writing and Sexual Difference.* Chicago: U of Chicago P, 1982.

Abel, Elizabeth, and Emily K. Abel. *The Signs Reader: Women, Gender & Scholarship.* Introduction. Chicago: U of Chicago P, 1983.

Auerbach, Nina. *Communities of Women: An Idea in Fiction.* Cambridge, MA: Harvard UP, 1978.

Baym, Nina. *Women's Fiction: A Guide to Novels by and about Women in America, 1820–1870.* Ithaca, NY: Cornell UP, 1978.

Beauvoir, Simone de. *The Second Sex.* 1949. Ed. and Trans. H. M. Parshley. New York: Modern Library, 1952.

Belsey, Catherine, and Jane Moore, eds. *The Feminist Reader: Essays in Gender and the Politics of Literary Criticism.* London: Macmillan, 1989.

Cixous, Hélène. "The Laugh of the Medusa." Trans. Keith Cohen and Paula Cohen. *Signs* 1 (1976): 875–94.

Cixous, Hélène, and Catherine Clement. *The Newly Born Woman.* Paris: Union Générale d'Editions, 1975.

Cohen, Ralph, ed. *New Literary History: A Journal of Theory and Interpretation.* vol. 19, 1 (Autumn 1987): special edition in Feminist Directions.

Donovan, Josephine, ed. *Feminist Literary Criticism: Explorations in Theory.* Lexington: Kentucky UP, 1975.

Eagleton, Mary, ed. *Feminist Literary Criticism.* New York: Longman, 1991.

——, ed. *Feminist Literary Theory: A Reader.* Oxford: Basil Blackwell, 1986.

Edwards, Lee, and Arlyn Diamond, eds. *The Authority of Experience: Essays in Feminist Criticism.* Amherst: U of Massachusetts P, 1977.

Eisenstein, Hester. *Contemporary Feminist Thought.* London: Unwin, 1984.

Eisenstein, Hester, and Alice Jardine, eds. *The Future of Difference.* Boston: G. K. Hall, 1980.

Ellmann, Mary. *Thinking About Women.* New York: Harcourt, 1968.

Felman, Shoshana. "Rereading Femininity." *Yale French Studies* 62 (1981): 19–44.

Fetterley, Judith. *The Resisting Reader: A Feminist Approach to American Fiction.* Bloomington: Indiana UP, 1978.

Fowler, Rowena. "Feminist Criticism: The Common Pursuit." *New Literary History* Vol. 19, 1 (Autumn 1987): 51–62.

French Feminist Theory. Special issue, *Signs* 7 (1981).

Gallop, Jane. *The Daughter's Seduction: Feminism and Psychoanalysis.* Ithaca, NY: Cornell UP, 1982.

Gilbert, Sandra M., and Susan Gubar. *A Classroom Guide to Accompany the Norton Anthology of Literature by Women.* New York: Norton, 1985.

———. *The Madwoman in the Attic: The Woman Writer and the Nineteenth-Century Literary Imagination.* New Haven: Yale UP, 1979.

Greene, Gayle, and Coppelia Kahn, eds. *Making a Difference: Feminist Literary Criticism.* New York: Methuen, 1985.

Irigaray, Luce. *This Sex Which Is Not One.* Trans. Catherine Porter. Ithaca, NY: Cornell UP, 1985.

Jacobus, Mary. *Reading Woman: Essays in Feminist Criticism.* New York: Columbia UP, 1868.

———, ed. *Women Writing and Writing About Women.* London: Croom Helm, 1979.

Jardine, Alice, and Paul Smith, eds. *Men in Feminism.* New York: Methuen, 1987.

Kauffman, Linda, ed. *Gender and Theory: Dialogues on Feminist Criticism.* New York: Basil Blackwell, 1989.

Kolodny, Annette. *The Lay of the Land: Metaphor as Experience in American Life and Letters.* Chapel Hill: U of North Carolina P, 1975.

———. "Some Notes on Defining a 'Feminist Literary Criticism.'" *Critical Inquiry* 2 (1975): 75–92.

Millett, Kate. *Sexual Politics.* New York: Doubleday, 1970.

Minnich, Elizabeth, Jean O'Barr, and Rachel Rosenfeld, eds. *Reconstructing the Academy: Women's Education and Women's Studies.* Chicago: U of Chicago P, 1988.

Moers, Ellen. *Literary Women: The Great Writers.* New York: Doubleday, 1976.

Moi, Toril. *Sexual/Textual Politics: Feminist Literary Theory.* New York: Methuen, 1985.

Newton, Judith, and Deborah Rosenfelt, eds. *Feminist Criticism and Social Change: Sex, Class and Race in Literature and Culture.* New York: Methuen, 1985.

Rich, Adrienne. *On Lies, Secrets, and Silence: Selected Prose 1966–1978.* London: Virago, 1980.

Ruthven, K. K. *Feminist Literary Studies: An Introduction.* New York: Cambridge UP, 1984.

Schriber, Mary Suzanne. *Gender and the Writer's Imagination: From Cooper to Wharton.* Lexington: UP of Kentucky, 1987.

Schuster, Marilyn R., and Susan R. Van Dyne, eds. *Women's Place in the Academy:*

Transforming the Liberal Arts Curriculum. Totowa, NJ: Rowman & Allanheld, 1985.

Showalter, Elaine. *A Literature of Their Own: British Women Novelists from Brontë to Lessing.* Princeton: Princeton UP, 1977.

——, ed. *The New Feminist Criticism: Essays on Women, Literature, Theory.* New York: Pantheon, 1985.

Spivak, Gayatri Chakravorty. *In Other Worlds: Essays in Cultural Politics.* New York: Methuen, 1987.

Todd, Janet. *Feminist Literary History.* New York: Routledge, 1988.

Tong, Rosemarie. *Feminist Thought: A Comprehensive Introduction.* Boulder, CO: Westview, 1989.

Weedon, Chris. *Feminist Practice and Poststructuralist Theory.* Oxford: Basil Blackwell, 1987.

Wittig, Monique. *Les Guerilleres.* Trans. David Le Vay. New York: Avon, 1973.

Woolf, Virginia. *Collected Essays.* London: Hogarth, 1966.

——. *A Room of One's Own.* London: Hogarth, 1929; London: Grafton, 1987.

——. *Women and Writing.* London: Women's Press, 1979.

CHAPTER 9

Adorno, Theodor W. *Prisms.* London: Neville Spearman, 1967.

Adorno, Theodor W., and Max Horkheimer. *Dialectic of Enlightenment.* London: Allen Lane, 1972.

Althusser, Louis. *For Marx.* New York: Pantheon, 1969.

Arvon, Henri. *Marxist Aesthetics.* Trans. H. Lane. Ithaca, NY: Cornell UP, 1973.

Baxandall, Lee, and Stefan Morowski, eds. *Marx and Engels on Literature and Art.* New York: International General, 1973.

Benjamin, Walter. *Illuminations.* New York: Schocken, 1970.

Bennett, Tony. *Formalism and Marxism.* London: Methuen, 1979.

Craig, David, ed. *Marxists on Literature.* Harmondsworth, England: Penguin, 1975.

Demetz, Peter. *Marx, Engels and the Poets: Origins of Marxist Literary Criticism.* Chicago: U of Chicago P, 1967.

Dowling, William C. *Jameson, Althusser, Marx: An Introduction to the Political Unconscious.* Ithaca, NY: Cornell UP, 1984.

Eagleton, Terry. *Criticism and Ideology: A Study in Marxist Literary Theory.* London: New Left Books, 1976.

——. *The Function of Criticism: From The Spectator to Post-Structuralism.* London: Thetford, 1984.

——. *Literary Theory: An Introduction.* Minneapolis: U of Minnesota P, 1983.

——. *Marxism and Literary Criticism.* Berkeley: U of California P, 1976.

Fekete, John. *The Critical Twilight.* Boston: Routledge & Kegan Paul, 1976.

Frow, John. *Marxism and Literary History.* Ithaca, NY: Cornell UP, 1986.

Goldmann, Lucien. *The Hidden God.* London: Routledge & Kegan Paul, 1964.

——. "Marxist Criticism." *The Philosophy of the Enlightenment.* Cambridge, MA: MIT, 1973, pp. 86–97.

Hicks, Granville. *The Great Tradition.* New York: Macmillan, 1933; rev. 1935.

James, C. Vaughan. *Soviet Socialist Realism: Origins and Theory.* New York: Macmillan, 1973.

Jameson, Fredric. *Marxism and Form: Twentieth-century Dialectical Theories of Literature.* Princeton: Princeton UP, 1971.

———. *The Political Unconscious: Narrative as a Socially Symbolic Act.* Ithaca, NY: Cornell UP, 1981.

———. *The Prison-House of Language: A Critical Account of Structuralism and Russian Formalism.* Princeton: Princeton UP, 1972.

Jay, Martin. *The Dialectical Imagination: A History of the Frankfurt School.* London: Heinemann, 1973.

Lentricchia, Frank. *Criticism and Social Change.* Chicago: U of Chicago P, 1983.

Lukacs, Georg. *The Historical Novel.* London: Merlin, 1962.

———. *The Meaning of Contemporary Realism.* London: Merlin, 1963.

———. *Writer and Critic and Other Essays.* London: Merlin, 1970.

Macherey, Pierre. *A Theory of Literary Production.* Trans. G. Wall. London: Routledge & Kegan, 1978.

Marcuse, Herbert. *The Aesthetic Dimension: Toward a Critique of Marxist Aesthetics.* Boston: Beacon, 1978.

McMurtry, John. *The Structure of Marx's World-View.* Princeton: Princeton UP, 1978.

Sartre, Jean-Paul. *What Is Literature?* New York: Philosophical Library, 1949.

Willett, John, ed. *Brecht on Theatre.* London: Methuen, 1964.

Williams, Raymond. *Culture and Society: 1780–1950.* London: Chatto and Windus, 1958.

———. *Marxism and Literature.* Oxford: Oxford UP, 1977.

Wilson, Edmund. *Axel's Castle.* New York: Scribner's, 1961.

CHAPTER 10

Collier, Peter, and Helga Geyer-Ryan, eds. *Literary Theory Today.* Ithaca, NY: Cornell UP, 1990.

Cooper, Barry. *Michel Foucault: An Introduction to the Study of His Thought.* New York: Edwin Mellen, 1982.

Cousins, Mark, and Athar Hussain. *Michel Foucault.* New York: St. Martin's, 1984.

Dollimore, Jonathan. *Radical Tragedy: Religion, Ideology, and Power in the Drama of Shakespeare and his Contemporaries.* Chicago: U of Chicago P, 1984.

Dollimore, Jonathan, and Alan Sinfield, eds. *Political Shakespeare: New Essays in Cultural Materialism.* Manchester, England: Manchester UP, 1985.

Foucault, Michel. *Madness and Civilization.* Trans. Richard Howard. New York: Pantheon, 1965.

———. *The Order of Things.* New York: Pantheon, 1972.

Gane, Mike, ed. *Towards a Critique of Foucault.* London: Routledge & Kegan Paul, 1987.

Goldberg, Jonathan. *James I and the Politics of Literature: Jonson, Shakespeare, Donne, and Their Contemporaries.* Baltimore: Johns Hopkins UP, 1983.

Graff, Gerald, and Reginald Gibbons, eds. *Criticism in the University.* Evanston, IL: Northwestern UP, 1985.

Greenblatt, Stephen. Introduction. "The Forms of Power and the Power of Forms in the Renaissance." *Genre* 15 (Summer 1982): 3–6.

———. *Renaissance Self-Fashioning: From More to Shakespeare.* Chicago: U of Chicago P, 1980.

Lindenberger, Herbert. "Toward a New History in Literary Study." *Profession: Selected Articles from the Bulletins of the Association of Departments of English and the Association of Departments of Foreign Languages.* New York: MLA, 1984. 16–23.

MaGann, Jerome. *The Beauty of Inflections: Literary Investigations in Historical Method and Theory.* Oxford: Oxford UP, 1985.

———. *Social Values and Poetic Act: The Historical Judgment of Literary Work.* Cambridge, MA: Harvard UP, 1988.

Morris, Wesley. *Toward a New Historicism.* Princeton: Princeton UP, 1972.

Rabinow, Paul, ed. *The Foucault Reader.* New York: Pantheon, 1984.

Robertson, D. W. "Historical Criticism." *English Institute Essays: 1950,* ed. Alan S. Downer. New York: Columbia UP, 1951. 3–31.

Sheridan, Alan. *Michel Foucault.* New York: Horwood and Tavistock, 1985.

Thomas, Brook. "The Historical Necessity for—and Difficulties with—New Historical Analysis in Introductory Literature Courses." *College English* 49 (Sept. 1987): 509–22.

Vesser, H. Aram, ed. *The New Historicism.* New York: Routledge, 1989.

Index

A

Absolutist critic, 3, 166
Aesthetic experience, 34
Aesthetic reading, 49, 166
Aesthetics, 8, 166
Affective fallacy, 36, 166
Ambiguity, 38, 166–67
Anal stage, 90, 167
Applied criticism, 3, 167
Aquinas, St. Thomas, 107
Archetypal criticism, 92–93, 167
Archetype, 92, 167
Archiécriture (arch-writing), 78, 167
Aristotle, 3, 8, 13–16, 26, 107
    reader-response criticism and, 47
Arnold, Matthew, 3, 25–27, 29
Aspirated, 73, 167
Autonomy of text (See New Criticism)

B

Barthes, Roland, 51, 65
Base, 119–20, 167 (See also Superstructure)
Beauvoir, Simone de, 104, 105
Binary oppositions/operations, 66, 76,
    77, 78
    textual analysis and, 79–82
Blackmur, R. P., 33
Blake, William, 88
Bleich, David, 53
Bourgeoisie, 115, 167–68
Brooks, Cleanth, 33, 38
Browning, Robert, 39, 122
Bunyan, Paul, 88

C

Castration complex, 90–91, 168
Catalyst, 35, 168
Catharsis, 15, 168

Chopin, Kate, 105
Close reading, 34
Coleridge, Samuel Taylor, 21, 88, 104
Collective unconscious, 92, 168
Condensation, 91, 168
Connotation, 37, 168
Conscious, 92, 168
Criticism (See Literary criticism; specific
    schools)
Culler, Jonathan, 51, 65–66

D

Dante Alighieri, 17–18, 26, 88
Darwin, Charles, 23, 25
Deconstruction, 53, 71–82, 168–69
    assumptions, 75–77
    historical development, 72–75
    methodology, 77–82
Denotation, 37, 169
De Quincy, Thomas, 88
Derrida, Jacques, 71–72, 75–80
Diachronic, 59, 169
Différance, 78–79, 169
Difference, as basis of language, 61–62,
    74–75
Discourse, 129, 133, 169
Displacement, 91, 169
Dollimore, Jonathan, 130
Dreams, 87–88, 91, 94–95
Dryden, John, 19–20

E

Eagleton, Terry, 118
Écriture féminine, 106, 169
Efferent reading, 49, 169–70
Ego, 90, 170
Eliot, T. S., 35
Emes, 73, 170

Engels, Friedrich, 115–17
Episteme, 131–32, 170
Esoteric work, 14, 170
Exoteric work, 14, 170
Expressive school, 32, 170
Extrinsic analysis, 32, 170

F

False consciousness, 119
Feminism, 53, 102–9, 170–71
    assumptions, 106–8
    historical development, 104–6
    methodology, 108–9
Formalism, 33, 171
Foucault, Michel, 131–32
Freeman, Mary E. Wilkins, 108
Freud, Sigmund, 88–96, 107, 109
Frye, Northrop, 89, 93

G

Gallagher, Catherine, 130
Geertz, Clifford, 132
Genette, Gerard, 51, 65
Glaspell, Susan, 66, 109
Goethe, Johann Wolfgang von, 88
Grammar, 63, 171
Greenblatt, Stephen, 129, 130
Gynocriticism, 171
    biological model, 105, 109
    cultural model, 106, 109
    linguistic model, 105–6, 109
    psychoanalytic model, 106, 109

H

Hamartia, 15, 171
Hawthorne, Nathaniel, 80, 135
Hegemony, 120, 171
Heresy of paraphrase, 37, 171
Hermeneutics, 89, 171
Holistic approach, 29, 172
Holland, Norman, 53
Horace, 16–17
Hume, David, 8

I

Id, 89, 172
Ideology, 116, 119, 121–22, 172
Imitation, 12–13, 14–15, 16, 19, 21
Impressionistic critics, 32, 172
In medias res, 16, 172

Intentional fallacy, 35, 172
Irony, 38, 172
Iser, Wolfgang, 52

J

Jakobson, Roman, 51
James, Henry, 27–28
Jauss, Hans Robert, 52
Johnson, Samuel, 19
Jung, Carl, 89, 92

K

Kekule, Friedrich August, 87–88

L

Lacan, Jacques, 89, 93–94, 109
Language, 59, 172–73
    Dante and, 17–18
    deconstruction and, 75–77
    feminism and, 105–6
    New Historicism and, 133–34
    structuralism and, 59–63, 72–75
    Wordsworth and, 22
Langue, 61, 63, 65, 73, 173
Latent content, 95, 173
Lentricchia, Frank, 118, 130
Lessing, Doris, 105
Lévi-Strauss, Claude, 51, 64
Libido, 90, 173
Linear, 81, 131, 173
Linguistic sign, 74, 173
Literacy experience, 49, 173
Literary criticism, 173
    defined, 3
    historical survey, 11–30
    schools, 6–7
    types, 3
Literary theory, 173
    conceptual framework, 4–5
    schools of criticism, 6–7
Literature, attempts at defining, 7–9
Logocentrism, 76, 77, 82, 173
Longinus, 16–17

M

Mailloux, Steven, 53
Manifest content, 95, 173–74
Marx, Karl Heinrich, 115–17
Marxism, 6, 53, 114–22, 174
    assumptions, 118–20

historical development, 115–18
  methodology, 121–22
McGann, Jerome, 130
Metaphor, 39, 174
Metaphysics of presence, 77, 174
Metatheory, 6, 175
Mimetic theory, 21, 60, 74, 175
Modernism, 32, 175
Monomyth, 93, 175
Montrose, Louis, 129
Mythemes, 64, 175

N

Narratology, 64, 175–76
Naturalism, 32, 176
Neurosis, 91–92, 94
New Criticism, 29, 31–40, 48, 176
  assumptions, 34–37
  historical development, 32–34
  methodology, 37–40
New Historicism, 6, 29, 53, 127–35, 176
  assumptions, 130–33
  historical development, 129–30
  methodology, 133–35
New Humanists, 32, 176
Novels, theory/criticism of, 27–28

O

Objective correlative, 34, 176
Objective theory of art, 35, 177
O'Connor, Flannery, 135
Oedipus complex, 90, 95, 177
Old historicism, 128, 130, 134, 135
Ontological, 9, 177
  critic, 31
Oral phase, 90, 177
Organic unity, 37, 38, 177

P

Paradox, 38, 177
Parole, 61, 63, 64, 65, 73, 177
Parrington, Vernon Louis, 117
Patriarchal, 104, 177
Peirce, Charles Sanders, 62
Penis envy, 91
Personal unconscious, 92, 177–78
Personification, 39, 178
Phallic stage, 90, 178
Phenomenology, 52, 178
Philologists, 59, 178

Philology, 59, 178
Phonemes, 64, 73, 178
Phonocentrism, 76, 77, 178
Plato, 3, 8, 11–13
  reader-response criticism and, 47
Pleasure principle, 90
Poe, Edgar Allan, 88
Poem, 31, 178
Poetic diction, 37–40
Pope, Alexander, 20–21
Poststructuralism, 71, 178
Poulet, George, 52
Practical critic, 3, 178–79
Practical criticism, 3, 34, 178–79
Prince, Gerald, 51
Privileged, 76, 179
Proletariat, 115, 179
Propp, Vladimir, 64
Prosody, 39, 179
Psychoanalytic criticism, 87–96, 179
  assumptions, 94–95
  historical development, 89–94
  methodology, 95–96

R

Ransom, John Crowe, 31, 33
Reader-response criticism, 45–54, 179–80
  assumptions, 50–51
  eclectic nature, 53
  historical development, 47–49
  methodology, 51–54
Reader-response critics
  phenomenologists, 52
  structuralists, 51–52
  subjectivists, 53
Reading process
  contextual nature of, 48–49
  Culler's theory of, 65–66
Reality principle, 91
Referent, 60, 180
Reflection theory, 119, 180
Relativistic critic, 3, 180
Rhetoric, 21, 180
Richards, I. A., 33, 34, 48
Romanticism, 32, 180
  British, 21–23
Rosenblatt, Louise M., 5, 48–49, 52

S

Saussure, Ferdinand de, 51, 59, 60–62, 64,
  72–75, 93

Schools of criticism, 6–7, 180
Semiology, 62, 180–81
Semiotics, 62, 181
Shor, Ira, 122
Showalter, Elaine, 105–6
Sidney, Sir Philip, 18–19
Sign, 61, 181
Signification, 75, 181
Signified, 61, 74, 75, 181
Signifier, 61, 74, 75, 181
Simile, 181
Slips of language, 81
Southwick, E. D. N., 108
Speech, phonocentrism and, 76–78
Stevenson, Robert Louis, 88
Structuralism, 51–52, 58–66, 72–75,
     181–182
  assumptions, 62–64
  historical development, 59–62
  literature and, 63–66
  methodology, 64–66
Structuralist narratology, 64, 182
Structural linguistics, 59, 72–75, 182
Sublime, 17, 26
Superego, 90, 182
Superstructure, 119–120, 182
Supplement, 78, 182
Synchronic, 60, 182

T

Taine, Hippolyte Adolphe, 23–25
Tartini, Guiseppe, 88
Teleological, 131, 182
Tension, 38, 182

Theoretical criticism, 3, 183
Todorov, Tzvetan, 65
Tompkins, Jane, 102, 107
Touchstone theory, 27
Traditional historic approach, 116–17
     (*See also* Marxism)
Tragedy, 15, 183
Transactional event/experience, 5, 49, 52,
     183
Transcendental signified, 75–76, 79, 183
Tropes, 65, 183
Turner, Victor, 132
Twain, Mark 1–3

U

Unconscious, 89, 183
Unprivileged, 76, 183
Unvoiced, 74, 183

V

Voiced, 74, 183
Vulgar Marxism, 119, 184

W

Warner, Susan, 108
Warren, Robert Penn, 33
Wellek, René, 33
Wimsatt, W. K., 33
Wittig, Monique, 105
Woolf, Virginia, 104, 105
Wordsworth, William, 21–23, 25
Worldview, 4, 184